TRADITIONAL
SPANISH
COOKING

Traditional Spanish Cooking

Janet Mendel

F

FRANCES LINCOLN LIMITED

PUBLISHERS

Frances Lincoln Ltd
4 Torriano Mews
Torriano Avenue
London NW5 2RZ
www.franceslincoln.com

British Library Cataloguing in Publication Data
A catalogue record for this book is available from the British Library.

First published in hardback by Garnet Publishing Ltd 1996
First paperback edition published by Frances Lincoln Ltd 2006

ISBN 10: 0 7112 2677 6
ISBN 13: 978 0 7112 2677 7

Printed and bound in Singapore

1 2 3 4 5 6 7 8 9

In memory of my mother, Shirley Laverne Mendel

CONTENTS

A Melting Pot   2

Ingredients, Utensils and Procedures   12

I Breakfast   19

      Our daily bread   24

II Dinner at Midday   29

    First Course

      Salads   31

      Gazpacho soups   39

      Soup   44

      Stews and soups with pulses   54

      Seafood soups   60

      Vegetable starters   69

      Seafood starters   92

      Dry salt cod   108

      Meat starters   118

    Main Dishes

      Rice   120

      Sturdy one-pot dishes   133

      Fish   140

      Poultry and small game   165

      Pork   183

      Lamb   193

      Beef and veal   203

III Lunch, Tea and Supper   211

      Eggs   213

      Snacks and sandwiches   222

IV Appetizers   228

    Deep-fried tapas   235

    Salads and cold tapas   246

    Hot tapas   251

V Desserts   262

    Fruit desserts   264

    Puddings   270

    Cakes, biscuits, tarts and pastries   279

    Confections   300

Glossary of Spanish words   303

Bibliography   306

Index   307

Traditional Spanish Cooking

A MELTING POT

Situated on a peninsula bordered by both the Mediterranean Sea and the Atlantic Ocean, Spain occupies a place on the crossroads of civilizations. Since the earliest records of mankind, different peoples and cultures settled here, waged wars, raised families, painted pictures, herded sheep, grew wheat and made bread. Spain's cooking is a true 'melting pot' of many cultures.

Spanish food today reflects these diverse traditions. Recipes, handed down through many generations, are like an historical outline through which we can trace the development of agriculture, migrations of people, wars and invasions, new trade routes, exploration and conquest. It's all in the *olla*, the big cooking pot which is the symbol of Spanish cooking.

At the dawn of civilization, a people of the Old Stone Age, the Magdelanian culture, hunters and gatherers with simple tools, roamed through the northern part of the Iberian peninsula. They left their mark for us to marvel at 15,000 years later. In the Altamira grottoes near the Bay of Biscay, close to what is now Santander, are extraordinary paintings of animals made on the cave walls by those ancient people. The Ice Age creatures depicted include bison, boar and a stag. Is this art for art's sake? Icons of a primitive religion? Or,

perhaps, the menu on the wall, a picture of what was, hopefully, for dinner?

Eons later, by 3000 BC, New Stone Age people, ancestors of the Iberians, were populating coastal Spain. These Neolithic folk, who migrated from the Middle East across North Africa, brought the germs of agriculture. Grain planted in one season could be harvested and stored to feed a tribe's hungry families when nature's pickings were slim. By then a type of wild olive was gathered for its oil, used for oil lamps.

The growth of agriculture had enormous implications for the development of civilizations. Those who depended on growing crops for food were less nomadic; they had to stick around to reap what they had sown. Then they had to protect their harvests from hostile intruders. Small settlements came first, and then villages; much, much later, cities. All these structures developed because of the way people gathered their food.

By 1500 BC, at the height of the Bronze Age, one thriving area of civilized life was in the region at the mouth of the Guadalquivir River, encompassing parts of what are now Seville, Cádiz and Huelva provinces, in the south-west corner of Spain. Somewhere here, now buried beneath the sands of time – literally silted over – lies the lost civilization of Tartessos. No mythical kingdom, though archaeological evidence of its site still eludes us, Tartessos was a kingdom renowned for the wealth of its silver and copper mines, and for having plenty to feed its people, thanks to fertile land and the wealth of the sea. According to a later historian, the Tartessians used silver feeding troughs and wine goblets. Tartessos probably endured until the sixth century BC. It disappeared leaving only tantalizing traces.

Although we have to fill in the gaps with imagination and speculation, recorded history shows that by 1000 BC, Celtic tribes were moving in to spread across north and central Iberia, while on the coasts the intrepid Phoenicians, traders to the core, established numerous beachheads. The Phoenicians already had a taste for Spanish products: silver, certainly, but almost as important, the tuna that made its way from the Atlantic to the Mediterranean, where it was captured in anchored nets by a method almost identical to that used today. The tuna appears on Phoenician coins of the era. The Phoenicians called the land 'Shapan', from which derive the names Spania, Hispania, España. One of the meanings attributed to the Phoenician word is 'land filled with rabbits', an apt description, then as now, when hunters carry home game for the stew pot or the paella. The city of Cádiz (then Gadir) was founded by the Phoenicians in 1100 BC, making it perhaps the oldest city in Europe, older even than Rome.

The Greeks, another trading nation, came this way, too, and introduced the production of *garon*, a fermented fish sauce, which later (as *garum*) the Romans were to take to in a big way. Then the Carthaginians ruled for two centuries. They are credited with bringing the vine and wine-making to Spain, about the sixth century BC, as well as the *malum punica*, the pomegranate. Prior to this, the Celtiberians made a fermented beer from grains. The Romans defeated Hannibal to push out the Carthaginians in 218 BC and went on to subjugate the Celtiberian settlements.

The Romans came to conquer and stayed for lunch. For six centuries, Hispania was Rome's best larder, a source of olive oil, wheat, wine, raisins and salt-fish, products shipped back to Rome in quantity. Baetica in the south of Spain became one of the richest provinces in the entire Roman Empire.

The Romans extended the plantings of olive trees in a wide swath across what is now Jaén, Córdoba and Seville. Hundreds of oil mills were situated on the banks of the Genil and Guadalquivir Rivers, from where the oil was easily transported down-river to the sea, to be shipped to Rome. The oil was carried in earthenware amphorae each containing about 50 litres of oil, with seals describing the olive grove, shipper and date. To give an idea of the magnitude of this transaction: a small hill near Rome was discovered to consist of the crumbled remains of 40 million Spanish oil vats with seals dating between the years 140 and 260 AD. Latin poets extolled Spanish oil and, in what may be the first cookery book, Roman gastronome Apicius gives recipes specifying olive oil from Hispania, while a recipe for mustard calls for mustard seed to be ground with honey, vinegar and oil from Baetica, southern Spain.

On the south coasts, the salting of fish became an important industry, especially the production of *garum*, fish paste. At Bolonia, a Roman site on the beach near Tarifa (Cádiz) in the Straits of Gibraltar, you can see the vats where this favoured condiment was made. One of the most sought-after was the *garum* from Cartagena (Murcia), the caviare of the ancient world. The Romans, powerful partisans of garlic, were probably responsible for introducing this flavour into Spanish cooking.

After the fall of the Roman Empire, the Visigoths, who were early Christians, filled the power vacuum, but not very well. They seem hardly to have left a mark on the culinary arts of Spain.

Then in 711, the Moors swarmed across the Straits of Gibraltar, taking over most of the country, as far as France, until being pushed back. While most of Europe was still languishing in the Dark Ages, subsisting on coarse gruels and game, in the kingdoms of Al-Andalus, people supped in flower-scented courtyards where fountains bubbled and musicians played. The foods were served in a special order on fine plates. There were vegetable dishes spiced from a tantalizing palette; meats carefully cooked and finished with egg and a dusting of cinnamon and almonds; sweetmeats and pastries perfumed with orange blossom and rose water, soaked in honey and sprinkled with crystalline sugar; a variety of fine fruits.

While not everyone in Al-Andalus enjoyed a life like a scene from Hollywood's rendition of Arabian Nights, the society was, if we can believe the records left by poets and historians of the era, highly refined at the height of the Moorish period.

The Moors took over a land already famed for its olive oil, grapes, wine and wheat. Settling in for a long stay – eight centuries, as it turned out – they extended and improved irrigation methods, adding hydraulic systems to transport water over great distances and raise it to higher fields. Some of the waterways and water tribunals are still in place today.

The Arabs planted wheat on non-irrigated land, allowing fields to lie fallow every alternate year, providing pasture for sheep, which also fertilized the ground. Areas near Granada, Murcia and Toledo were acclaimed for the quality of their wheat and bread.

New crops were planted in Al-Andalus: rice, sugar cane, aubergines, bitter oranges and lemons (the sweet orange came later, via the Portuguese who discovered it in China), almonds, pomegranates, saffron. Fruit orchards of cherries, apples and pears were planted. Vegetables cultivated and used in cooking included four kinds of broad beans (the haricot bean or kidney bean came from the New World, after Columbus), lettuce, cabbage, chard, turnips, escarole, purslane, carrots, radishes, onions, garlic, leeks, celery, cardoons, artichokes, asparagus, cucumber and aubergine.

The Arabs, who came from the crossroads of the great Spice Routes to the East, brought to Al-Andalus the exotic spices of cinnamon, nutmeg, pepper, aniseed, sesame, cumin, coriander, ginger, caraway, and more, all of which were and are used extensively in cooking. Many dishes today could almost have come straight out of a Moorish recipe book: such as a Catalan dish of stuffed aubergine with cinnamon; Andalusian meatballs, *albondigas* (a word derived from the Arabic), with nutmeg in a sauce of ground almonds and saffron and, most especially, Andalusian pastries and sweets spiked with aniseed.

The Arabs planted sugar cane along the Granada, Almería and Málaga coasts – where it still thrives today, just beyond Málaga's international airport – and introduced the process of refining sugar from the cane juice. With spices and sugar, even simple flour porridges – and there were many variations – became special. Many of these, such as *gachas*, are still part of Andalusia's culinary repertoire. Al-Andalus also produced superb honey – as it still does.

The flavouring ingredient *garum* remained important, and by Moorish times this had been refined considerably, constituting a sort of 'salad dressing', made from grains as well as fish guts.

Lamb and mutton were the popular meats. Both Muslims and Jews were prohibited from eating pork, though their Christian neighbours, the *mozarabes*, raised pigs. This was the beginning of Spain's great sheep-raising era, when huge flocks ranged across vast areas of the country in the *trashumancia*, or migrations from high summer pastures to lowland winter pastures. The Mesta, a shepherds' guild, was created in 1273 both to regulate the wool trade and to levy taxes on it. Cattle were primarily used for ploughing, though beef was available, as well as goats' meat. Cheese and fermented milk were used in cooking.

The fishing of big tuna was practised at Málaga, Almuñecar and Tarifa much as it is today, by the *almadraba* anchored nets. Smaller fish were captured with *jhabak* nets, from which derives the Spanish *jábega*, nets hauled in from the beach.

Legend has it that the Hebrew peoples have lived in Spain since the time of King Solomon and the voyages of the Phoenicians. Records indicate that Jewish refugees may have found asylum in the Iberian Peninsula after the first temple of Jerusalem was destroyed by the Babylonians in 586 BC. It is certain that these tribes lived in Spain from the first century AD, during the time of the Roman Empire. They called their country Sepharad, meaning Spain. By 300 AD their numbers were fairly substantial –

sufficient to cause the nascent Spanish Church to worry about living next door to Jews. It was during periods of benevolent Moorish rule, after the eighth century, that Spain's Jews enjoyed a 'golden age' of philosophy, science, medicine and statesmanship. The Jews were expelled from Spain in 1492 by the same Catholic monarchs, Ferdinand and Isabella, who, having defeated the last of the Moors in the kingdom of Granada, funded Columbus's wild scheme to sail west to look for the Spice Islands.

The dispersion of the Spanish Jews created communities of Sephardim in many parts of the world where, today, their members still speak Ladino, a fifteenth-century Spanish. The Jews took with them not only the language but the culture and the food. Much of it is still vital today. In fact, it is said that if Columbus were to come back to life today he would find it easier to converse with the Sephardic Jews of Istanbul than with modern-day *Madrileños*, inhabitants of Madrid. And, if the great explorer wanted a nostalgic taste of the food he remembered from the fifteenth century, he would find that many dishes of the Sephardim are little changed from the Spanish cuisine of his time.

Although the Jews maintained a separate identity, they are credited with contributing the national dish, *cocido*, a one-pot meal, to Spanish cookery. The *cocido* derives from the *adafina*, a dish of meat and pulses put to cook all night in the coals to serve on the Sabbath. After the expulsion of the Jews and the Inquisition,

converts to Christianity – known as *marranos*, swine – proved their faith by adding pork, which was forbidden by Jewish law, to the dish.

Spain's rich heritage of sweets, not just Moorish, but Jewish as well, is amazingly well preserved in Catholic convents: here nuns make the same sweets, by the same names, that are made by Sephardic families in Israel.

The reconquest of the peninsula by Christian forces from the north began early in the eleventh century and continued until the taking of the last Moorish kingdom of Granada by Ferdinand and Isabella at the end of the fifteenth century. A potent symbol of the Reconquest was the image of the apostle St James, Santiago, the Moor-slayer, whose shrine is at Santiago de Compostela in Galicia. The shrine became a destination for pilgrims from all over Europe, and by the twelfth century was as important as Rome and Jerusalem.

The pilgrims' route attracted not just the pious and penitent, but tradesmen, builders, salesmen, artisans, artists, thieves, prostitutes and the like. This was, in effect, Spain's first tourist route, with inns, hostels, hospitals, monasteries and soup kitchens, where merchants and purveyors of food and other goods plied their wares.

Though vineyards and wine-making had been established in the regions of Rioja and Navarre since Roman times, the coming of numerous monasteries did much to further the development of viticulture. Monks and pilgrims brought in grape varietals from elsewhere in

Europe. The Rioja *tempranillo* may be descended from Burgundy's *pinot noir*, while the Galician *albariño*, from which is made what is arguably Spain's best white wine, is reputed to be the original Rhine wine grape.

Granada's capture freed up money and energy for other pursuits, such as the funding of Christopher Columbus's first voyage in search of a quick route to the Spice Islands.

Although it's hard to imagine, five hundred years ago when King Ferdinand and Queen Isabella sat down to dinner, there was not a potato, bean, pepper or tomato in sight. These and many other now-familiar foods were unknown in the Old World.

On 4 November 1492, Columbus's party exploring the eastern end of what is now Cuba found great expanses of tilled land sown with a sort of bean (Europeans knew broad beans but not the haricot), a grain the natives called *mais*, 'which tasted well made into flour', and what was identified as a 'gourd' called *calabaza*, which today we know as squash.

At a feast hosted by the king of the island given the name of St Thomas, Columbus was served several varieties of sweet potatoes, called *batatas*, whence comes our word for potatoes. Columbus probably brought sweet potato plants back to Spain, for they were growing here by 1493. The white potato was several years down the line, discovered around 1530 by Pizzaro's men near Quito, Ecuador. Potatoes were cultivated by monks in Seville by 1539 and are

said to have arrived in Ireland around 1586, possibly from ships of the Spanish Armada wrecked on the Irish coast.

Early chroniclers really believed that Columbus had reached the Indies, the Spice Islands in the East where the treasured spice, pepper, came from. So when served a fiery spice on his food, Columbus naturally called it 'pepper', thus confusing the issue for centuries. The pepper of the New World is the capsicum, from which come the chilli, the sweet bell pepper, and the spices paprika and cayenne.

It was on his fourth voyage in 1502 that Columbus discovered in Nicaragua the cocoa bean, which was duly brought back to Spain. It aroused little interest at the time. It wasn't until 1519 that Hernando Cortez tasted it, prepared as a drink by the Aztecs, flavoured with vanilla – the fruit of a native orchid – and sweetened with cane sugar, which Columbus had carried to the New World and planted there in 1494. Spain and Portugal then enjoyed a century-long monopoly on chocolate, which became exceedingly popular.

Columbus did not find tomatoes in the Caribbean. They were probably brought from Peru or Mexico to Spain around 1520 and passed on to the kingdom of Naples, which came under Spanish rule about the same time. The Italians were early pioneers in the use of the tomato in cooking while other Europeans shunned it for another 200 years. It wasn't until the twentieth century that most people dared to consume tomatoes raw.

The avocado, *aguacate* in Spanish, was first described in 1519 by a Spanish explorer who discovered it in Columbia. The name comes from *ahuacatl*, derived from the Aztec word meaning 'testicle tree'. Nor did Columbus enjoy that native American bird, the turkey, for it is too heavy a bird to make flights between the islands. A chronicler of Cortez, around 1519, reported seeing turkeys in Mexican markets and said they were cooked daily for Montezuma's table. All of this incredibly enriched the Spanish diet, which by the sixteenth century was probably the most varied in Europe.

During the sixteenth century Spanish galleons plied two great oceans so that eventually they opened up trade routes to the real Spice Islands. Spain grew staggeringly rich and lived high off the hog. In this Golden Age, aristocrats built fine mansions, patronized the arts and made much of their culinary wizards. Spanish cooking, based on this rich larder, was sumptuous and refined.

With the ascent to the Spanish throne in the mid-eighteenth century of the first Bourbon king, gastronomic traditions underwent another profound change. The nobility quickly took to French language, style and culture. Food served by French chefs at court was copied by the upper classes, though ordinary rural folk, hardly touched by city life, still ate simply – stews of dry mutton or beef, bread with onion for dessert. It was during this 'French period' that Spanish food came to be thought inferior. During the nineteenth century, travellers to Spain wrote scathing accounts of meals suffered in the inns and country *ventas*.

In the twentieth century, with the Civil War and its aftermath came intense poverty in many regions of Spain. People starved to death. Those who lived ate unmentionable things. They ate foods that previously they had only fed to pigs. Through the 1950s the country slowly recovered from devastation. In the 1960s, tourism brought new prosperity.

The most revolutionary change in Spanish food has come with refrigeration, making it unnecessary to preserve and keep foods in the old-fashioned ways. That and modern transport mean that *pueblos* in isolated valleys now are supplied with frozen fish; strawberries served in southern Spain are topped with whipped cream, almost unknown not so many years ago, and fresh meat can be eaten throughout the year. Incredibly, neither refrigerated lorries, nor television commercials, nor the tourist invasion have created a unified Spanish kitchen – the cooking is still the food of the village. Prosperity has brought a renewed pride in the richness of traditional cooking and an enormous interest in keeping it alive and simmering in the big *olla*. Even many of those who cook in the modern kitchens of a city apartment maintain the flavours and style of traditional dishes.

REGIONAL STYLES

En enero, pedir pepinos es desatino.

In January, to ask for cucumbers is nonsense.

While Spanish cooking easily divides into broad regional styles, clichés almost – as, 'in the north, you stew; in the centre, you roast; in the south, you fry' – in fact, traditional Spanish cooking is less regional, and more a multitude of micro-cuisines. Essentially it is the cooking of the *patria chica*, one's own village and immediate region, much of which has come down to us virtually unchanged.

Until very recently, the village was dependent on resources immediately to hand, so the cooking was intensely local. For example, certain Galician villages, surrounded by chestnut groves, invented a repertoire of dishes, sweet and savoury, based on chestnuts. Where walnuts thrived, this nut added substance to local dishes, while in the south, the almond was the secret ingredient. While seafaring Basques and Galicians from northern coastal villages were famous for their fish dishes, people in villages and on isolated farms hardly 150 kilometres inland seldom ate fresh fish. Instead, they were known for the flavour of their corn-fed, free-range chickens. Similarly in the south, villages near the Bay of Cádiz could revel in a proliferation of prawns and other shellfish, but, until refrigeration became prevalent, interior towns had to depend on *bacalao*, dried salt cod, during Lenten fasts.

Pueblo food was also totally seasonal. There were no oranges in summer because oranges ripen in winter; no tomatoes, a summer crop, at Christmas; nor artichokes, which bud in early spring, to be had in the autumn.

THE TRADITIONAL KITCHEN

Cuando el mortero llama, O Dios, ¡Que buena mañana!

When the mortar rings, Oh Lord, what a great morning!

In the north and central plains, most kitchens are dominated by a hearth inside a great chimney. A cauldron set on a tripod over the coals bubbles away from early morning. Hung to one side in the chimney are ropes of sausages, drying in the fragrant wood smoke. There are clay pots filled with lard or salted bacon, and jugs full of olive oil. A table and chairs lined up against the wall will be pulled to the centre of the kitchen when meals are served.In the airy pantry, hams hang from the beams and slabs of dry salt cod dangle, like grey bats, from pegs. There are strings of dried peppers and garlic braided into long strands. Wild mushrooms, strung on thread, hang next to strands of green beans, which have been blanched and sun dried. Melons slung in nets are also suspended from the rafters. A sack of lentils, a bin of onions, newly dug potatoes stand on the floor. On the shelves are jars of fruit jams, fruits preserved in grape syrup, homemade fruit and herb liqueurs and honey in combs.

On country *cortijos*, farms, in southern Spain, often the kitchen occupies a building separate from the house, so the cooking fire doesn't heat the house. Instead of the hearth, a tiled counter has an inset covered with a grid over a charcoal fire. Deep niches in the whitewashed walls hold big clay jars for oil, for wine, for water. Pots of herbs and geraniums adorn a sunny windowsill and an unglazed water jug, beaded with droplets of water, keeps drinking water fresh and cool by evaporation. Colourful pottery bowls and copper pans are lined up on a shelf over the hob. The *almirez*, a brass mortar and pestle for grinding spices, has a place of honour. So beloved is the ringing sound of the mortar that it's used as a rhythm instrument to accompany folk dances.

Outside the kitchen a grape arbour shades the terrace. A domed bread oven, built in a style hardly changed since Roman times, can be found at the end of the terrace. Hens peck in the dirt near the house and a cock crows from his perch atop the chicken coop.

In the storeroom are clusters of raisins hung from a beam, dried apricots and figs packed in baskets, sun-dried tomatoes and aubergines. The briny smell of olives in clay vats prickles the taste buds.

Olive oil, bread and rice, fish, fresh fruits and vegetables, pulses and wine – these are the fundamentals of Spanish food, which traditionally was low in red meat and dairy products. This is what today is called 'The Mediterranean Diet', the healthiest way to eat.

THE RHYTHM OF THE DAY

Después de comer, duerme la siesta, y después de cenar, vete de fiesta.

After dinner, have a nap, and after supper, a party.

Meal times mark the rhythm of the day. Up at dawn, a light breakfast and off to work. A pause at mid-morning for a snack, in the shade of a tree or at a corner café. *La comida*, dinner, the main meal of the day, comes at two in the afternoon. Some enjoy the luxury of a siesta, while field labourers return to work until six in the evening. That's the hour for a *merienda*, tea-time refreshment. In town, when shops and businesses close at eight o'clock, friends and colleagues meet at a local bar or *tasca* for a few *copas* of wine or glasses of draught beer and the titbits of food, *tapas*, that traditionally accompany them. After that, it's home for supper, as late as nine or ten o'clock or even later in the summer. On weekend evenings, the tapa hour might stretch on much longer, and on Sunday nights, the whole family goes out, small children in tow, for a *paseo* around the plaza punctuated with stops in several tapa bars.

A fiesta day or a village *feria* shakes up the rhythm. Then there are all-night revels, chocolate and *churros*, fritters, at dawn, midnight Mass, candlelit processions, dancing in the plaza, *romerías*, pilgrimages to country shrines, with picnics and all the special foods and sweets that accompany the special days.

Ingredients, utensils and procedures

Beans, dry. See pulses.

Biscuits (*galletas*). A plain, not too sweet biscuit, *galleta Maria*, is sometimes used, finely ground, as a thickening agent for sauces. *Galletas Marias* are also served for breakfast, where they are dipped in coffee.

Brandy (Brandy de Jerez; *aguardiente*). Spain makes excellent brandy, most of which comes from the Sherry region of Jerez. In small quantities, brandy adds depth of flavour to sauces. If food is to be flambéed, place the brandy in a soup ladle, heat it slightly, then set alight. Pour over the food and shake the pan until the flames subside. Another type of brandy which is used in the kitchen is anise brandy, *aguardiente de anis*, both dry, *seco*, and sweet, *dulce*. Any anise-flavoured drink could be substituted.

Bread, breadcrumbs (*pan, pan rallado*). Stale bread to be used for thickening may either first be fried crisp before grinding, or else soaked in water, then squeezed out and mashed or puréed in a processor. Use only Spanish, Italian or French-style loaves which do not contain texturizers.

Breadcrumbs (for breading croquettes, fish, etc.) can be made by grating stale bread, or use packaged fine dry crumbs.

Casserole (*cazuela*). Traditional earthenware casseroles are used both in the oven and – with care – on a gas or electric hob. They should be unglazed on the bottom. Bring them up to temperature slowly. Don't set a hot *cazuela* on a cold surface. The earthenware holds heat for a while after being removed from the heat, so foods will continue to cook. Any flameproof casserole or cooking pan can be used in place of a *cazuela*.

Cheese (*queso*). About 36 different cheeses are made in Spain, from cows', goats' and ewes' milk, though many are made in such small quantities that they are not found outside their region of origin. Some traditionally made cheeses now carry labels of *denominación de origen*, designation of origin. Best-known cheeses are Manchego, Cabrales, Burgos, Idiazàbal, Roncal and Villalón.

Cheeses may be fresh, semi-cured or well aged. Some aged cheeses are preserved in pots of olive oil. Fresh cheeses are soft and usually white. Keep them refrigerated and use within a week. Some of these are used in cooking, particularly for desserts. Manchego, or other semi-cured yellow cheese, can be used whenever a recipe calls for 'grated cheese'.

Serve aged cheeses as an aperitif with Sherry or at the end of the meal with red wine. *Requesón* is a type of fresh cheese, like a dry cottage cheese, served with fruit and honey as a dessert or made into cheesecake.

Chorizo. See sausages.

Cod, Dry Salt Codfish (*bacalao*). Except where otherwise noted in a recipe, dry salt cod is soaked in water for 24–36 hours, changing the water four or five times. After soaking, remove bones (and usually skin too) before proceeding with cooking (see page 110).

Flour (*harina*). Use plain flour, except where cake flour or bread flour is specified. Do not use self-raising flour.

Garlic (*ajo*). A favourite flavour in Spanish food. When used raw in salads, it is finely minced. When incorporated in sauces, the whole cloves of garlic are usually lightly fried, then mashed smooth. For sauté dishes (such as *pollo al ajillo,* chicken with garlic), either the coarsely chopped garlic has to be skimmed out before it burns, or else whole, unpeeled cloves of garlic, lightly smashed, are fried. The skin protects the garlic from burning.

Yet another treatment for garlic is roasting. **To roast garlic:** spear a whole head of garlic on a fork or grasp with tongs and turn it over a gas flame or put it under the grill, turning, until it is black and charred on all sides. Rub off the skin and peel the garlic cloves. Add them whole to stews or pulse dishes.

Ham (*jamón*). Spain has a very special ham, *jamón serrano*, which means 'mountain' ham, because it is frequently made in mountain regions where cold winters and hot summers contribute to the curing process. These hams are salt-cured, but not smoked, and served raw. Serrano ham, if made from the native Iberian pig, which is fed on acorns, is called *jamón ibérico* or *pata negra*, 'black hoof'. Ibérico ham is very expensive. Enjoy it, thinly sliced, as an aperitif.

Serrano ham, its fat and the bone are all used in cooked dishes as well. If serrano ham is not available, substitute Parma ham or unsmoked lean bacon or gammon.

Herbs, for cooking (*hierbas de cocina*). Fresh flat-leafed parsley (*perejil*) is used lavishly, chopped into salads, sprinkled over cooked foods before serving. Mint (*hierba buena*) is also used fresh in some soups and stews. Other herbs which play a part in Spanish cooking are bay leaf (*laurel*), celery (*apio*), wild fennel (*hinojo*), oregano (*oregano*), tarragon (*estragon*) and thyme (*tomillo*).

Dry herbs can be crumbled to a powder and added to the pot. Fresh herbs on the stalk can be tied with string into a herbal bouquet, which is removed before serving the food.

Lard (*manteca*). Rendered pig fat, pure white and soft, is used in some dishes for sautéing and for basting roast chicken and meat. If preferred, olive oil can be used instead. Lard is also popular for pastry making. For pastry dough, butter can be substituted.

Manteca colorada is lard coloured bright orange by the addition of paprika or the pulp of sweet peppers. It's served spread on bread or toast or used for frying eggs.

Leavening (*levadura*). Yeast (*levadura de pan*) is usually sold in fresh, cake form. Keep it refrigerated or in the freezer. Proof it in warm water before incorporating with flour and other ingredients. If dry yeast is substituted, use one tablespoon for 17 grams fresh pressed yeast. Also used in bread making is starter dough (*levadura de masa*), a piece of fermented dough from the previous baking. This can sometimes be purchased from a bakery. Baking powder (*levadura en polvo* or *polvo Royal*) and bicarbonate of soda (*bicarbonate sodico*) are used in some breads, fritter batters and cakes.

Morcilla. See sausages.

Mortar (*mortero* or, of brass, *almirez*). Before electric appliances such as blenders were available, the mortar was used for grinding whole spices, for crushing nuts to thicken sauces, for mashing tomatoes and garlic for gazpacho. It's still a handy tool. The brass or granite mortars are better than wood for pulverizing hard spices.

Nuts. Almonds (*almendras*), walnuts (*nueces*), hazelnuts (*avellanas*) and chestnuts (*castañas*) are much used in savoury dishes to thicken and enrich sauces. Usually the nuts are skinned, then sometimes toasted or fried, then finely ground or crushed.

To skin almonds: blanch in boiling water for one minute. Drain, cool and slip skins off.

To skin hazelnuts: spread them in an oven tin and toast in a medium oven for 12 minutes. Remove and wrap in a towel until cooled. Rub the nuts in the towel to remove skins.

To skin chestnuts: after peeling off shells, drop the chestnuts, which still have a thin brown skin, into boiling water for five minutes. Drain. Use a knife to scrape off the skin.

Almonds, hazelnuts and peanuts (*cacahuetes*) are also combined with honey and egg white to make nougat candy, *turrón*.

Oil, Olive oil (*aceite, aceite de oliva*). Spain produces more olive oil than any other country in the world. For more than two millennia it has been the preferred cooking fat. Olive oil is one of the few oils which can be consumed straight from the presses, without further refining and purification. Modern research has shown that olive oil, a mono-unsaturated fat, is also the healthiest of fats and oils, because it raises 'good' cholesterol levels and lowers 'bad' ones, and because it contains natural anti-oxidants.

All olive oils are equally 'light'. None contain cholesterol; all have the same calories as other vegetable oils. They do, however, vary considerably in flavour and colour. Some have fruity overtones, others are spicy or nutty. Some are green, others golden. Olive oil is essential to

Spanish cooking and, in the recipes in this book, oil always means olive oil.

Types of olive oil:

Extra virgin olive oil is the 'juice' extracted from olives which have been crushed and cold-pressed without the use of heat. The oil is filtered, but not refined in any way. Extra virgin oil cannot exceed 1 per cent of oleic acid. It is expensive, but the flavour is exquisite: use it in salad dressings and mayonnaise and exactly as you would use butter: brushed on toast, spooned over cooked fish, vegetables, potatoes, pasta.

Virgin olive oil is produced in the same way as the extra virgin, but contains up to 1.5 per cent oleic acid. It is likely to be somewhat stronger in flavour. This oil is ideal for fried foods: chips, fish, croquettes and fritters emerge from the bubbling oil crisp and golden. Foods fried in olive oil absorb less fat than foods fried in other oils and olive oil is more stable at high temperatures than other fats. Virgin oil is also perfect for sautéing as well as for salads.

Ordinary non-virgin olive oil, like most other vegetable oils, is the result of a refining process. The refined oil is then combined with a small percentage of virgin oil, which contributes flavour. It's less expensive than virgin oil, a good 'everyday' oil for salads, cooking, frying.

Olives (*aceitunas*). Seville Manzanilla green olives, whole or stuffed, are the best known

because they're widely exported in tins and jars. They are big, sweet and meaty with a fine texture. Another commercially prepared variety is the *gordal*, 'queen' olive, sometimes as fat as a small plum. It has a more sour taste and coarser texture than the Manzanilla.

Most prevalent in Spain are home-cured olives, *aceitunas aliñadas caseras*. These are usually cracked, but not stoned, slightly bitter, and flavoured with garlic, lemon, thyme, fennel and strips of red pepper, and kept in brine. They can be served as an aperitif, with a meal, or used in cooking.

Paella pan (*paella*). A shallow, two-handled pan of rolled steel used for cooking paella rice. It comes in various dimensions, from a small (26 cm/10¼ inches) one adequate for two or three servings up to those big enough to serve a party of 20. Large pans are unwieldy on a hob, are best used out-of-doors on a woodfire or on a special large gas ring. After use, scour the pan well and dry it thoroughly. Store in a dry, airy place.

Paprika (*pimentón*). Paprika is made from ground sweet red peppers. It sometimes comes in both mild and strong varieties. It is extensively used in Spanish cooking to give colour and flavour to soups and sauces. *Pimentón de la vera* is smoked paprika.

Peppers (*pimientos*). Several members of the capsicum pepper family are used in Spanish cooking: both red and green bell peppers; small pointy green peppers for frying; *piquillo* red peppers which are slightly piquant, prized for stuffing; dried sweet peppers, such as *ñora*, which is plum-sized; and *choricero*, long and skinny; hot chillies, *guindillas*, both fresh and dried.

To skin peppers: roast whole or halved peppers over a gas flame, under a grill or over a charcoal fire, turning them until blackened and charred on all sides. Wrap them in a towel or paper bag until cool enough to handle. Then peel off the charred skin and discard the stem and seeds. Tinned or bottled pimiento can be substituted.

Paprika can be substituted for dried sweet peppers.

Pulses, legumes (*legumbres secas*). Dry beans and lentils play an important part in the Spanish diet. Dried beans (*alubias, fabes, habichuelas*) are usually white, but pinto, red and black ones are also used. *Fabes* are big white beans, similar to butter beans, used for the Asturian bean dish, *fabada*. Chickpeas (*garbanzos*) are essential to the *cocido* or boiled dinner. Lentils (*lentejas*), brown, green and black, are used in various soups. Black-eyed peas (*chicharo, figüelo*) can be used interchangeably with beans.

Most pulses should be soaked overnight in ample water (lentils need not be soaked). Before cooking, drain the water and cover with fresh water. A pinch of bicarbonate of soda added to very hard water helps cook tender beans. Most beans cook in one hour. Chickpeas take two hours. A pressure cooker can be used.

Rice (*arroz*). Spanish rice is a medium-short grain variety, not long-grain pilaf-type rice. If Spanish rice is not available, use Italian *arborio* or risotto rice. Rice for paella or pudding is not washed before cooking. The usual cooking procedure for paella and other rice dishes is to add the rice to boiling liquid, allowing approximately double the volume of liquid to rice. Remove the rice from the heat when it is just barely tender. Let it rest ten minutes to finish cooking.

Saffron (*azafrán*). A very costly spice, because it takes the stigmas of 75,000 autumn-blooming crocuses to make 450 g (1 lb), saffron is grown in La Mancha and Murcia. Deep-orange coloured threads should first be pulverized in a mortar, then dissolved in a little liquid before adding to cooking rice, soup or sauce. Because it is expensive, artificial yellow colouring or paprika is frequently substituted for real saffron. Do not use turmeric as a substitute.

Salt-pork (*tocino*). Pigs' belly fat or fat back is preserved in salt, then cut into chunks to cook with soups and stews. If not available, either use unsmoked ham or bacon fat or omit it altogether.

Sausages (*embutidos*). A wide range of sausages is produced in Spain. The distinctive red *chorizo* is probably the best known, and is in many UK supermarkets. It is made of chopped or minced pork (and sometimes beef) with pork fat, macerated with sweet and hot paprika or the pulp from red peppers, plus pepper, garlic, oregano. *Chorizo* comes in two types: hard, aged sausage, which is sliced and served as cold cuts; and soft sausage, tied off in links, which is cooked with beans and chickpeas for thick soups. Soft *chorizo* is harder to find outside Spain, though a recipe appears on page 190.

Morcilla is black pudding, made from pigs' blood and seasoned with cinnamon, cloves and nutmeg. Some regional types may contain onion, anise, fennel, rice or pine nuts. Asturian *morcilla*, which goes into *fabada* beans, is smoked. *Morcilla* is usually stewed with pulses and vegetables. *Butifarra negra* is Catalan blood sausage.

Butifarra blanca is a white Catalan sausage made of minced pork and spices and cooked before curing.

Salchichón is a hard sausage similar to salami, lightly garlicky and studded with peppercorns. Skinny ones can be called *longaniza* or *fuet*. *Salchicha* is fresh pork sausage links, either plain or spicy. *Sobrasada* is a soft, spreadable sausage from Mallorca, flavoured similarly to *chorizo*. Use it as a spread for hot toast or serve with fried eggs. *Lomo embuchado* is cured pork loin in sausage casing.

Many of these sausages can be found outside Spain in specialist delicatessens or food departments of large stores.

Spices (*especias*). Spices most commonly used in Spanish cooking are aniseed (*matalahuga*), in many Christmas sweets; cinnamon (*canela*), on puddings and custards; cloves (*clavo de comer*), in stews; ground coriander (*cilantro*), in a spice blend for marinating meat; cumin (*comino*), in meat and poultry dishes or gazpacho; nutmeg (*nuez moscada*), for meatballs and minced meat stuffings; paprika (*pimentón*); pepper (*pimienta*); saffron (*azafrán*), with rice, fish, potatoes; sesame seeds (*ajonjolí*), with pastries. A mixture of spices for marinating meat to be skewered and grilled is *especia para pinchitos* and contains cumin, coriander, ginger, pepper, cayenne, and turmeric.

Spices should be purchased whole, in small quantities and freshly ground before using. They can be ground in a mortar or in an electric spice mill or coffee grinder. Cinnamon can be purchased already ground. Nutmeg is best if freshly grated.

Tomato, Tomato Sauce (*tomate, salsa de tomate*). One of the plants brought to Europe from the New World by Spanish explorers. Sweet, vine-ripened tomatoes are one of the glories of the Spanish summer. They go into salads, fresh tomato sauce and, of course, gazpacho. These are big, beef tomatoes – a medium-sized one weighs 180 g (more than 6 oz); a large one weighs in at a quarter of a kilo (more than half a pound). In the winter when good quality tomatoes are not available in the markets, substitute canned plum tomatoes, very well drained.

In recipes which call for tomato sauce, either use canned tomato sauce (in Spain it is called *tomate frito*, fried tomato sauce) or make it as follows.

Tomato sauce: Fry a small chopped onion and chopped garlic clove in 3 tbsp of olive oil until softened. Add 2 kg (4 lb 6 oz) tomatoes, which have been peeled and chopped (dip tomatoes in boiling water and skins slip off easily). Fry them on a high heat for several minutes. Then add 1 tsp salt, ¼ tsp ground cumin, ¼ tsp ground black pepper, bay leaf, a sprig of parsley and 100 ml (3 ½ fl oz) white wine, stock or water. Simmer, partially covered, stirring occasionally, for 45 minutes. Sieve the sauce, or purée it in a blender. Makes about 750 ml (1¼ pints) of sauce.

Vinegar *(vinagre)*. Use wine vinegar whenever vinegar is called for in these recipes. Speciality vinegars, such as the mellow Sherry vinegar from Jerez, add flavourful variations.

Wine *(vino)*. Wine is produced in almost every region of Spain (except for Asturias, where apple cider is drunk). Most are quite good, some are exceptional. Labels designate the origin, *denominación de origen* (D.O.), of the wines. Some of the best table wines come from the regions of the Rioja, Ribero del Duero, Rueda, Navarra, Rias Baixas-Galicia and Penedés-Cataluña. Red wine is *tinto*; white is *blanco*; rosé is *rosado*.

Wines meant to be drunk young and fresh are labelled with the year the wine was made, the *cosecha*. Wines aged a minimum of two years in wooden casks and bottles are labelled *crianza*. Red wines labelled *reserva* must be aged at least three years with one year in oak.
A *gran reserva* wine is aged even longer.

Sherry, made in the region of Jerez (Cádiz), and Montilla wine from Córdoba are both made in the *solera* process, which blends younger wines with aged wines. They are fortified wines, meaning they have a higher alcohol content than table wines. Sherry *fino* is dry and smooth, the perfect foil for Spanish tapa foods, shellfish, ham, nuts. Sweeter *oloroso* and cream Sherry, Pedro Ximenez and sweet Málaga muscatel make excellent dessert wines.

Cava, sparkling wine made by the Champagne method, comes mainly from the Penedés-Cataluña region.

In cooking, white wine and Sherry or Montilla are the most frequently used.

Note:

Throughout this book **flour** always means plain flour; **ham** is always Spanish salt-cured serrano; **oil** is olive oil unless otherwise noted, and **vinegar** is wine vinegar.

1

BREAKFAST

BREAKFAST

Breakfast happens twice in Spain. The worker, businessman or schoolchild has a first breakfast early, before leaving in the morning: bread or toast served with coffee with lots of milk and sugar, or cocoa with milk. People who do hard physical work might start the day with something more substantial: a garlic soup or thick porridge. In a custom left over from leaner times, a man might have a *copa* of strong anise brandy, *para matar el gusanillo* – to kill the little 'worm' of hunger that gnaws the insides. Schoolchildren and workers alike set off with a bag containing a second *desayuno*, to eat between 10 and 11 o'clock. The businessman or office worker probably slips out to the corner café. This second breakfast may be *café con leche*, coffee with milk, with a sweet roll or biscuits, *galletas*, dunked in the coffee, or *una tostada*. A *tostada* is much more than a thin slice of toasted bread; it's usually a small roll split lengthwise and toasted on a grill, sometimes rubbed with garlic and tomato, then served with a plate of olive oil for dipping. I have even seen country folk dip the garlic toast in plenty of oil, then place it in sweetened, milky coffee and eat it like soup.

The worker probably carries in his bag a *bocadillo*, a sandwich consisting of bread roll split and filled perhaps with *manteca*, paprika-flavoured lard, or sausage, canned tuna or maybe half a potato omelette. This repast is accompanied by coffee or a beer and may finish with a piece of fruit. Thus sustained, he can work until dinner at 2 o'clock.

Sunday breakfasts are more leisurely, with all the family at home. Papá might bring home *churros*, fritters, for the family to dunk in coffee or thick hot chocolate.

FRITTERS
CHURROS

Churros, fried strips of dough, are usually made by street vendors who set up cauldrons of oil in the early mornings near a bustling market place or at fiesta fairgrounds, where it's traditional to buy them at the end of a night of *alegría*. Ring-shaped *churros* might be strung on a loop of reed for carrying to the nearest café. Sprinkle the *churros* with sugar and dunk in coffee or thick hot chocolate.

250 ml (8 fl oz) water

5 tbsp olive oil

1 strip of lemon rind

½ tsp salt

200 g (7 oz) plain flour

deep oil for frying

caster sugar

Put the water in a pan with the oil, lemon rind and salt and bring to the boil. Remove the lemon rind. Add the salt to the flour, then add it to the pan all at once and beat vigorously with a wooden spoon, working it over a low heat for 1–2 minutes until it forms a ball. The mixture will be very stiff. Put it in a piping bag. Heat the oil to 185°C (365°F) (when a piece of dough is dropped in it should brown in 60 seconds). Force out long strips or rings of the batter into the hot oil, a few at a time. Fry for a few minutes until golden brown, then remove from the oil and drain. Sprinkle generously with sugar.

MAKES 30

DRINKING CHOCOLATE
CHOCOLATE A LA TAZA

200 g (7 oz) plain chocolate, chopped
4 tsp cornflour
1 litre (1¾ pints) milk and/or water
3 tbsp sugar
ground cinnamon (optional)

Place the chopped chocolate in a pan. Dissolve the cornflour in a little of the milk or water, then whisk into the remaining milk. Add to the chocolate with the sugar. Heat the mixture, whisking continually to keep it smooth as the chocolate melts. As it begins to boil, remove from heat and keep whisking for 1–2 minutes. Thin with a little more milk or water if preferred, and pour into cups. Dust with cinnamon if desired.

SERVES 4

MALLORCAN SWEET ROLLS
ENSAIMADAS

These rolls, made with *saim*, lard in the Catalan language, are one of the glories of the cooking of Mallorca. So popular are they, that they can now be bought all over Spain. Small ones are served for breakfast, with hot chocolate or coffee, while huge wheels are special for feast days. Then the *ensaimada* would be split in half and filled with whipped cream, a fruit preserve such as angel's hair, pastry cream, or, for Carnival, a layer of the soft Mallorcan sausage, *sobrasada*.

If possible, use hard-wheat bread flour for these rolls. Otherwise, use any plain white flour. The quantity needed varies with the type of flour. Do not be over-generous with the yeast, as these rolls stay fairly flat.

15 g (½ oz) fresh yeast or 2½ tsp dried yeast
270 ml (9½ fl oz) hand-hot water
215 g (7½ oz) sugar
900 g (2 lb) flour mixed with 1 tsp salt
4 small to medium eggs
5 tbsp oil (any cooking oil is suitable)
175 g (6 oz) lard (room temperature)
icing sugar

Place the yeast in a bowl and dissolve it in the warm water. Add 1 teaspoon of the sugar and 125 g (4¼ oz) of the flour. Beat the mixture. Cover with a dampened cloth and put in a warm, draught-free place until the mixture is bubbly and spongy, about 30 minutes. In a large bowl, beat the eggs with 3 tbsp of the cooking oil and the remaining sugar. Add the yeast sponge, then add 600 g (1 lb 5 oz) of the flour, beating it in gradually with a wooden spoon. Spread some of the remaining flour on a board and turn out the dough. Knead it, adding flour as necessary, until the dough is very smooth and elastic. Oil a bowl, place the ball of dough in it and turn to coat the dough with oil. Cover with a damp cloth and put in a

warm place to rise for 4 hours or at room temperature overnight. Before shaping the rolls, beat the lard until soft and creamy. Then punch the dough down, knead it into a ball and divide it in half. On a lightly floured board roll one half out to a rectangle approximately 25 × 50 cm (10 × 20 in). Spread it with half the lard. Starting on the short side of the rectangle, roll the dough into a log approximately 7 cm (3 in) thick. Pinch the seam together to seal the roll. Trim off the ends, then cut the roll crosswise into about 15 pieces of 1 cm (½ in). Place them, spaced apart, on a baking tray, brush with oil and cover with a damp cloth (or a box). Roll out the remaining dough and shape in the same manner. Use the bits of dough trimmed off the ends to roll into long cords. Starting at one end, wind each strip into a flat coil. Let the rolls rise in a warm place for 2–3 hours. Bake in a hot oven (190°C, 375°F, gas 5) for 8–10 minutes, until the rolls are golden on top. Remove and cover with a damp cloth and let them cool. Dust the tops with icing sugar.

MAKES 25

OUR DAILY BREAD

Ni mesa sin pan, ni mocita sin galán.

No table without bread, nor girl without a suitor.

No other single food is as important to the Spanish diet as bread, and this is as true today as it was centuries ago. In Roman times, Spain was known for the excellence of its wheat. Romans introduced methods of ploughing, reaping, winnowing and milling which changed very little until recently. They also perfected ovens and bread-making, and made a variety of leavened breads.

Country families traditionally grew their own wheat, threshing it on cobbled threshing floors with sleds pulled round and round by mules, and winnowing the grain by pitching it into the wind. They carried it to a local mill, paying the miller a percentage of the grain, and carried home the flour, with which the womenfolk made the family's bread.

In Moorish times it was customary for every household to make its own bread, mark it with the family insignia, and send it to the village baker to be baked, a custom which continued in many towns until the twentieth century. During the medieval era, Christians were prohibited by the Church from purchasing bread from Muslim or Jewish bakers, so the trade of *panadero*, baker, came to be a very Christian profession. Not always an honourable one, however: dozens of Spanish proverbs attest to the fact that, in the old days, you couldn't trust the miller or the baker not to give false weight!

'Twenty kilos at a time – enough bread to last a whole week,' says Ana. She is kneeling on the floor, in front of the hearth, where a big *olla*, soup pot, bubbles over a fire, her arms elbow-deep in a mass of dough which she is kneading in a *lebrillo*, a huge, earthenware bowl. Bread-making, which she learned from her mother, was part of the self-sufficient life of *campesinos*, country folk.

To the flour she adds starter dough, *masa de levadura*. This starter is simply some of the dough from the previous baking which is left to ferment. Some salt is added – a *puñado*, a little handful – and nothing else. No sugar, no fat, no milk. She makes a well in the centre of the heap of flour and her daughter pours in some water, heated in a blackened kettle near the coals. Ana starts kneading and the daughter stays close by and seems to know just when to add a little more water. The dough is worked for more than half an hour. It is strenuous work.

The two women begin shaping the loaves. Ana pulls free a big handful of dough, kneads it briefly and hands it to her daughter, who pats and shapes it quickly into a flattened circle, the typical *hogaza* or round loaf. The loaves are placed on top of a doubled cloth on a wooden table and kept covered, so as not to 'catch a cold'. When all the loaves are shaped they are 'put to sleep', tucked snugly in a folded blanket. The bread will be left to snooze about two hours. It doesn't quite double in bulk.

Meanwhile, Ana and her son start the fire in the bread oven which, typically, is situated separate from the house. Made of brick, the inside is vaulted to provide the best circulation of heat. A mortar of clay and lime holds the bricks together. Firewood such as olive, almond and grape prunings and wild brush such as gorse, furze and broom fuel the oven. As brittle twigs burn down, more are added. It takes nearly two hours for the wood to burn down to coals and ash. It is the heat retained in the bricks and clay which bakes the bread – or roasts meat or cooks a casserole.

The floor of the oven is raked clean of ash. The loaves are unwrapped from their blanket and, after a *benedición*, a blessing, Ana uses a long-handled paddle to slide the loaves on to the floor of the oven. Her son closes the air-inlet hole with a brick and the oven door with a sheet of metal.

The large, one-kilo loaves take an hour to bake. Using the paddle, the daughter pulls the loaves out one by one. Ana catches them in her apron, brushes off the ash, and places them again on the table. The bread is kept wrapped until partially cooled, to sweat out excess humidity. Properly baked and cooled, the bread keeps for a week or more. The crust becomes rock-hard, but the crumb is still edible. And this long before the advent of preservatives! Stored in a wooden chest, a wicker basket or a *talega*, linen bag, it lasts a family until the next baking. Traditionally, nothing is ever wasted – stale bread would be added to soup or soaked in water to thicken gazpacho and various sauces.

Ana lays out a shallow dish of olive oil and fetches a knife. She picks up a still warm loaf and, with the tip of the knife, makes the sign of the cross on it and kisses the bread. She cuts it into thick slices and hands them around. The bread is a deep golden colour with a thick, hard crust. Inside, the crumb is a little moist, very dense and fine-textured. And the fragrance: faintly smoky, with a subtle, sour-sweet yeasty aroma and the soul-satisfying smell of toasted grain. Dipped in olive oil, this is filling stuff, indeed, the staff of life.

De los olores, el pan; de los sabores, la sal.

For aroma, bread; for flavour, salt.

Until not so many years ago, bread was made fresh every day – seven days a week, 364 days a year – only New Year's Day was a *panadero's* day off! While bakers now take Sundays and holidays off, everywhere in Spain bread is still made locally: wonderful, fresh, crusty, sustaining stuff. Mainly it is white wheat bread, though some regions, such as Menorca, enjoy wholewheat breads. In northern Spain, where wheat doesn't thrive, the Galicians make huge wheels of maize and rye bread. Shepherds in La Mancha traditionally made a hard, unleavened bread, *torta*, used as plate, spoon and thickener for local stews. While today's bakers have frequently converted to electric or gas-fuelled ovens, bread baked in an *horno de leña*, wood-fired oven, is highly prized.

From basic bread derive many variations. In Andalusia, extra bread dough is made into *torta de aceite*, sweet, anise-flavoured flat-breads, enjoyed for breakfast or snacks. In the Levante, the *coca*, a Spanish version of pizza, is a favourite snack. In Galicia, the dough is baked into *empanadas*, a thick pie filled with anything from pork loin to eel, rabbit to sardines (see chapter on Snacks and Sandwiches for some of these recipes). From Mallorca comes one of Spain's favourite breakfast breads: *ensaimada*, a sweet roll enriched with lard.

COUNTRY BREAD
PAN DE CAMPO

The best flour for bread-making is a hard-wheat (high gluten), unbleached flour. If stoneground, so much the better. Buy it fresh and keep it refrigerated. In Spain, you can buy *harina para pan*, bread flour, at any bakery. Elsewhere, if not available in supermarkets, check a health-food shop. Otherwise, use plain (not self-raising) flour.

If you can, buy 'starter dough', a natural yeast, from a local bread bakery. Otherwise, start with fresh, pressed yeast (this can be kept in the refrigerator for several weeks, or frozen for several months).

Add as little water as possible to the dough. Knead it for 20–30 minutes. Shape the loaves and let them rise only once. One of the most typical country loaves is the *hogaza*, a big, round bread.

In country ovens, bread is baked on the floor of the oven. In my home oven, I place loaves in earthenware casseroles or on clay tiles.

40 g (1½ oz) fresh yeast or 2 tbsp dried yeast
about 250 ml (8 fl oz) hand-hot water
1 kg (2 lb 3 oz) bread flour
4 tsp salt

Dissolve the yeast in the warm water and allow to stand for 10 minutes. Combine the flour and salt in a large bowl. Make a well in the centre and add the yeast mixture. Work the dough, adding more water as needed, to make a very stiff dough. Knead it (in the bowl or on a board) for 20–30 minutes, until the dough is very smooth and elastic. Take 1 kg (2 lb 3 oz) of dough and roll it into a ball. Flatten and shape into a round about 23 cm (9 inches) across. Use the remaining dough to make small *bollos*, buns, or one *viena*, an oval-shaped loaf, slashed diagonally, or use it to make Sweet Oil Breads (see page 28). Cover the loaves with a towel and place in a warm place to rise for 1½–2 hours.

Pre-heat the oven to 230°C (450°F, gas 8). Place the bread in the oven, then reduce oven temperature to 200°C (400°F, gas 6). The 1 kg (2 lb 3 oz) loaf needs about 1¼ hours to bake, but depends on oven temperature.

MAKES 1 × 1 KG (2 LB 3 OZ) LOAF
PLUS 1 SMALL LOAF OR BUNS

Sweet Oil Breads
Tortas de Aceite

These anise-scented breads are delicious at breakfast, with afternoon tea or with sweet wine. The dough can also be used to make *hornazos*, *toñas* or *mones*, little buns with an egg baked in the centre. At Easter time, these are given by godparents to their godchild. The identical roll with egg is also given to children of Sephardic Jewish families for the early spring festival of Purim.

120 ml (4 fl oz) olive oil

1 strip of orange rind

1 tbsp aniseed

½ tsp bicarbonate of soda

500 g (1 lb 2 oz) bread dough (see page 27)

110 g (4 oz) sugar

about 55 g (2 oz) flour

1 egg, beaten

12 almonds, blanched and skinned

Heat the oil in a small frying pan with the orange rind until the rind just browns. Remove from heat and skim out the rind. Add the aniseed to the hot oil; leave it to cool. Add the bicarbonate of soda. Put the bread dough in a bowl and knead the flavoured oil into it little by little, until it has all been absorbed. Then add all but 2 tbsp of the sugar. Cover the bowl with a damp cloth and put in a warm place to rise for about 2 hours until dough has doubled in bulk.

Preheat the oven to 200°C (400°F, gas 6). Punch down the dough. Oil baking sheets and sprinkle with flour or line with baking parchment. Take a ball of dough about the size of an egg and knead it briefly on a floured board. Pat each ball of dough into a round, then flatten it very thinly on the baking sheet to 14 cm (5½ inches) in diameter. Brush the tops with beaten egg, sprinkle with remaining sugar and press an almond in the centre of each. Bake immediately in the hot oven for about 15 minutes until golden.

To make Easter buns, take a slightly larger piece of dough (about 100 g, 3½ oz), flatten it slightly and pull it apart from the middle to make a small hole. Tuck a hard-boiled egg, shell and all (tinted yellow, if desired) into the hollow. Roll thin cords of the dough and cross them over the top of the egg, pinching the cords into the dough on the bottom of the bun. Let the buns rise, covered, for about 30 minutes. Paint them with beaten egg and bake in a hot oven for about 15 minutes until golden.

Makes 12

2

DINNER AT MIDDAY

DINNER AT MIDDAY

Not so many years ago it was common to see, every day at midday, women with parasols walking along the country lanes carrying lunch to their husbands working in the fields. Lunch, though, is not the right word. This was *la comida*, dinner. Packed in carrying tins were a first course of soup, still hot from the big *olla*, a main course of meat, sausage, vegetables and chickpeas, a whole loaf of fresh bread and a piece of fruit. While the day's rhythm has picked up in modern times, Spain still sticks to its ancient pace of meal hours – the principal meal of the day, dinner, is served between 1 and 3 o'clock in the afternoon, usually followed by a siesta hour. To accommodate these old patterns most shops, businesses and offices close between 2 and 4 pm in the afternoon.

Because it is the principal meal of the day, the *comida* always consists of at least two courses, sometimes three, plus dessert, which is normally fruit. The first course might be a salad, soup, vegetable or egg dish; the main course, fish, poultry or meat with potatoes. It's not unusual to see working men polish off a good-sized bowl of lentils or beans with sausages and then a pork steak with a heap of chips. More extravagant dinners would start with *entremeses*, a plate of cold cuts, salads, olives and the like, followed by a fish or shellfish entrée and then a meat course, with both pudding and fruit.

First Course

Salads

La ensalada, bien salada, poco vinagre y bien aceitada.

Salad: well salted, little vinegar, plenty of oil.

At the family table and amongst friends, salad, heaped on a big platter, is set in the centre of the table and everyone eats from the same dish. When finished, chunks of bread are used to mop up the delicious 'broth' at the bottom of the dish. More salads are to be found in the chapter devoted to *tapas*. These are served as starter or supper dish.

MIXED SALAD
ENSALADA MIXTA

Serve cruets of good olive oil and wine vinegar with the salad and dress it at the table.

2 heads leafy lettuce

1–2 tomatoes (not too ripe)

½ cucumber, peeled and sliced

1 small onion

200 g (7 oz) tinned tuna, drained

6 spears tinned white asparagus, drained

2 hard-boiled eggs, quartered

12 olives

salt and pepper

extra virgin olive oil

vinegar

Wash the lettuce and drain it. Tear the leaves into bite-sized pieces and spread them across a large platter. Cut the tomatoes into wedges and arrange on top with the sliced cucumber. Slice the onion thinly from stem to root and arrange on top. Lay chunks of tuna over all the salad and top with asparagus, quartered eggs and olives. At the table, sprinkle with salt and pepper and drizzle liberally with oil and lightly with vinegar. There's no need to toss the salad. Serve with bread.

SERVES 6

ANDALUSIAN SALAD
ENSALADA ANDALUZA

This salad dressing is much like a *gazpacho*, without the bread thickening. It's delicious with a salad of cooked vegetables, such as potatoes, green beans, cauliflower, artichokes, as well as Batavian endive, or escarole. A Catalan version, *xato*, includes ground hazelnuts and almonds in the dressing and is made with curly endive and artichokes.

FOR THE DRESSING

450 g (1 lb) ripe tomatoes, peeled and seeded

2 garlic cloves

2 tsp paprika

1 tsp ground cumin

1 tsp salt

120 ml (4 fl oz) olive oil

120 ml (4 fl oz) wine vinegar

FOR THE SALAD

2 heads Batavian endive or lettuce

2 hard-boiled eggs, sliced

2 spring onions, sliced

100 g (3½ oz) serrano ham, thinly sliced and cut into strips

55 g (2 oz) green or black olives

In a blender or processor, purée the peeled tomatoes, garlic, paprika, cumin and salt. With the motor running, add the oil and vinegar. Tear the endive or lettuce into pieces and toss with some of the dressing. Arrange on a platter and top with the eggs, onions, strips of ham and olives. Spoon the remaining dressing over the salad.

SERVES 8

SIERRA SALAD
ENSALADA DE LA SERRANÍA

Garnished with sweet-sour pomegranate pips, this salad is a lovely autumnal dish. Served at room temperature, it is a fine accompaniment to pork or game. But try it any time of the year with a little chopped apple instead of the pomegranate.

2 ñoras (dried sweet pepper) or 1 tbsp
    paprika

5 tbsp boiling water

1 small cabbage or cauliflower

½ tsp cumin seed

2 tbsp olive oil

2 garlic cloves

1 slice bread

10 peppercorns

5 tbsp wine vinegar

140 g (5 oz) shelled walnuts, coarsely
    chopped

seeds from 1–2 pomegranates

Soak the *ñoras* in the boiling water for 20 minutes (or mix the paprika to a paste with a little water). Cut the cabbage into fine shreds or cut the cauliflower into small florets. Blanch the cabbage in boiling water for about 5 minutes just until wilted, or cook the cauliflower until crisp-tender. Drain and refresh in cold water, then drain again. In a frying pan, toast the cumin seed until fragrant, then remove from the pan. Heat the oil in the pan and fry the garlic and slice of bread until golden. Remove. Scoop out the flesh from the *ñoras*. Combine the *ñora* flesh or paprika paste in a mortar with the peppercorns, cumin seed, garlic and bread. Grind to a paste, adding the vinegar and enough water from soaking the peppers to make a smooth dressing.

Immediately before serving, combine the blanched cabbage or cauliflower with the dressing, chopped walnuts and pomegranate seeds.

SERVES 6–8

PARTRIDGE SALAD
ENSALADA DE PERDIZ

Siempre perdiz, hasta el rey cansó, y un gazpacho apetició.

Even the king got tired of partridge every day, and craved gazpacho.

So plentiful are partridge in parts of Jaén and La Mancha that the meat is served chopped in salad. Either use birds cooked *en escabeche* (see page 182) or poach them in water with a little oil, salt, bay leaf, onion and a little vinegar. The salad can also be made using turkey.

2 partridges, cooked (or turkey)

2 tomatoes, finely chopped

2 spring onions, chopped

1 garlic clove, crushed

4 tbsp mayonnaise

vinegar

salt and pepper

1–2 heads leafy lettuce, separated into leaves

Remove and discard the skin and bones from the partridges and chop the meat. Combine it with the chopped tomatoes and onions. Combine the garlic, mayonnaise and a little of the reserved cooking liquid with vinegar to taste to make a dressing, seasoning it with salt and pepper. Arrange a bed of lettuce on a platter or on individual salad plates. Top with the partridge salad and spoon over the dressing.

SERVES 8

MURCIA SALAD
MOJETE

Murcia, in eastern Spain, is a market garden, the source of fine peppers and tomatoes. This salad can be served as a supper dish, with lots of bread for sopping up the juices – which is why it is called *mojete*, or 'soak'. In springtime, wild greens, blanched in boiling water, are gathered for the salad and *ajos tiernos*, fresh garlic shoots, would be used. In winter, tinned tomatoes can be substituted.

1 kg (2 lb 3 oz) ripe tomatoes, chopped

1 onion, chopped

1 green or red pepper, roasted and skinned (see page 16) or 1 tin pimientos

2 garlic cloves, crushed

55 g (2 oz) black olives

3 tbsp olive oil

1 tsp salt

200 g (7 oz) tinned sardines or tuna, drained

lemon juice

Combine the chopped tomatoes and onion. Chop the roasted and skinned pepper and add to the tomatoes with the garlic, olives, oil and salt. Arrange the salad on a platter and top with pieces of sardine or tuna. Squeeze a little lemon juice over the top. Serve with bread.

SERVES 6

Summer Salad from Jaén
Pipirrana Jienense

In southern Spain, where summers are hot indeed, this fresh salad of chopped tomatoes and peppers is often served as a first course or a light supper dish, with bread to accompany it. In the Balearic Islands, a very similar salad, *trempó*, without the ham and eggs, has a little chopped mint added and is garnished with quartered ripe figs and served with bread for dipping.

1 kg (2 lb 3 oz) medium tomatoes, chopped

1 small onion, chopped

200 g (7 oz) green peppers, chopped

1 garlic clove, finely chopped

1 tsp salt

1 tbsp chopped parsley

2 hard-boiled eggs

6 tbsp olive oil

3 tbsp vinegar

diced ham

Combine the tomatoes, onion and peppers in a bowl. Add the garlic, salt and parsley. Separate the egg yolks from the whites and chop the whites into the salad. Mash the yolks in a small bowl, then beat in the oil a little at a time, then beat in the vinegar. Add the dressing to the salad and toss lightly. Serve garnished with ham.

Serves 6

CATALAN SALAD
AMANIDA

1 head Batavian endive

3 stalks celery, diced

6 spring onions, chopped

100 g (3½ oz) serrano ham, diced

1 small tin anchovies, rinsed and drained

120 ml (4 fl oz) mayonnaise

1 garlic clove, crushed

1 tbsp wine vinegar

salt

2 hard-boiled eggs

150 g (5¼ oz) *butifarra*, white Catalan
    sausage, coarsely chopped

Cut the endive into bite-sized pieces and place in a salad bowl. Add the celery, spring onions and ham. Mince the anchovies and add to the salad. In a bowl mix the mayonnaise with the garlic, vinegar and salt. Toss the dressing with the salad and garnish with sliced egg and pieces of sausage.

SERVES 6

ROASTED PEPPER SALAD
ENSALADA DE PIMIENTOS ASADOS

Mejor pan y pimiento y dormir con un buen mozo, que no comer chocolate con un viejo pegajoso.

Better bread and peppers and sleep with a good lad than to eat chocolate with an old creep.

Red peppers are incredibly sweet, and green ones just slightly bitter, so they make a good combination. While often served as a starter, this salad is also a *tapa* and a side dish, especially good with fried or grilled fish.

1 kg (2 lb 3 oz) red and green peppers
2 garlic cloves, minced
½ tsp salt
3 tbsp olive oil
3 tbsp wine vinegar
2 tbsp chopped parsley

Traditionally, the peppers would be roasted in the embers of the cooking fire or turned over a gas flame. Otherwise remove stems and seeds, cut the peppers in half lengthwise and flatten them. Place on a grill pan in a single layer and place skin-side up under a hot grill until the skin is charred and the peppers soft. Remove and wrap in a tea towel until cool enough to handle. Peel the skin from the peppers and tear them into strips, saving all the juice. Put in a bowl and add the garlic, salt, oil, vinegar and parsley. Toss lightly. Serve at room temperature.

SERVES 6

GAZPACHO SOUPS

De gazpacho no hay empacho.

No such thing as too much gazpacho.

Halfway between salad and soup, *gazpacho* fills a unique category in Spanish cookery. It belongs to Andalusia, where labourers in vineyards, olive plantations, citrus groves, wheat fields or cork forests received rations of bread and oil for their meals. Bread soaked in water made a simple gruel, to which was added oil, garlic and salt for flavour, and whatever fresh vegetables were available – tomatoes, peppers and cucumbers in the summer –

everything pounded together in a mortar or *dornillo*, a large wooden bowl. Gazpacho provided nourishment, quenched the thirst, and sustained a body working in the hot sun. Although today it is speedily made in a blender, gazpacho hasn't changed much from its peasant roots. It is still made without cooking. It is still served, day in and day out, in Andalusian homes, for the midday meal, for the afternoon *merienda* or for supper.

Andalusian Gazpacho
Gazpacho Andaluz

Tomatoes are one of the summer-time glories of the Spanish *huerta*, vegetable garden. Vine-ripened, they are wonderfully fragrant and sweet. Spanish housewives prefer the solid, slightly underripe tomatoes for chunking into salads, but for gazpacho, the ripe, juicy ones are best. The bread must be 'real' white bread, Spanish, French or Italian-style loaf, not packaged bread. The oil, of course, only the 'juice of the olive'.

In restaurants gazpacho is usually accompanied by additional chopped tomatoes, onions, peppers, cucumbers and breadcrumbs. Each diner spoons some into their bowl. At home, other typical garnishes are chopped eggs, diced apples or melon, grapes, mint, olives, ham, figs, raisins, peanuts. Gazpacho can also be served in a drinking glass, with no garnish. If there is no time to chill the gazpacho before serving, add ice cubes in place of water in the final stages.

75 g (3 oz) bread, crusts removed

1 kg (2 lb 3 oz) ripe tomatoes

3 garlic cloves

2 tsp salt

¼ tsp ground cumin

6 tbsp olive oil

5 tbsp wine vinegar

about 300 ml (½ pint) water

FOR THE GARNISH

100 g (3½ oz) green peppers, finely chopped

100 g (3½ oz) cucumber, peeled and finely chopped

1 small onion, finely chopped

1 small tomato, finely chopped

2 slices bread, toasted and diced

Put the bread to soak in enough water to cover for 15 minutes. Squeeze out excess water and put the bread in a blender or processor. Peel the tomatoes, cut them into chunks and add to the blender with the garlic, salt and cumin. Process until puréed. With the motor running, add the oil in a slow stream, then add the vinegar. The mixture will thicken and change colour as the oil emulsifies. Add a little of the water and transfer to a serving bowl. You can rub the gazpacho through a sieve for a finer texture. Stir in water to the desired consistency; it should be neither thick nor thin. Chill until serving time. Place the chopped peppers, cucumber, onion, tomato and breadcrumbs in small bowls or a divided dish and serve as accompaniments.

SERVES 6

GAZPACHO CREAM
SALMOREJO CORDOBES

This is essentially gazpacho without the water. In Córdoba and Seville it is served in individual earthenware ramekins, topped with ham and chopped egg, with a spoon and bread for dipping. It makes an excellent dip for raw vegetables – carrot sticks, red pepper strips, celery.

450 g (1 lb) stale bread, crusts removed

600 g (1 lb 5 oz) tomatoes, peeled
    and chopped

55 g (2 oz) green peppers

3 garlic cloves

1 tsp salt

2 eggs

120 ml (4 fl oz) extra virgin olive oil

4 tbsp wine vinegar

100 g (4 oz) serrano ham, cut in strips

2 hard-boiled eggs or 6 hard-boiled
    quail eggs

Soak the bread in enough water to cover for 15 minutes. Squeeze it out. Put in blender or processor with the tomatoes, pepper and garlic. Process until smooth. Then add the salt and eggs. With the motor running, add the oil in a slow stream until it is incorporated. Blend in the vinegar. Serve the cream smoothed into soup plates or a wide dish, topped with strips of ham and sliced eggs.

SERVES 6

White Garlic Soup with Grapes
Ajo Blanco con Uvas

Like a gazpacho without tomatoes, this refreshing soup certainly existed as a hot-weather antidote way back in Moorish times. If the combination of garlic and grapes seems unusual, I can only urge you to try it, for it's wonderful.

200 g (7 oz) stale bread, crusts removed

100 g (3½ oz) almonds, blanched and skinned

3 garlic cloves

150 ml (¼ pint) extra virgin olive oil

5 tbsp wine vinegar

2 tsp salt

1 litre (1¾ pints) water

200 g (7 oz) muscatel grapes, seeded

Soak the bread in water until softened, squeeze it out and put in a blender or processor with the almonds and garlic. Blend to a smooth paste, adding a little water, if necessary. With the motor running, add the oil in a slow stream, then the vinegar and salt. Beat in some of the water, then pour the mixture into a tureen, wooden bowl or pitcher and add the remaining water. Taste for seasoning, adding more salt or vinegar if needed. The soup should be fairly tangy. Serve immediately or chill the soup. Stir before serving into bowls garnished with grapes.

Serves 6

TOASTED GAZPACHO
GAZPACHO TOSTADO

This is a winter gazpacho, served warm or room temperature. If Seville oranges are not available, use the juice of a sweet orange.

450 g (1 lb) stale bread, crusts removed

1 litre (1¾ pints) water

1 tomato

1 tinned red pimiento, puréed or mashed

2 tsp salt

2 garlic cloves

2 tsp paprika

6 tbsp olive oil

4 tbsp sour (Seville) orange juice or 2 tbsp orange juice and 2 tbsp wine vinegar

Slice the bread thinly and toast it. Break it into bits and put in a tureen. Put the water in a pan and bring to the boil. Drop in the tomato for 1 minute, then remove. Skin the tomato and mash it with the red pimiento, salt, garlic and paprika. Stir in the oil. Add this mixture to the boiling water with the orange juice or juice and vinegar, then remove from the heat. Pour the water over the bread in the tureen. Cover and leave to stand until the bread has soaked up all the water.

SERVES 6

SOUP

Sopa comes from *sopas*, bread used to soak up liquid (just as in English, soup derives from sop). Many simple peasant soups and gazpachos are just that – bread soaked in liquid. Spanish garlic soup, a soul-satisfying winter dish, is the best example. While any soup is better if made with a good stock (made by simmering bones of meat or fish with herbs, onion and carrot), Spanish housewives rarely go to the trouble. The basic starting point for many soups is the *caldo*, broth, from the *cocido*, boiled meat dish. Rich with the flavours of ham and chicken, it's also served on its own in little cups at tapa bars.

Soup often precedes the main course for the midday dinner, but it's also served as the principal dish for supper (though not the ones with pulses, considered too heavy at night). Before refrigeration, the evening meal usually recycled leftovers from midday, so dinner's fried fish turned up in the evening's fish soup.

BROTH WITH CHOPPED HAM
SOPA DE PICADILLO

Because this soup reputedly has great restorative powers, it is traditionally consumed after a night of partying, such as New Year's Eve or at a bachelor's party before a wedding. It's made with leftover broth from the *cocido* or *puchero*, the meal-in-a-pot. For a 'quickie' method, boil any good chicken broth with a ham bone or piece of bacon for 20 minutes, then strain. *Añejo* is the name for an old ham bone.

FOR THE BROTH

> **30 g (1 oz) salt pork or unsmoked bacon**
>
> **1 piece of ham bone**
>
> **1 meaty beef bone or 100 g (3½ oz) of stewing beef**
>
> **chicken carcass or piece of boiling fowl**
>
> **1 carrot**
>
> **1 turnip**
>
> **1 onion**
>
> **1 stalk celery**
>
> **2 bay leaves**
>
> **2.5 litres (4½ pints) water**
>
> **1 tbsp salt**
>
> **10 peppercorns**

FOR THE GARNISH

> **3 tbsp olive oil**
>
> **100 g (3½ oz) bread, diced**
>
> **100 g (3½ oz) serrano ham, chopped**
>
> **2 hard-boiled eggs, chopped**
>
> **4 tbsp dry Sherry**
>
> **sprigs of mint**

Into a large soup pot, put the salt pork or bacon, ham bone, beef bone or stewing beef, chicken, carrot, turnip, onion, celery, bay leaves and water. Bring to the boil, then skim off any froth. Add salt and pepper and simmer the stock, partially covered, for 2 hours. Strain it into a clean pot. (If desired, the broth can be refrigerated overnight, then any solidified fat removed from the top.) Heat the oil in a small pan and fry the bread until crisp. Heat the soup. Immediately before serving the soup, add the chopped ham, chopped eggs, Sherry and fried bread. Serve each bowl of soup with a sprig of mint.

Variations: Chopped and fried chicken livers can be added to the soup with the ham. Two egg yolks can be mixed with the Sherry and added to the soup (any eggs inside the hen, resembling eggs' yolks without shells, are usually poached whole in the broth).

SERVES 6

BROTH
CALDILLO

2 partridges or 1 chicken
    (about 1.5 kg, 3¼ lb)

2.5 litres (4½ pints) water

2 tsp salt

1 large onion, peeled and quartered

10 garlic cloves, peeled

1 bay leaf

¼ tsp thyme

2 hard-boiled eggs

salt and pepper

2 tbsp vinegar, preferably Sherry vinegar

3 tbsp olive oil

1 tin red pimientos, chopped (90 g/3 oz)

1 tbsp chopped parsley

Clean the partridges or chicken and put to cook in the water with the salt, onion, garlic, bay leaf and thyme. Skim off any froth when the water boils, then simmer for 1 hour, partially covered, or until the birds are very tender. Strain and reserve the broth. Remove the bones and skin and dice the meat. Mash the egg yolks with the salt and pepper, vinegar and oil and whisk into the broth. Add the finely chopped egg whites, chopped pimiento, parsley and reserved meat. Add additional vinegar to sharpen the flavour, if desired.

SERVES 6

Egg Soup

Gazpachuelo

This is sometimes called *sopa de duelo*, a soup eaten at a wake, because it can be quickly prepared. Though simple, it is delicious. There is also another version, much more luxurious, made with prawns, fish, ham and Sherry.

750 g (1 lb 10 oz) potatoes, peeled
    and diced

2 litres (3½ pints) water

1 tbsp salt

2 eggs

350 ml (12 fl oz) olive oil

4 tbsp lemon juice

In a soup pot, cook the diced potatoes in the water with the salt until the potatoes are tender. Put the eggs in a blender or processor and, with the motor running, very slowly add the oil until the sauce is emulsified and thick. Then beat in the lemon juice. Very slowly beat 1 cup of the hot liquid into the sauce, then whisk the sauce into the hot soup. Do not boil.

SERVES 6

Savoury Almond Soup

Sopa de Almendras

A sweet version of almond soup, with cinnamon, is served on Christmas Eve in many homes in Castille. This is a soup from Granada, hardly changed since the Moors lived in the Alhambra, their sumptuous palace. Typically it is served in the autumn, after the almonds have been gathered.

3 tbsp olive oil

200 g (7 oz) almonds, blanched and skinned

2 garlic cloves

100 g (3½ oz) bread, diced

10 peppercorns

¼ tsp ground cumin

¼ tsp saffron

salt

1.5 litres (2½ pints) chicken stock

1 tsp wine vinegar

chopped parsley

Heat the oil in a large soup pan and in it brown the almonds, garlic and bread. Skim them out when golden, saving a few of the croûtons of bread for garnish, and grind in a mortar, blender or processor. Crush the peppercorns, cumin and saffron in a mortar and add to the almond mixture with salt to taste. Add a little of the stock and the vinegar. Heat the remaining stock in the pan, stir in the puréed almond mixture and bring to the boil. Simmer for 15 minutes, then serve hot, garnished with chopped parsley and the reserved croûtons.

SERVES 6

MALLORCAN 'DRY' SOUP WITH CABBAGE
SOPAS MALLORQUINAS

For centuries this has been the mainstay of the Mallorcan peasant diet, eaten at dawn, at midday, at supper, sometimes cooked in the field in a pot resting on three stones over a fire. The soup would be served from a deep bowl, everyone helping themselves. It's delicious and very nourishing. Slice leftover bread, then let it dry for two days.

6 tbsp olive oil

2 leeks, chopped

1 onion, chopped

100 g (3½ oz) green peppers, chopped

2 tomatoes, peeled and chopped

3 garlic cloves, chopped

a few red pepper flakes (optional)

2 tbsp chopped parsley

1 tbsp paprika

1 bay leaf, crumbled

1 medium-sized cabbage, chopped

1 tbsp salt

1.5 litres (2½ pints) boiling water (approximately)

450 g (1 lb) stale wholewheat bread, sliced

Heat the oil in a large pan and sauté the chopped leeks, onion and green peppers until soft. Add the tomatoes and garlic and fry a few minutes more, then add the red pepper flakes, parsley, paprika, bay leaf and chopped cabbage. Season with salt, pour over half the water, cover and simmer until the vegetables are tender. In a large *cazuela*, casserole, layer the bread and vegetables with their liquid. Add enough more water barely to cover the ingredients. Cover the *cazuela* and leave to stand for about 15 minutes until the liquid is absorbed. Serve warm or cold.

SERVES 6

CANARY ISLANDS 'SCALDED' SOUP
ESCALDÓN

The Spanish *conquistadores* used the Canary Islands as a jumping-off point for the New World. There they found a simple people, whose diet consisted of barley, goats' meat, milk and fish. The barley was first toasted, then ground to a coarse meal, *gofio*, now more usually made of maize. Kneaded with water in a goat skin, this 'porridge' was the basis of the everyday diet. Flour may be toasted in the oven (180°C, 350°F, gas 4) for 30 minutes, stirring frequently, or in a heavy pan over low heat, stirring constantly.

250 g (9 oz) *gofio* or maize or wholewheat flour, toasted in an oven

1 litre (1¾ pints) meat stock or water

140 g (5 oz) salt pork or bacon, diced

1 onion, chopped

1 tomato, peeled and chopped

a few red pepper flakes

3 garlic cloves, crushed

½ tsp chopped thyme

1 tsp paprika

1 tbsp salt

Put the toasted flour in a large bowl, breaking up any lumps. In the stock or water, boil the diced salt pork or bacon, onion, tomato, red pepper flakes, garlic, thyme, paprika and salt until the onion is soft. Gradually pour the boiling liquid into the flour, working it with a wooden spoon to keep it very smooth. When all of the liquid has been absorbed, serve the *gofio* with the following sauce.

SERVES 4–6

CANARY ISLAND GREEN SAUCE
MOJO VERDE

3–4 fresh or bottled green chilli peppers

10 garlic cloves

1 tsp ground cumin

3 tbsp chopped parsley

1 tbsp coriander leaves

2 tbsp olive oil

2 tbsp wine vinegar

1 tsp salt

water

Put all the ingredients except the water in a mortar, blender or processor and process until you have a smooth sauce. Thin it with water to taste. The sauce keeps, tightly covered and refrigerated, for a long time. You can also serve it with boiled or grilled fish.

Serves 4–6

GALICIAN CHESTNUT SOUP
SOPA DE CASTAÑAS

Chestnuts were basic to the Galician diet until disease wiped out vast stands of chestnut trees at the end of the 18th century, causing widespread famine. Eventually, potatoes replaced chestnuts as sturdy, daily fare, but chestnuts are still widely used.

450 g (1 lb) fresh chestnuts (or 300 g/10½ oz tinned, without sugar)

2 litres (3½ pints) water

1 tbsp salt

1 onion

1 garlic clove

100 g (3½ oz) serrano ham

100 g (3½ oz) salt pork

3 tbsp olive oil

3 tbsp chopped onion

3 tbsp wine vinegar or lemon juice

100 g (3½ oz) bread, thinly sliced and toasted

Shell the chestnuts. Boil them in a small quantity of the water for 15 minutes. Drain and peel off the inner brown skins and cut them in half. Return to the pan with the remaining water, salt, onion, garlic, ham and salt pork. If using tinned chestnuts, place them in the pan. Bring to the boil and simmer for 2 hours, partially covered, until very well cooked. In a frying pan, heat the oil and sauté the chopped onion until soft. Add the vinegar or lemon juice and stir it into the soup. Arrange the sliced bread in a *cazuela* or in individual soup bowls. Ladle the boiling soup over it.

Serves 6

GARLIC SOUP
SOPA DE AJO

A Spanish classic, ever so heart-warming on a blustery winter's day, this soup has many variations. In the Balearic Islands, *oliaigua*, literally garlic water, contains tomatoes and green peppers; in Galicia, it's made with the local rye bread and, made with eggs, is traditional for newlyweds; in Andalusia, *maimones* is said to be the perfect food for weaning a baby. This is the Madrid version.

6 tbsp olive oil

6 garlic cloves, coarsely chopped

300 g (10½ oz) bread, cubed

1 tsp paprika

1.75 litres (3 pints) boiling water or broth

2 tsp salt

4 eggs

chopped parsley

Heat the oil in a soup pot or *cazuela* and add the chopped garlic and bread cubes. Fry until lightly golden, then stir in the paprika. Immediately add the boiling water or broth and salt. Cover and simmer gently for 5–10 minutes. The bread should almost dissolve in the broth. Place the soup in four individual earthenware bowls and add one egg per bowl. Poach the eggs in the soup (in the oven or on the hob) until the whites are just set, but the yolks still liquid. Serve with a garnish of chopped parsley.

SERVES 4

LEEK SOUP
PURRUSALDA

8 leeks (about 750 g/1 lb 10 oz)

3 tbsp olive oil

2 garlic cloves

450 g (1 lb) potatoes, peeled and cut into
  small pieces

1 bay leaf

salt and pepper

dry salt cod, soaked overnight in several
  changes of water (optional) (see page 110)

1 litre (1¾ pints) water or stock

½ tsp paprika

Clean the leeks very well and slice them, including a little of the green part. Heat the oil in a pan and fry the whole garlic cloves until golden, then remove. Add the sliced leeks to the oil and sauté very gently for 2 minutes. Add the potatoes to the oil with the bay leaf, salt and pepper. Add the pieces of salt fish, if using. Then add water or stock. In the mortar crush the fried garlic with the paprika and add to the vegetables. Cook slowly for about 45 minutes, until the leeks are very tender and the potatoes almost disintegrated.

SERVES 4–6

Stews and Soups with Pulses

These soups are generally served as a first course, but many are substantial enough, with salad and bread, to make a whole meal.

Spinach with Chickpeas
Espinacas con Garbanzos

In Seville, this is served as a tapa.

4 tbsp olive oil

2 slices bread (55 g/2 oz)

4 garlic cloves

1 tsp cumin seeds or ground cumin

10 black peppercorns

1 piece chilli pepper

1 tsp salt

1 tbsp paprika

1 tbsp wine vinegar

250 ml (8 fl oz) water

750 g (1 lb 10 oz) cooked chickpeas

300 g (10½ oz) cooked or frozen spinach

Heat the oil in a pan and fry the bread and 2 garlic cloves until golden. Remove. In a mortar or processor, grind toasted bread and garlic with the cumin, peppercorns, chilli and salt. Dissolve in a little water and reserve. Into the same oil, chop the remaining 2 garlic cloves. Stir in the paprika and immediately add the vinegar, water and the mixture from the mortar. Add the cooked chickpeas and spinach. Simmer for 20 minutes.

Serves 8

POTAGE WITH WHEAT AND FENNEL
OLLA DE TRIGO CON HINOJO

In the damp of early spring the wild fennel sends up tender new shoots, which are gathered by the handful to add to this hearty potage with whole wheat berries. This dish is typical of Almería and Murcia. Though wild fennel might not be available, the soup works with cultivated fennel bulb, purchased from your greengrocer. Add a little of the finely chopped ferny leaf at the very end of cooking. *Chorizo* is a spicy Spanish sausage available from the supermarket or delicatessen.

200 g (7 oz) wheat berries, soaked overnight, or cracked wheat, such as bulgur

200 g (7 oz) white beans, such as cannellini, soaked overnight

300 g (10½ oz) pork

2 litres (3½ pints) water

200 g (7 oz) fennel bulb, cut into slivers

¼ onion

2 tsp salt

½ tsp ground black pepper

140 g (5 oz) *morcilla de cebolla* (black pudding with onion)

140 g (5 oz) *chorizo*

Drain wheat and beans and place in a pan with the pork and water. Bring to the boil, then skim off any froth and add the fennel, cut into slivers, and the piece of onion. Cook, covered, for 1 hour. Then add the salt and pepper, *morcilla* and *chorizo,* and the cracked wheat, if using. Cook until the beans are tender, another 40 minutes. The wheat remains a little chewy. Cut the piece of pork and sausages into small pieces and serve the soup sprinkled with a little of the fennel leaf, finely chopped.

Variation: Chopped potatoes and green peppers are often added to the dish.

SERVES 6

Lentil Pot
Cazuela de Lentejas

500 g (1 lb 2 oz) lentils, soaked overnight

2 litres (3½ pints) water

1 ham bone (optional)

3 tbsp olive oil

200 g (7 oz) large tomatoes, cut into chunks

1 onion, quartered and stuck with 2 cloves

1 green pepper, cut into strips

2 carrots, sliced

1 bay leaf

1 head garlic, roasted (see page 13)

1 tbsp salt

2 large potatoes, diced

½ tsp ground cumin

½ tsp paprika

¼ tsp ground black pepper

140 g (5 oz) *chorizo*, cut into short pieces

140 g (5 oz) *morcilla*, cut into short pieces

1 tbsp wine vinegar or lemon juice

Drain the soaked lentils and put them in a large pan with the water, ham bone if using, oil, tomato, onion stuck with cloves, peppers, carrots, bay leaf and garlic. Bring the lentils to the boil, then simmer gently for 40 minutes. Then add the salt, potatoes, cumin, paprika, pepper and sausages. Cook for a further 30 minutes until the potatoes are tender. Immediately before serving, stir in the vinegar or lemon juice.

SERVES 6

Uncle Lucas's Bean Pot
Judías a lo Tío Lucas

3 tbsp olive oil

200 g (7 oz) salt pork or bacon, diced

450 g (1 lb) white beans, such as cannellini, soaked overnight

1 onion, quartered

1 head garlic, roasted (see page 13)

1 bay leaf

1 tsp paprika

¼ tsp ground cumin

1 sprig of parsley

2 litres (3½ pints) water (approximately)

salt and pepper

Heat the oil in a soup pot and fry the salt pork until lightly browned. Drain the beans, then add to the pan with the onion, garlic, bay leaf, paprika, cumin and parsley. Add enough water to cover, bring to the boil, then simmer for 1 hour. Add a cup of cold water and the salt and pepper and continue cooking until the beans are quite tender, about 30 minutes more.

SERVES 6

CATALAN POTAGE
POTAJE A LA CATALANA

450 g (1 lb) chickpeas or white beans, such as cannellini, soaked overnight

55 g (2 oz) salt pork or bacon

2 litres (3½ pints) water

½ onion

1 bay leaf

2 tsp salt

55 g (2 oz) lard

1 onion, chopped

4 tomatoes, peeled and chopped

55 g (2 oz) pine nuts

175 g (6 oz) *butifarra* (white sausage), cut into chunks

salt and pepper

2 hard-boiled eggs, chopped

Drain the chickpeas or beans and place them in a pan with the salt pork or bacon, water, the ½ onion and the bay leaf. Bring to the boil, then simmer for 30 minutes. Add the salt and continue cooking until tender (1 hour more if you are using chickpeas; 30 minutes for beans). Meanwhile, heat the lard in a frying pan and sauté the chopped onion. When softened, add the tomatoes, pine nuts and sausage. Cook this mixture on a medium heat for about 15 minutes until reduced. Season with salt and pepper and place this *sofrito* in a *cazuela* or flameproof casserole dish. Add the cooked chickpeas and enough of their cooking liquid to make a thick soup. Cook for another 20 minutes and serve garnished with the hard-boiled eggs.

SERVES 6

PURÉE OF WHITE BEANS
PURÉ DE JUDÍAS BLANCAS

450 g (1 lb) white beans, such as haricots or
    cannellini, soaked overnight

2 litres (3½ pints) water

4 garlic cloves

2 bay leaves

½ tsp chopped thyme

2 tsp salt

6 tbsp olive oil

100 g (3½ oz) bread, diced

55 g (2 oz) serrano ham, chopped

1 onion, sliced

2 tsp paprika

Drain the beans then simmer them in the water with 3 garlic cloves, the bay leaves and thyme for 30 minutes. Add the salt and another cup of water. Meanwhile, heat half the oil in a frying pan and fry the diced bread with the remaining garlic clove, chopped. Skim out and reserve. Fry the ham and reserve. Add the remaining oil to the pan and sauté the sliced onion. Stir in the paprika, then add to the cooking beans. When they are tender, drain and reserve the liquid. Either purée them in a processor or rub through a sieve. Return the bean purée to the pot and add enough of the liquid to make a smooth soup. Heat and serve with the fried bread, garlic and ham.

SERVES 6

ARAGÓN-STYLE BEANS AND RICE
RECAO DE BINEFAR

**300 g (10½ oz) white or red beans,
 soaked overnight**

2 litres (3½ pints) water

5 tbsp olive oil

10 garlic cloves

½ onion

1 bay leaf

1 tsp paprika

½ tsp cayenne

2 tsp salt

300 g (10½ oz) potatoes, peeled and diced

175 g (6 oz) medium-grain rice

Drain the beans and place them in a pan with the water. Bring to the boil, skim, then simmer for 30 minutes. Add the oil, garlic, onion, bay leaf, paprika, cayenne and salt and cook 15 minutes more. Add the potatoes and simmer for 10 minutes, then add the rice. Cook until rice is just tender, about 15 minutes. The dish should still be soupy.

SERVES 6

SEAFOOD SOUPS

From the Bay of Biscay to the Mediterranean, from the Atlantic to the plains of Spain, seafood soups occupy an important place in the daily fare. These are mainly simple soups, made with what's at hand on any one day.

While a housewife doesn't go to special trouble to confect a *fumet* or *court bouillon* to enrich a soup, what usually happens is that a simple *caldo*, fish broth, is made first. This makes it easy to remove, using the fingers, all the skin and bones, reserving the flesh to return to the finished soup.

For a simple fish stock, use about 250–500 g (or 9 oz–1 lb 2oz) fish or fish trimmings (rock fish, white fish), 3 litres (5¼ pints) water, 1 tbsp salt, 2 bay leaves, a strip of lemon rind, ½ onion, a few parsley stems and a little white wine. Bring to a boil, then simmer, partially covered, for 1 hour. Strain the broth. Strained liquid from mussels or clams can be added to the broth. Prawn or lobster shells can be cooked with it. This should make slightly more than 2 litres (3½ pints) of stock, which can be used in any of the following recipes. Or freeze it in two or three containers for future use.

FISH SOUP WITH ORANGE
CACHORREÑAS

Cachorreña is the name in Andalusia for the bitter Seville orange, the type used for English marmalade. The peel is bitter, the juice is sour. If these are out of season and not readily available, use sweet oranges with vinegar. A similar soup in Cádiz is called *caldillo de perro* – 'dog's soup'.

350 g (12 oz) white fish fillet

250 g (9 oz) small clams or *coquinas* (wedgeshells)

1.5 litres (2½ pints) water or fish stock

2 tsp salt

2 bitter (Seville) oranges

1 tomato

2 slices bread (about 55 g/2 oz)

2 garlic cloves

1 tsp ground cumin

2 tsp paprika

3 tbsp olive oil

Cut the fish into bite-size pieces and set aside. Wash the clams in running water and reserve. Put the water or stock to boil with the salt. With a vegetable peeler, skin one of the oranges in a spiral strip. Add it to the soup pan with the whole tomato. Soak the bread in water. In a mortar, processor or blender, crush the garlic cloves with the cumin and paprika. Squeeze out the bread and add. Take the tomato from the pan, skin it and purée it with the garlic. Add the olive oil. Skim out the pieces of orange peel from the soup and discard. Put the pieces of fish and clams into the soup. Add the mashed mixture. Simmer for 8–10 minutes or until the fish flakes and the clams open. Meanwhile, squeeze the juice from the peeled orange and half the second orange. Stir into the soup 5 tbsp of sour orange juice or 3 tbsp sweet orange juice with 3 tbsp of wine vinegar. Serve the soup with thin slices of the remaining half-orange.

SERVES 4

WHITE FISH SOUP
EMBLANCO

Use almost any white fish for this soup. Small hake are perfect, but cheaper, bony fish work fine too because, after cooking, you flake the fish and discard bones.

500–750 g (about 1–1½ lb) whole fish

2.5 litres (4½ pints) water

1 tsp salt

250 g (9 oz) potatoes, thinly sliced

1 tomato, peeled and chopped

1 green pepper, diced

1 garlic clove, crushed

3 tbsp olive oil

lemon juice to serve

Clean and scale the fish and cut them crosswise into thick pieces. Bring the water with salt to a full boil and put in the fish heads. Boil for 10 minutes, then add the pieces of fish and simmer, uncovered, until the fish flakes easily, about 8 minutes. Pour the fish and broth through a strainer into a bowl. Return the broth to the pan and bring back to the boil. Put in the sliced potatoes, chopped tomato, pieces of green pepper, crushed garlic and oil. Simmer, uncovered, until the potatoes are very tender. Meanwhile, with the fingers, remove and discard all skin and bones from the cooked fish. Set the boned, cooked fish aside. When the potatoes are tender, return the fish to the soup to reheat. Serve with a squeeze of lemon juice.

SERVES 4–6

RED GARLIC FISH SOUP
AJO COLORADO

This is a soup from Almería in Andalusia. Rockfish, monkfish, skate or bass are all excellent for this dish.

400 g (14 oz) fish fillets

1.5 litres (2½ pints) water or fish stock

2 tsp salt

600 g (1 lb 5 oz) potatoes, peeled and sliced

1 tomato, left whole

2 dried sweet peppers

3 garlic cloves

3 tbsp olive oil

½ tsp ground cumin

1½ tbsp paprika

cayenne (optional)

a few threads of saffron

1 tbsp wine vinegar

strips of green pepper

Cut the fish into chunks. Put the water in a pan with the salt and bring to the boil. Add the potatoes, tomato and dried peppers. Cook, covered, just until the potatoes are tender (reserve the broth). In a mortar, blender or processor, purée the garlic cloves, oil, cumin, paprika, cayenne and saffron with the cooked tomato, peppers and potato. Add a ladle or two of the broth. Add the fish to the soup pan, then add the purée mixture. Cook for another 10–15 minutes until fish is done. Stir in the vinegar and serve the soup with strips of green pepper.

SERVES 4

Clam and Pine Nut Soup from Las Marismas
Sopa de Almejas con Piñones, Las Marismas

This soup was invented by hunters camping in Las Marismas, the marshlands of the Guadalquivir. They dig clams and gather nuts from pine trees in the area to make this soup. Cockles or mussels could be used instead of clams.

1 kg (2 lb 3 oz) clams, well scrubbed

1 litre (1¾ pints) water

200 g (7 oz) pine nuts

4 tbsp olive oil

4 garlic cloves, thinly sliced

1 tbsp flour

6 tbsp dry Sherry

500 ml (¾ pint) water or fish stock

**4–6 slices bread, crusts removed
    (100 g/, 3½ oz)**

3 eggs, beaten

Put the clams in the water and cook on a high flame, stirring, just until the shells open. Remove from the heat. Drain, reserving the liquid. Remove most of the clams from the shells, discarding any that have not opened, and reserving a few in their shells for garnish. Toast the pine nuts lightly in a dry frying pan or in the oven. Remove and grind them in a mortar or processor. Heat the oil in a pan and add the garlic. Then stir in the flour and let it cook briefly. Add the ground pine nuts, then the Sherry, the water or fish stock and the reserved clam liquid. Cook for 15 minutes. Preheat the oven to 220°C (425°F, gas 7). Add the clams to the soup. Ladle the soup into an ovenproof casserole, adding a few of the clams in their shells. Toast the bread slices lightly and place on top of the casserole. Pour the beaten egg on top. Put in a hot oven until the top is set and slightly browned. The soup can also be ladled into 4–6 individual casseroles, each topped with a slice of bread and a whole egg, baked until the white is set and the yolk still runny.

Serves 4–6

CRAB BISQUE
SOPA DE CANGREJOS DEL MAR

If you enjoy the flavour of crab, this will taste sublime. Versions of this soup are made from Asturias (*crema de andariques*) to Mallorca to Andalusia. Made with small crabs – too small to bother with extracting the shreds of meat – the soup is a concentrated essence of their flavour. In Mallorca, the soup is made with toasted brown bread rather than egg yolks.

1 kg (2 lb 3 oz) small crabs (depending on size, from 1–6 dozen)

3 tbsp olive oil or butter

1 carrot, chopped

1 leek, chopped

1 onion, chopped

1 garlic clove, chopped

400 g (14 oz) tomatoes, chopped

4 tbsp brandy

1.5 litres (2½ pints) fish stock (plus de-boned bits of fish)

herb bouquet of thyme, fennel, bay leaf, parsley

2 egg yolks

1 tsp paprika

120 ml (4 fl oz) cream (optional)

dash of brandy or white wine

Wash the crabs in several changes of water. In a large soup pan, heat the oil or butter. Sauté the chopped carrot, leek, onion and garlic until softened. Add the crabs and the tomatoes and cook on a high heat for several minutes. Put the brandy in a soup ladle, heat slightly, then set it alight. Pour it over the crabs. Tilt the pot until the flames subside. Add 1 litre (1¾ pints) of the fish stock and the herb bouquet. Bring to the boil, then cover and simmer for 30 minutes. Drain, reserving the liquid.

Pop the shells off the crabs, scooping the bit of soft, dark meat out of them and discarding the shells. Put the remainder of the crabs, the vegetables and the soft crab meat through a mincer, or purée it in several batches in a processor. Press through a coarse sieve, then combine with the reserved liquid and the remaining 500 ml (¾ pint) of stock. Now put the soup through a fine sieve, pressing hard on the solids. Return to the soup pan (with any bits of fish or crab meat) and heat. Beat the egg yolks with paprika and a little of the hot liquid, then whisk the mixture into the hot soup. Heat, but do not boil. Add the cream, if desired, and a dash of brandy or wine.

SERVES 6

CATALAN FISHERMEN'S SOUP
SUQUET DEL PESCADOR

1.5–2 kg (3 lb 5 oz–4 lb 6 oz) whole fish or 750 g (1 lb 10 oz) fillets

4 tbsp olive oil

3 garlic cloves, crushed

1 tomato, peeled and chopped

2 onions, thinly sliced

450 g (1 lb) potatoes, peeled and thinly sliced

2 litres (3½ pints) water or stock

6 tbsp white wine

1 tsp salt

3 tbsp chopped parsley

alioli sauce (see page 199)

Typically the fish would be cut into crosswise slices, bones and all, but, if preferred, use bone-free fillets. Save the head and trimmings to make the stock. Place the oil, garlic, tomato, onions and potatoes in a deep *cazuela* or soup pot. Cover with the water or stock and add the wine. Bring to the boil and cook for 5 minutes. Add the pieces of fish and sprinkle with salt. Cook on a very high flame until the fish flakes and the potatoes are tender, a further 12 minutes or so. Sprinkle with the chopped parsley and serve the soup from the same *cazuela*. Accompany with alioli sauce.

SERVES 6

SEAFOOD SOUP
SOPA DE PESCADOS Y MARISCOS

Use two or more kinds of fish to make this soup especially rich in flavour. Like the French *bouillabaisse*, this soup is improved with rock fish, such as scorpion fish, rascasse, bluemouth and gurnard. Solid-fleshed fish such as monkfish and grouper are good because they don't disintegrate in cooking.

2 kg (4 lb 6 oz) fish

1 kg (2 lb 3 oz) any combination of crustaceans: prawns, langoustines, lobster, crab

1 kg (2 lb 3 oz) any combination of bivalves: clams, mussels, scallops

350 g (12 oz) squid, cleaned and diced (optional)

3 litres (5¼ pints) water

120 ml (4 fl oz) white wine

salt and pepper

½ onion, chopped

1 carrot

1 stalk celery

herb bouquet of bay, thyme, parsley, fennel and orange peel

4 tbsp olive oil

1 garlic clove, crushed

3 tbsp brandy

100 g (3½ oz) bread, toasted or fried, or plain biscuits

½ tsp saffron

10 peppercorns

cayenne

175 ml (6 fl oz) tomato sauce

chopped parsley

triangles of fried bread

In the simplest version of this soup, the fish is simply sliced and everything cooked in the pot. Each person fishes out the bones at table. Easier to serve is fish that has been filleted, in which case, save all the heads, bones and trimmings to make stock.

Cut the fillets into chunks and set aside. Shell the prawns or slice the halved lobster, remove from the shell and hack the shell and head into pieces. Scrub the clams or mussels and steam them open over a high heat in a covered pan. Remove and discard the shells. If using scallops, prise them open and remove the white flesh. Strain and reserve the liquid.

Put all the fish trimmings and crustacean shells into a large pan with the water, wine, salt and pepper, half the onion, carrot, celery and herb bouquet. Bring to the boil, skim the froth and simmer, partially covered, for 1 hour. Meanwhile, in another pan or a deep flameproof casserole, heat the oil and sauté the remaining chopped onion and the garlic. Add the pieces of fish and squid and sauté them, then add the peeled prawns or pieces of lobster. Pour over the brandy, set it alight and tilt the pan until the flames subside. Crush the toasted bread or biscuits in a mortar with the saffron, peppercorns and cayenne. Dissolve in some of the fish stock, then add to the fish with the tomato sauce. Strain the stock and add about 2 litres (3½ pints) of it to the fish. Simmer the soup for 15 minutes. Serve with chopped parsley and triangles of fried bread.

Serves 6–8

MENORCA-STYLE LOBSTER POT
CALDERA DE LANGOSTA A LA MENORQUINA

1 onion, quartered

1 tomato, quartered

6 garlic cloves

3 tbsp chopped parsley

1 tbsp paprika

1 chilli pepper

1 or 2 lobsters (about 500 g/1 lb 2 oz)

alioli sauce (see page 199)

bread

Bring a large pan of water to the boil with the onion, tomato, garlic, parsley, paprika and chilli. Boil for 10 minutes, then add the lobsters and cook over a brisk heat, about 5 minutes. Remove the lobsters from the pot and serve them with alioli sauce. Ladle the broth into soup bowls with bread.

SERVES 4

VEGETABLE STARTERS

Las habas de abril para mí; las de mayo, para el caballo.

April's beans, for me; those of May, for the horse.

This is a very special category in Spanish cooking. While Spaniards, typically, turn up their noses at vegetables served plain, boiled – English style – they enjoy vegetables in dozens of combination dishes, most usually as a starter or light luncheon or supper dish. A few could double as a side dish with a main course of fish, poultry or meat.

BROAD BEANS WITH HAM
HABAS CON JAMÓN

Broad beans, also called fava beans, have been part of European food since long before haricot beans were brought from America. They are widely grown in Spain, as food both for people and for animals. This is a Granada speciality, a spring-time dish, when broad beans are at their best. Broad beans are best young and freshly picked. Older ones might need to be first shelled, then blanched and skinned. Frozen beans can be used.

800 g (1 lb 12 oz) shelled broad beans (2 kg/4 lb 6 oz in their pods)
150 ml (¼ pint) olive oil
200 g (7 oz) serrano ham, chopped
6 garlic cloves, chopped
salt and pepper
chopped parsley, mint or fennel

If the beans are small and freshly picked (or frozen), they can be sautéed directly with the ham. Otherwise, shell them and par-boil in boiling water for 8 minutes. Drain and refresh in cold water. In a frying pan or *cazuela*, heat the oil and add the chopped ham, garlic and the shelled beans. Stew the beans on a low heat until the beans are cooked, about 30 minutes, adding a little water if necessary. Season with salt and pepper. To serve, sprinkle with chopped parsley, mint or fennel.

SERVES 4

CATALAN-STYLE BROAD BEANS
HABAS A LA CATALANA

4 kg (9 lb) broad beans (or 1 kg/2 lb 3 oz, frozen shelled beans)

2 tbsp lard

150 g (5 oz) streaky salt pork

6 spring onions, chopped

3 garlic cloves, chopped

200 g (7 oz) piece of *butifarra* (white Catalan sausage)

200 g (7 oz) piece of *butifarra negra* (black pudding)

salt and pepper

bouquet of thyme, bay, rosemary, mint and cinnamon stick

4 tbsp medium Sherry

1 tbsp rum or brandy

chopped parsley

Shell the beans. Heat the lard in a soup pot or *cazuela*. Cut the piece of salt pork into 6 or 8 pieces and brown in the lard. Then add the onions and garlic and let them brown. Add the shelled beans and the two kinds of sausage (unsliced). Season with salt and pepper and add the herb bouquet. Add the Sherry, rum or brandy and enough water just to cover the beans. Cook, covered, until very tender, about 45 minutes. Discard the bouquet. Cut the sausages into pieces and arrange on top of the beans. Sprinkle with the chopped parsley.

SERVES 6

Spring Vegetable Stew
Menestra de Primavera

Peas, artichokes and broad beans all come in to season in the spring. In summer, a similar stew can be made with green beans, potatoes, courgettes and pumpkin. In Navarre and Aragón, lamb is sometimes cooked with the vegetables.

300 g (10½ oz) shelled peas

300 g (10½ oz) shelled broad beans

500 g (1 lb 2 oz) artichokes

lemon juice

3 tbsp olive oil

2 spring onions, chopped

2 garlic cloves, chopped

200 g (7 oz) ham, diced

1 tinned red pimiento, chopped

1 tbsp flour

salt and pepper

½ tsp paprika

3 tbsp tomato sauce (see page 17)

6 tbsp water or stock

1 sprig of parsley or mint

Cook the peas and broad beans separately in water until tender, then drain and reserve. Trim the artichokes down to the bottoms, or quarter them, rub with lemon juice and cook them in boiling water until tender. Heat the oil in a *cazuela* and fry the onions and garlic. Add the ham and pimiento and fry a few minutes more. Then add the cooked and drained vegetables and sauté briefly. Sprinkle with the flour, season with salt, pepper and paprika and stir in the tomato sauce and water or stock. Cook on a medium heat for 15 minutes, then serve garnished with a sprig of parsley or mint.

Serves 4–6

STUFFED ARTICHOKES
ALCACHOFAS RELLENAS

8 artichokes

lemon juice or wine vinegar

250 g (9 oz) pork, minced

55 g (2 oz) pork fat, minced

1 garlic clove, crushed

2 tbsp chopped parsley

70 g (2½ oz) bread, soaked in water
then squeezed

grating of fresh nutmeg

½ tsp salt

1 egg, beaten

20 g (¾ oz) fine breadcrumbs

olive oil

salt and pepper

120 ml (4 fl oz) white wine

¼ onion, sliced

1 bay leaf

tomato sauce (optional, see page 17)

Cut the stems off the artichokes, remove the outer leaves and cut off the tops about a third above the base, dropping each one into water with a squeeze of lemon juice or vinegar to prevent darkening. In a bowl, combine the minced pork and pork fat, garlic, parsley, bread, nutmeg and salt. In a small bowl, beat the egg with a spoonful of water. Add 1 tbsp of the beaten egg to the meat mixture and combine well. With the fingers, spread open the artichoke leaves slightly. Use the tip of a spoon to scoop out the centre leaves and fuzzy choke. Fill the centres with the meat mixture, mounding it smoothly. Dip each one in the remaining beaten egg, then in breadcrumbs. Fry them, topside down, slowly in a little oil until golden. Remove from the oil and place the artichokes, topside uppermost, in a *cazuela* or large pan. Pour in hot water to ¾ depth of the artichokes. Add the salt and pepper, white wine, onion and bay leaf. Bring to the boil, cover and simmer until the meat filling is cooked, about 1 hour, adding more water if necessary. Serve hot or room temperature. If desired, a little tomato sauce can be stirred into the remaining liquid, then sieved and served as a sauce to accompany the artichokes.

Variation: *alcauciles a la gaditana*, Cádiz-style artichokes. Use flaked cooked fish and chopped egg instead of minced pork, and reduce the cooking time to about 40 minutes.

SERVES 8

ARTICHOKES SAUTÉED WITH HAM
ALCACHOFAS SALTEADAS CON JAMÓN

Frozen artichokes could be used in this recipe.

1.5 kg (3 lb 5 oz) fresh artichokes

lemon juice

1 tsp salt

225 g (8 oz) serrano ham, chopped

4 tbsp olive oil

1 garlic clove, chopped

Cut the artichokes in half or quarters and trim the leaves. Rub with lemon juice. Cook them in boiling water with salt and a squeeze of lemon juice until tender (a leaf will pull off easily), about 15 minutes. Drain well. In a frying pan or *cazuela*, fry the ham in the oil. Add the chopped garlic and the cooked artichokes and sauté for several minutes.

SERVES 8

ANDALUSIAN-STYLE ASPARAGUS
CAZUELA DE ESPARRAGOS A LA ANDALUZA

In the early spring in the Andalusian countryside, folks go out to stalk the wild asparagus, which pushes up through damp soil around wheat fields, even by roadways. The thin, green stalks have a slightly bitter taste and are much appreciated for omelettes and cooking in this *cazuela*.

400 g (14 oz) slender, green asparagus

3 tbsp olive oil

3 garlic cloves

**2 slices bread, crusts removed
(about 40 g/ 1½ oz)**

¼ tsp saffron

½ tsp paprika

8 black peppercorns

½ tsp salt

2 tbsp wine vinegar

2 eggs

4 tbsp water

Preheat the oven to 180°C (350°F, gas 4).
Cut the asparagus into 4–5 cm (about 2 inch) lengths. Cook them in boiling salted water for 8 minutes and drain, reserving the liquid. Heat the oil in a frying pan or *cazuela*, fry the garlic and slices of bread until golden, then remove them from the pan. In the same oil, fry the drained asparagus. In a mortar crush the saffron, paprika, peppercorns and salt with the fried garlic and fried bread. Dilute with 1 cup of the reserved liquid. Stir this mixture into the asparagus with the vinegar and cook another few minutes, adding additional liquid if the sauce is too thick. Beat the eggs with the water and a pinch of salt. Pour the eggs over the top of the asparagus in the casserole (or divide the asparagus and eggs between four small ovenproof ramekins) and bake in the oven until the egg mixture is set, about 20 minutes.
Serve hot.

SERVES 4

JAÉN-STYLE SPINACH
ESPINACAS ESTILO JIENENSE

With an egg topping, this is served as a supper dish. Without the egg, it makes a fine starter or side dish.

1 kg (2 lb 3 oz) fresh spinach (or 400 g/14 oz frozen spinach)

4 tbsp olive oil

4 garlic cloves

2 sweet dried peppers, de-seeded, or 1 tsp paprika

70 g (2½ oz) stale bread

1 tbsp wine vinegar

55 g (2 oz) serrano ham or unsmoked bacon, diced

½ onion, chopped

piece of orange peel

1 tsp salt

250 ml (8 fl oz) water

¼ tsp caraway seeds

2–3 eggs (optional)

Trim the spinach stems and wash in several changes of water. Put in a large pan and steam until wilted. Drain and set aside. In a frying pan, heat the oil and fry the garlic, dried peppers (though not paprika), and bread until they are browned. Remove and grind them in a mortar or processor with the vinegar and paprika, if using. In the remaining oil in the frying pan, sauté the ham and onion until onion is soft. Stir in the chopped spinach, the piece of orange peel, the ground garlic mixture, the salt and water. Simmer for 10 minutes. Stir in the caraway and serve.

For a supper dish, preheat the oven to 180°C (350°F, gas 4). Place the spinach in an ovenproof casserole. Beat the eggs together and pour over the spinach. Bake until eggs are set, about 15 minutes. The spinach can also be spooned into 6 individual baking dishes and one egg per serving broken on top of each, then baked until the whites are set.

SERVES 6

CATALAN-STYLE GRILLED VEGETABLES
ESCALIVADA

Serve this at room temperature as a starter or as a side dish with grilled meat or chicken. It can be cooked under the grill or on the barbecue.

450 g (1 lb) aubergines

2–3 red and green peppers

1 onion

1 tomato

3 tbsp extra virgin olive oil

2 tbsp lemon juice

salt

Prick the aubergines so they don't burst as steam builds up. Place them in one layer with the peppers, onion and tomato under a hot grill, turning them to grill all sides. (If necessary, grill the vegetables in two or three batches.)

Remove the tomato when the skin splits, but let the other vegetables get fairly charred on all sides. Remove them and cover with a cloth until cool enough to handle. Peel off all the skin and, with the fingers, tear the aubergines and peppers into strips. Cut the onion and tomato into thin wedges. Combine all the vegetables and their juices in a bowl. Add the oil, lemon juice and salt. The vegetables can be served immediately or left to marinate several hours.

SERVES 6

STEWED PEPPERS WITH TUNA
RIN RAN

This Levante dish can be served hot or cold, as a starter or a light supper dish. *Bacalao*, salt cod, which has been cooked and flaked, can be substituted for the tuna.

4 red or green peppers (or tinned pimientos)

3 tbsp olive oil

2 garlic cloves, chopped

450 g (1 lb) tomatoes, peeled and chopped

½ tsp salt

70 g (2½ oz) black olives

225 g (8 oz) tinned tuna, drained

Roast the peppers over a gas flame or under the grill, turning, until charred on all sides. Remove, cover and cool. Then peel the peppers, discard the stem and seeds and cut the flesh into strips. In a *cazuela* or pan, heat the oil and sauté the garlic. Add the tomatoes, then the skinned peppers. Season with salt and cook until thick, 15 minutes. Add the olives and drained tuna.

SERVES 4

MÁLAGA-STYLE CHARD
ACELGAS A LA MALAGUEÑA

Acelgas en la comida y en la cena ó válganos, Cristo, con tantas acelgas?

Chard at midday and for supper too – are we worthy, Lord, of so much chard?

Chard, or Swiss chard, also known as spinach-beet, has a fleshy white stalk and a big, green leaf, which can be used interchangeably with spinach. Because the two parts are often served separately – for instance, the stalks in a midday stew, and the greens in a supper's omelette, chard 'overkill' has resulted in the saying above.

This is called Málaga-style because it's made with the incomparably sweet Málaga muscatel raisins. The same dish with spinach in Cataluña is known as Catalan style.

1.5 kg (3 lb 5 oz) chard

3 tbsp olive oil

50 g (1¾ oz) pine nuts

3 garlic cloves, chopped

100 g (3½ oz) Málaga muscatel raisins, seeded

salt and pepper

lemon juice

Wash the chard, remove any strings from the stalks and chop the stalks and leaves together. Heat the oil in a deep frying pan and fry the pine nuts until lightly browned, then skim them out and reserve. Add the chard to the pan with the chopped garlic and turn it in the oil for several minutes. Add the raisins and salt and pepper. Cover and cook the chard in its own liquid until tender, about 15 minutes. (You may need to add a little water.) Immediately before serving, add the roasted pine nuts and a squeeze of lemon juice.

SERVES 6

MULE-DRIVER'S-STYLE GARLIC CAULIFLOWER
COLIFLOR AL AJO ARRIERO

Muleteers were the lorry drivers of old, before the internal combustion engine. They transported fish inland from the sea; wool and wheat from the interior to port.

1 cauliflower

150 ml (¼ pint) olive oil

1 tsp salt

4 garlic cloves, chopped

1 tbsp paprika

1 tbsp wine vinegar

pinch of cayenne

Separate the cauliflower into florets. Cook them in boiling salted water until tender. Drain and place in a serving bowl. Heat the oil and salt in a small pan. Add the chopped garlic to the hot oil. Remove from heat and stir in the paprika, vinegar and cayenne. Pour this mixture over the cauliflower.

SERVES 6

AUBERGINE PUDDING
CUAJADO DE BERENJENAS

750 g (1 lb 10 oz) aubergines

1 tbsp onion

1 tsp salt

75 g (3 oz) breadcrumbs

2 eggs

140 g (5 oz) cheese, grated

olive oil

Grill the aubergines until they are easily pierced with a skewer (timing depends on size). Remove and cool. Preheat the oven to 180°C (350°F, gas 4). Cut off and discard the stem ends. Cut the aubergines in half lengthwise. With a knife, scrape the flesh away from the skin, reserving the skins. Chop or purée the flesh with the onion, salt, breadcrumbs, eggs and grated cheese. Oil a 20 cm (8 inch) round baking tin. Line it with the reserved skins, shiny side down. Fill with the aubergine purée. Cover with foil and bake in the oven until the pudding is set and a skewer comes out clean, about 45 minutes. Unmould the pudding. Serve hot or cold.

Variation: *cuajado* or *fritada de calabacín*, courgette pudding. Grate 1 kg (2 lb 3 oz) courgettes, salt them and stand for 30 minutes. Squeeze out the pulp. Mix it with 3 eggs, 3 tbsp oil, 20 g (¾ oz) breadcrumbs, 70 g (2½ oz) grated cheese, salt and pepper. Put in a greased baking dish, cover and bake at the above temperature for 1 hour.

<small>SERVES 8</small>

MALLORCAN AUBERGINE CASSEROLE
TUMBET

Typically in Mallorca, this would be made at midday and served later as a light supper dish. With the addition of fish or lamb, it makes a main dish.

4 medium aubergines (1.2 kg/2 lb 10 oz)

salt

5 tbsp olive oil

750 g (1 lb 10 oz) potatoes, peeled and sliced

1 onion, chopped

1 red pepper (150 g/5¼ oz), cut in strips

320 ml (11 fl oz) tomato sauce (see page 17)

1 garlic clove, crushed

pinch of thyme

pinch of oregano

If desired, peel the aubergines. Slice them and layer in a colander with a sprinkling of salt. Leave to sweat out the juice for 2 hours. Preheat the oven to 180°C (350°F, gas 4). In a frying pan, heat 2 tbsp of oil and slowly fry the sliced potatoes, turning them in the oil. Add the chopped onion and strips of red pepper. The potatoes shouldn't brown, but cook until partially tender. Transfer them to an ovenproof casserole.

Place the aubergine slices on a baking tin and brush them on both sides with the remaining oil. Bake in the oven for 5 minutes. (Or, flour the slices and fry.) Layer the aubergines in the casserole with the potatoes. Combine the tomato sauce with crushed garlic, thyme and oregano. Pour over the aubergines. Cover the casserole with foil and bake for 35 minutes until bubbly and the vegetables are soft. Serve hot or cold.

<small>SERVES 8</small>

CATALAN STUFFED AUBERGINES
BERENJENAS RELLENAS A LA CATALANA

Aubergines were one of the vegetables contributed to Spanish cooking by the Moors. This dish is hardly changed today from one found in a cookbook of the thirteenth century.

4 medium aubergines (1.2 kg/2 lb 10 oz)

olive oil

200 g (7 oz) minced beef, lamb or pork

1 onion, finely chopped

½ tsp cinnamon

3 tbsp white wine

1 tbsp plain flour

100 ml (3½ fl oz) milk

grating of nutmeg

salt and pepper

2 eggs, beaten

50 g (1¾ oz) fine breadcrumbs

Preheat the oven to 180°C (350°F, gas 4). Cut the aubergines in half lengthwise. With a sharp knife cut out the pulp, leaving the shells about 1 cm (½ inch) thick. Place the shells on a baking tin, brush with oil and bake until soft (about 20 minutes). Chop the pulp and reserve it. Heat 3 tablespoons of oil in a frying pan and sauté the minced meat until browned. Add the chopped onion and aubergine pulp and continue to fry for a few minutes. Stir in the cinnamon and wine and a little more water if needed. Cook until all the liquid has been absorbed. In a saucepan heat a tablespoon of oil, stir in the flour to a paste, then whisk in the milk. Stir over a low heat until thickened. Season with nutmeg and salt and pepper. Add the sauce to the meat mixture with one of the eggs, well beaten. Arrange the aubergine shells in a casserole. Spoon the stuffing mixture into them. Beat the remaining egg and spoon a little of it over each, top with breadcrumbs and drizzle with oil. Put in the oven for 20 minutes.

SERVES 8

AUBERGINES WITH CHEESE
BERENJENAS CON QUESO

Four centuries ago, a poet, Baltásar del Alcázar, wrote:

Tres cosas me tienen preso
de amores el corazón –
la bella Inés, el jamón
y las berenjenas con queso.

Three things hold
my heart a prisoner of love –
beautiful Inez, ham
and aubergines with cheese.

Here is one version to capture your heart.

2 medium aubergines (about 600 g/1 lb 5 oz)
30 g (1 oz) stale bread
olive oil for frying
100 g (3½ oz) onion, finely chopped
1 sprig of mint leaves, chopped
½ tsp salt
grating of fresh nutmeg
pinch of ground cloves
pinch of pepper
1–2 eggs, beaten
55 g (2 oz) cheese, chopped
flour or fine breadcrumbs

Cook the aubergines in boiling water until they are easily pierced with a skewer, about 10 minutes. Drain and cool. Soak the bread in water to cover until softened, then squeeze out. Cut the aubergines in half lengthwise and scoop out the pulp, leaving a shell. In a frying pan sauté the chopped onion in a tablespoon of oil until softened. Chop the aubergine pulp (or purée in a processor) and add to the onion. Cook until the moisture has evaporated, about 5 minutes. Combine the aubergine flesh, bread, chopped mint, salt, nutmeg, cloves, pepper and enough beaten egg to moisten the mixture. Stir in the chopped cheese. Fill the aubergine shells with this mixture and press down. Dip them in beaten egg, then in flour or breadcrumbs and fry them, open side down, in some more hot oil. Turn to brown the skin side. If preferred, the aubergines can be finished under a hot grill until browned on top. Serve hot or at room temperature.

SERVES 4–6

GREEN BEANS WITH TOMATO
JUDÍAS VERDES CON TOMATE

A real summertime dish.

1.5 kg (3 lb 5 oz) green beans

1 kg (2 lb 3 oz) tomatoes

4 tbsp olive oil

1 onion, chopped

1 garlic clove, chopped

salt and pepper

1 tbsp chopped parsley

55 g (2 oz) serrano ham, chopped

2 hard-boiled eggs, sliced

Top and tail the beans and cook them in boiling salted water until tender. Drain and refresh in cold water. Dip the tomatoes in boiling water to loosen the skins. Remove as soon as the skins split and peel them. Chop (or purée in a blender). Heat the oil in a *cazuela* or frying pan and sauté the onion and garlic until softened. Add the tomatoes and fry on a fairly high heat until they begin to lose their juice. Season with salt, pepper and parsley. Cover and cook for about 15 minutes until reduced to a sauce, then add the beans. Serve hot or cold garnished with chopped ham and sliced eggs.

SERVES 8

GREEN BEAN AND SAUSAGE CASSEROLE
CAZUELA DE JUDÍAS VERDES CON CHORIZO

450 g (1 lb) green beans

1 bay leaf

3 tbsp olive oil

5 medium potatoes (750 g, 1 lb 10 oz),
 peeled and sliced

½ tsp salt

225 g (8 oz) *chorizo*, sliced

1 onion, chopped

2 garlic cloves, chopped

15 g (½ oz) flour

3 tbsp tomato sauce (see page 17)

salt and pepper

Top and tail the beans and snap them into regular size pieces, removing any strings. Cook them in boiling salted water with the bay leaf until tender, then drain, saving the liquid, and refresh them under cold water. Heat the oil in a *cazuela* or frying pan and fry the potatoes slowly, sprinkling them with the salt. When nearly tender, add the *chorizo*. Fry for a few minutes more then remove to another plate. In the same oil, fry the chopped onion until softened, then add the garlic. Stir in the flour, tomato sauce and about 3 tbsp of the reserved bean liquid. Stir until thickened, then return the potatoes, chorizo and beans to the pan. Season with salt and pepper and simmer for 10 minutes, adding a little more of the liquid if necessary.

SERVES 4

VEGETABLE SHAKE-UP
ZARANGOLLO

3 tbsp olive oil

450 g (1 lb) potatoes, peeled and cubed

1 onion, chopped

1 red pepper, chopped

1 garlic clove, chopped

600 g (1 lb 5 oz) tomatoes, peeled and chopped

750 g (1 lb 10 oz) courgettes, cubed

salt and pepper

½ tsp oregano or basil

Heat the oil in a heavy pan or *cazuela* and add the cubed potatoes. Cook them slowly until partially done. Add the chopped onion, pepper and garlic and fry for a few minutes. Add the chopped tomatoes and cubed courgettes. Season with salt and pepper and oregano or basil. Cover and cook until the courgettes are just tender, about 15 minutes. If necessary, add a little water.

SERVES 6

STEWED PUMPKIN
CALABAZA GUISADA

1 kg (2 lb 3 oz) pumpkin

2 red or green peppers, cut in strips

1 onion, sliced

2 tomatoes, sliced

2 garlic cloves, chopped

½ tsp ground cumin

1 tsp salt

1 bay leaf

4 tbsp olive oil

250 ml (8 fl oz) water

Peel the pumpkin and cut into slices about 2 cm (¾ inch) thick. Layer it in a casserole or *cazuela* with the peppers, onion and tomatoes. Sprinkle with the chopped garlic, cumin and salt. Add the bay leaf, broken into a few pieces, and drizzle with the oil. Add the water. Bring the vegetables to a simmer, cover the pan and simmer gently until very tender, about 45 minutes. Alternatively you can transfer to a preheated oven and bake at 180°C (350°F, gas 4).

SERVES 6

STUFFED PEPPERS
PIMIENTOS RELLENOS

Of all the sweet peppers grown in Spain, the *piquillo* is possibly the best. It's small, with a pointy bottom, and sweet but with a slight piquancy. Small red bell peppers can be substituted.

FISH-STUFFED PEPPERS

3 tbsp butter

2 tbsp finely chopped onion

1 garlic clove, minced

30 g (1 oz) plain flour

500 ml (16 fl oz) milk

grating of fresh nutmeg

salt and pepper

dash of cayenne

300 g (10½ oz) cooked fish, prawns or tiny squid, flaked or chopped

20–24 small red peppers, (about 450 g/1 lb) roasted and peeled, stems and seeds removed, or a jar of roasted and peeled peppers. Allow 3–4 peppers per person.

120 ml (4 fl oz) white wine

1 tsp paprika

Preheat the oven to 180°C (350°F, gas 4). Heat the butter in a pan and sauté the onion and garlic until softened. Stir in the flour and cook, stirring, for 2 minutes, then whisk in the milk and season with nutmeg, salt, pepper and cayenne. Cook, stirring constantly, until the sauce has thickened, about 8 minutes. Set aside about 5 tbsp of the sauce. Add the rest to the cooked fish or shellfish. Drain and rinse the peppers if using tinned ones. Very carefully fill them with the fish mixture and place in an oiled ovenproof dish. Combine the reserved sauce with the wine and paprika and simmer for 5 minutes, stirring. Pour over the stuffed peppers. Cover and bake in the oven for 15 minutes, until heated through.

MEAT-STUFFED PEPPERS

> **6 red and/or green peppers, roasted and peeled, stems and seeds removed.**
>
> **450 g (1 lb) minced pork and/or beef**
>
> **1 garlic clove, finely chopped**
>
> **5 tbsp olive oil**
>
> **1 onion, chopped**
>
> **3 tomatoes, peeled, seeded and chopped**
>
> **3 tbsp chopped parsley**
>
> **5 tbsp white wine**
>
> **salt and pepper**
>
> **70 g (2½ oz) bread, crusts removed**
>
> **grating of fresh nutmeg**
>
> **2 eggs, beaten**
>
> **flour**
>
> **olive oil**

Preheat the oven to 180°C (350°F, gas 4). Season the minced meat with the garlic and let it rest for 15 minutes. Heat 3 tbsp of the oil in a pan and sauté all but 1 tbsp of the onion until soft. Then add the tomatoes and fry for 5 minutes. Add 2 tbsp of chopped parsley, 3 tbsp of the wine and salt and pepper. Cook until the sauce is reduced, about 15 minutes. Sieve or purée in a blender and put to one side. Heat the remaining 2 tbsp of oil in a frying pan, add the meat and the remaining chopped onion and fry until the meat is browned. Meanwhile, soak the bread slices in water or milk until spongy. Squeeze out and add the bread to the meat, mashing it with a fork. Season with salt, pepper and nutmeg. Stir in the remainder of the wine and cook the meat for several minutes. Remove from the heat and stir in 1 beaten egg and the remaining parsley. Spoon the mixture into the prepared peppers, taking care not to split them. Dip the tops of the stuffed peppers in beaten egg, then in flour and fry them (tops down) in hot oil until the tops have browned. Place in an ovenproof dish and cover with the tomato sauce. Bake the peppers in the oven for 20 minutes.

SERVES 6

CHOPPED CABBAGE AND POTATOES
TRINXAT

This Catalan dish is much like 'bubble and squeak'. Serve it as a side dish with duck, pork, sausages, or as a sturdy supper dish.

1 medium cabbage (1 kg), sliced

1.25 kg (2 lb 3 oz) potatoes, peeled and quartered

½ tsp cumin seed

salt and pepper

4 thick rashers streaky bacon

6 tbsp olive oil

Parboil the cabbage in lots of boiling water. Drain and put into a large pan with the potatoes, 1 tsp salt and enough water to cover. Bring to the boil and cook until tender, about 30 minutes. Drain and return the cabbage and potatoes to the pan. Using the edge of a metal spatula or fish slice, chop them up (keep a low heat under the pan to evaporate excess liquid). Stir in the cumin seed and a sprinkling of salt and pepper. In a frying pan, fry the bacon rashers in half the oil until crisped. Remove and set aside. Put a spoonful of the chopped cabbage and potatoes into the oil and pat it into a smooth cake. Fry until browned on the bottom. Turn and brown the other side. Fry the rest of the mixture in the same way, adding the remaining oil as needed. The vegetables can also be kept warm in the oven.

SERVES 8

MEDLEY OF SUMMER VEGETABLES
PISTO

This dish derives from *alboronía*, a Moorish dish, the name of which is still used. However, in those times, before the discovery of the New World by Columbus, the dish must have been made only with aubergines, for peppers, tomatoes and courgettes all come from the Americas. This dish is sometimes served with fried eggs.

1–2 aubergines

salt

3–4 tbsp olive oil

1 large onion, quartered and sliced

2 green peppers, seeded and cut in pieces

1 garlic clove

800 g (1 lb 12 oz) large, ripe tomatoes, peeled, seeded and chopped

1–2 courgettes, diced

pinch of oregano or basil

pepper

lemon juice

30 g (1 oz) pine nuts, toasted

Peel the aubergines and cut in large dice. Place in a colander, sprinkle with salt and leave to drain for 1 hour. Rinse and pat dry. Heat the oil and sauté the onion, peppers and garlic with the pieces of aubergine until beginning to soften. Then add the tomatoes, courgettes, 1 tsp salt, oregano or basil, and pepper. Cover and simmer until the vegetables are tender, about 20 minutes (add a little water if vegetables tend to scorch). Serve hot or at room temperature with a little lemon juice and garnished with toasted pine nuts.

SERVES 6

STUFFED CABBAGE
BERTONS RELLENOS

Bertons are the heart and stalk of the cabbage plant left after the head of cabbage is cut. In Galicia, where housewives are known for their frugality, these are gathered and cooked with a stuffing at the end of the season when the field is being cleared for spring planting. The same stuffing is delicious for a head of cabbage. White, green or leafy cabbage may be used.

1 firm head cabbage

5 tbsp lard or olive oil

3 garlic cloves

1 onion, chopped

300 g (10½ oz) minced pork or beef

200 g (7 oz) fatty ham, minced

1 tsp salt

¼ tsp pepper

2 eggs, beaten

3 carrots, peeled and sliced

150 ml (¼ pint) meat stock

6 tbsp white wine

Blanch the whole head of cabbage in boiling water for 5 minutes. Drain. Remove the outer leaves and save them. With a sharp knife, cut out the core and inner stalks, leaving a deep hollow in the cabbage. Heat 3 tbsp of the lard or oil in a frying pan and sauté 1 clove of the garlic and half the chopped onion. Add the minced meat and ham and fry until the meat loses its pink colour. Season with salt and pepper. Remove from the heat and stir in the eggs. Use this mixture to stuff the cabbage. Cover the opening with several of the reserved leaves. Tie with thread to hold them in place. In a pan large enough to hold the cabbage, heat the remaining fat and brown the remaining chopped onion and garlic with the sliced carrots. Put in the cabbage, add the stock and wine, cover and simmer the cabbage until tender, about 1½ hours. Remove the thread and let the cabbage rest 10 minutes, then slice it thickly. Sieve the sauce and spoon over the cabbage.

Variation: After blanching the cabbage, remove all the leaves. Place a spoonful of stuffing on a leaf, fold and roll it and tie with thread.

SERVES 6

POTATOES

When vegetables are served as a starter, they probably don't reappear as a side dish with the main course. Potatoes usually are the only accompaniment to a main dish of fish, poultry or meat. They're usually served fried. *Patatas fritas* are not quite the same thing as chips, however – fried in olive oil, they are at the same time 'light', meaning not greasy, but flavourful. They're not necessarily intended to be crisp and are, in fact, often added to a sauce.

Below are recipes for several other potato dishes which, while they come in the category of 'first dish', can also be served alongside meat.

POOR FOLKS' POTATO CASSEROLE
PATATAS A LO POBRE

'Poor' probably was used for this tasty preparation because it could serve as a main dish, without meat or fish, whereas now it's a favourite side dish with fish, with roast meat and chicken. It's likely to be oven-baked nowadays, but can be slow-cooked in a casserole on the hob too.

120 ml (4 fl oz) olive oil

2 kg (4 lb 6 oz) potatoes, peeled and cut
    into slices 50 mm (⅜ inch) thick

2 onions, sliced

1 small green pepper, cut in strips

3 garlic cloves, chopped

200 g (7 oz) tomatoes, peeled and chopped

1 tbsp chopped parsley

½ tsp ground cumin

½ tsp paprika

1 tbsp salt

½ tsp ground black pepper

120 ml (4 fl oz) white wine

120 ml (4 fl oz) water

Preheat the oven to 180°C (350°F, gas 4). Pour half the oil into a flameproof casserole and put in the potatoes, onions, green peppers and garlic. Add the pieces of tomato and chopped parsley. Combine the cumin, paprika, salt, pepper, wine and water with the remaining oil and pour over the potatoes. Put on a medium heat just until the liquid begins to boil, then cover and place in the oven until the potatoes are fork-tender, about 1 hour.

SERVES 10

'WIDOWED' POTATOES
PATATAS VIUDAS

As with the previous recipe, these potatoes can be served alone, making a fine supper dish. Sometimes the 'widow' entertains a few clams and bits of fish. This type of dish would be eaten for Lenten meals, when meat is prohibited.

1 kg (2 lb 3 oz) potatoes, peeled and chopped

1 tsp salt

500 ml (16 fl oz) water

1 tbsp wine vinegar

450 g (1 lb) tomatoes, peeled and chopped

100 g (3½ oz) green peppers, chopped

1 head garlic, roasted (see page 13)

1 onion, sliced in thin wedges

½ tsp oregano

1 bay leaf

½ tsp paprika

pinch of cayenne

¼ tsp pepper

4 tbsp olive oil

chopped parsley

Put the potatoes in a *cazuela* or large pan with the salt and water and vinegar. Bring to a boil and add the tomatoes, peppers, cloves of roasted garlic and onion. Season with oregano, bay leaf, paprika, cayenne and pepper. When the liquid comes to the boil again, add the oil. Let the potatoes bubble until very tender, but not disintegrated, about 40 minutes. The dish will be somewhat soupy. Serve in the same casserole, sprinkled with chopped parsley.

SERVES 6

POTATOES IN GREEN SAUCE
PATATAS EN SALSA VERDE

6 tbsp olive oil

1 kg (2 lb 3 oz) potatoes, peeled and thinly sliced

6 garlic cloves, chopped

2 tbsp chopped onion

1 tbsp plain flour

2 tbsp chopped parsley

200 ml (7 fl oz) water or stock

3 tbsp white wine

salt and pepper

1 hard-boiled egg, chopped

additional chopped parsley

In a heavy pan or *cazuela* heat the oil and add the sliced potatoes, turning them so they don't brown. Add the garlic and onion and continue frying gently. Stir in the flour, mixing it well. Add the chopped parsley and water or stock and wine. Bring to a boil, then reduce to a simmer. Season with salt and pepper. Cook until the potatoes are tender. Do not stir the potatoes, but shake the pan occasionally to prevent sticking. Garnish with chopped egg and more parsley.

SERVES 6

JAÉN-STYLE GARLIC POTATOES
AJOHARINA JIENENSE

The dried sweet peppers give the potatoes a wonderful, dusky flavour. If not available, use an additional spoonful of paprika plus just a pinch of cayenne.

2 dried sweet peppers, stems and seeds discarded

3 tbsp olive oil

1 kg (2 lb 3 oz) potatoes, peeled and sliced

2 tsp salt

250 ml (8 fl oz) water

4 garlic cloves

8 peppercorns

15 g (½ oz) plain flour

1 tsp paprika

Cover the dried peppers with boiling water and soak them for 30 minutes. Remove and either grind them in a mortar or else open them and scrape the flesh from the skin. Heat the oil in a frying pan or *cazuela* and fry the potatoes very gently without browning. Sprinkle with the salt and add the water. In a mortar, grind the garlic and peppercorns with the pulp from the dried peppers. Add the flour and paprika and dissolve the paste in some of the liquid from the potatoes. Stir this into the potatoes. Cook until the potatoes are tender, about 30 minutes. Let the casserole rest a few minutes before serving.

SERVES 6

SEAFOOD STARTERS

Almost any one of these dishes based on fish and shellfish could be served as a main dish for a lighter meal.

FISHERMAN'S WIFE'S VEGETABLE AND FISH DISH
PISTO A LA MARINERA

Necessity is said to be the mother of invention. Imagine a fisherman's wife inventing this delicious dish with the remains of the day's catch and fresh vegetables from her kitchen garden. With bread or rice it easily makes a luncheon dish, or can serve as the first course of a more substantial meal. This dish is from Sanlúcar de la Barrameda, where the Guadalquivir River empties into the Atlantic. Besides superb seafood, Sanlúcar is known for good vegetables and, of course, its particular style of Sherry wines.

2 mackerel, each approx. 450 g (1 lb), or other oily fish such as sardines, herring

¼ onion

2 sprigs parsley

2 tbsp wine vinegar

salt

250 g (9 oz) green beans

450 g (1 lb) pumpkin

300 g (10½ oz) carrots, peeled and diced

350 g (12 oz) courgettes, diced

3 tbsp olive oil

1 small onion, chopped

2 garlic cloves, chopped

3 tbsp medium dry Sherry, *palo cortado, amontillado* or *oloroso seco*

salt and pepper

finely chopped fresh mint

This dish can be made with flaked bits of leftover cooked fish. If starting with uncooked mackerel, poach them for 10 minutes in water boiled with the quarter onion, parsley, vinegar and salt. Let the fish cool in the broth, then drain and use your fingers to remove the flesh in chunks, discarding all skin and bone. Meanwhile, top and tail the beans and cut crosswise into short pieces. Remove the skin and seeds from the pumpkin and cut into dice. Add the carrots to boiling, salted water and cook for 2 minutes. Add the green beans and cook for 2 minutes. Add the courgette and pumpkin and cook another 5 minutes. The vegetables should be crisp-tender. Drain. (A frugal housewife would keep the liquid for another soup.)

In a frying pan or flameproof casserole, heat the oil and sauté the chopped onion and garlic until they are softened. Stir in the fish bits and the cooked vegetables and sauté for a few minutes, stirring occasionally. Add the Sherry and simmer just until the wine is absorbed. Season with salt and pepper. Serve hot or at room temperature with finely chopped fresh mint.

SERVES 8

MARINATED FISH
PESCADO EN ESCABECHE

Before most households had refrigerators, leftover foods could not readily be kept because of the danger of spoilage. Sometimes village housewives would fry fish so crisp that it was, essentially, dehydrated. These 'crisps' lasted a day or two and could be served to hungry children at snack time. Another traditional way to keep fish was in this vinegar marinade. So tasty is this preparation that I use it frequently as a very elegant starter. While inexpensive mackerel is the usual choice for *escabeche*, virtually any fish can be used – eel, trout, grey mullet and freshwater tench. In Cáceres, the tench's companions in the marinade are patties made of mashed potatoes.

2 kg (4 lb 6 oz) mackerel

30 g (1 oz) plain flour

olive oil

10 garlic cloves, slivered

4 bay leaves

1 sprig of thyme or ½ tsp dried

1 sprig of oregano or ½ tsp dried

2 cloves

10 peppercorns

2 tsp paprika

1 chilli pepper or red pepper flakes (to taste)

500 ml (16 fl oz) wine vinegar

250 ml (8 fl oz) white wine

250 ml (8 fl oz) water

2 tsp salt

sliced onions, tomatoes and olives, for garnishing

Clean the fish and either cut it into crosswise slices or fillet it. Dust the pieces lightly with flour and fry in just enough hot oil to cover the bottom of a frying pan. Remove them as they are cooked and transfer to a glass or crockery container with a lid. Add a further 6 tbsp oil to the pan and in it stew the garlic with the bay leaves, thyme, oregano, cloves and peppercorns for 2 minutes. Remove from the heat and stir in the paprika and chilli. Add the vinegar, wine, water and salt and boil for 5 minutes. Remove from the heat, allow to cool slightly, then pour over the fish. Cover and marinate, refrigerated, for at least 24 hours. Serve at room temperature garnished with sliced onions, tomatoes and olives.

FIRST COURSE SERVINGS 6–8

Asturias-Style Stuffed Sardines
Sardinas Trechadas a la Asturiana

La mujer y la sardina, cuanto mas chica, mas fina.

———————

Women and sardines, the smaller the better.

Spanish humorist and commentator on life, Julio Camba, once wrote that, with sardines, you should 'watch how you eat them, where you eat them and with whom you eat them'. Sardines, he says, are not to be consumed at home with a virtuous wife, but out with a shameless hussy not afraid to get her fingers greasy.

Indeed, the pungent, salty-smoky smell of grilled sardines clings to one's fingers, chin, moustache and clothing long after the feast is finished. But so popular is this fish that in Asturias and Galicia there are *sardinadas*, sardine festivals. On Mediterranean beaches, sardines are skewered and roasted by a driftwood fire in the traditional fishermen's meal.

Here is a slightly more dignified way of serving this delicious fish, but do turn on the kitchen extractor fan when you start frying!

You may be able to get the fishmonger to fillet the sardines. If not, you'll find very fresh ones are easier to work with if you leave them to soak in salted water for an hour. Then scales slide off with a scrape of a blunt knife and you can lift the spine with a knife tip and pull it free. Cut it off at the tail, leaving the fish 'butterflied'. If sardines are not available, small mackerel or herring can be used.

24 sardines (about 1.5 kg/3 lb 5 oz)

salt

55 g (2 oz) serrano ham (or bacon), finely chopped

¼ onion, minced

1 garlic clove, minced

100 g (3½ oz) fresh breadcrumbs

1 tbsp chopped parsley

1 tbsp lemon juice

2 eggs

200 g (7 oz) plain flour

150 ml (¼ pint) olive oil

lemon to serve

Remove the heads and innards from the fish and scale them. Slit them open and remove the spines. Salt lightly and allow to stand for 30 minutes, then rinse and drain. In a bowl, combine the ham, onion and garlic, breadcrumbs, parsley and lemon juice. Beat the eggs with a little water in a separate bowl. Add 2 tbsp of the beaten egg to the ham mixture. Pat the sardines dry and spread 12 of them opened on a flat surface. Spread a spoonful of the filling on each one and top it with another opened sardine. Press the edges together slightly. Dust each sardine with flour, dip in beaten egg and again in flour. Handling with care, fry them a few at a time, in the olive oil, turning so they brown evenly. Drain on kitchen paper and serve hot with lemon wedges.

Variation: add 1 tbsp of pine nuts and 1 tbsp of seeded Málaga raisins to the stuffing mixture. After frying, place the sardines in an ovenproof dish, add a glass of white wine and a little water and simmer until the liquid is reduced.

MAKES 12

SARDINES IN TOMATO SAUCE
SARDINAS CON TOMATE

In Spain this is made with fresh sardines, but it works well using tinned ones too.

400 g (14 oz) tinned sardines, preferably packed in olive oil

450 g (1 lb) tomatoes, peeled

90 g (3 oz) green pepper

1 small onion

2 garlic cloves

2 tbsp chopped parsley

3 tbsp olive oil

1 piece chilli pepper, finely chopped or red pepper flakes (to taste)

¼ tsp saffron, crushed

¼ tsp ground cumin

¼ tsp paprika

salt and pepper

2 tbsp white wine

lemon slices

toast

Drain the sardines, reserving the oil if they are packed in olive oil. In a processor, grind together the tomatoes, pepper, onion, garlic and parsley. Heat 3 tbsp of reserved or fresh oil in a pan and fry the tomato mixture for 10 minutes. Add the chilli, saffron, cumin, paprika, salt, pepper and wine. Simmer until the sauce is reduced. Add the drained sardines to the sauce and cook for 5 minutes. Remove from the heat. Serve the sardines, hot or cold, with lemon slices and toast.

SERVES 4–6

ELVERS SIZZLED WITH GARLIC
ANGULAS AL PIL PIL

In the luxury category with caviar and truffles, teensy baby eels are an expensive treat. Elvers, spawned in the Sargasso Sea, find their way across the Atlantic to the mouths of rivers in northern Spain. Some of them survive to grow to be real eels. But many are scooped up in nets, quickly cooked and frozen.

The fishing of baby eels was traditional in the area near San Sebastian, in the Urbion river. Basques, especially, love to serve elvers on special occasions such as Christmas. Unfortunately, supply cannot keep up with demand. So at holiday time supermarkets feature 'fake' *angulas*, made from *surimi* (fish paste), complete with the pale grey line down their backs.

In fact what makes *angulas* so delicious is their texture and the manner of preparing them, quickly sizzled in oil with garlic and a touch of chilli. *Surimi* elvers can be found at specialty stores. Or try this recipe with enokitake mushrooms in place of the elvers. They look the part, are similar in texture – but they don't have eyes.

3 tbsp olive oil

1 garlic clove, sliced

small piece chilli pepper or red pepper flakes to taste

150 g (5¼ oz) tiny elvers

1 tsp water

Heat the oil in a flameproof dish with the garlic and chilli. When oil is very hot, add the *angulas*. Toss them in the oil only until they are heated and the oil is bubbling. They should not fry. Add the water and serve immediately with a wooden fork. (Remove the chilli before eating.)

SERVES 1

GALICIAN-STYLE SCALLOPS
VIEIRAS A LA GALLEGA

Scallop shells were worn by those pilgrims who made the arduous journey to the shrine of St James at Santiago de la Compostela in Galicia. (Incidentally, Santiago, San Diego, St Jacques and San Jacobo are different versions of the same name, St James – hence the French term for scallops, 'Coquilles St Jacques'.) If you can get fresh ones, prepare them in their shells. Frozen scallops can be put into tiny ramekins if shells aren't available. Small scallops in their shells can be served as tapas or canapés. For a first-course serving, put three or four scallops into each shell.

1.5 kg (3 lb 5 oz) scallops in their shells or 12–16 scallops

lemon juice

5 tbsp olive oil

1 large onion, minced

50 g (1¾ oz) ham or bacon, chopped (optional)

2 tbsp white wine

2 tsp paprika

pinch of cayenne

salt and pepper

1 tbsp chopped parsley

30 g (1 oz) fine breadcrumbs

Preheat the oven to 190°C (375°F, gas 5). If using fresh scallops, open them by inserting a knife blade between the shells and prising them apart. Slice the scallop free of the flat shell and discard the flat half. With a knife tip, lift the mantle – the scalloped rim around the white centre muscle – and discard (it's tough to chew). Cut out the black sac. Leave both the white muscle and the coral 'foot' attached in the shell. Rinse under running water, drain and place the scallops in their shells in an oven tin. Put a drop or two of lemon juice on each. In a frying pan, heat the oil and cook the minced onion, and the chopped ham or bacon if desired, until the onion is very soft, about 15 minutes. Add the wine and cook until reduced. Remove from the heat and stir in the paprika, cayenne, salt, pepper and parsley. Spoon the onion mixture on to each scallop shell. Spoon breadcrumbs over each. Bake in the upper part of the oven for 15 minutes until the crumbs are slightly crisped and scallops are bubbling.

FIRST COURSE SERVINGS 4; INDIVIDUAL CANAPÉS 12–16

UNCLE JIM'S PRAWN CASSEROLE
CAZUELA TIO DIEGO

A lovely starter, this is usually prepared in individual earthenware ramekins, but you can sizzle all the ingredients in a frying pan.

750 g (1 lb 10 oz) king or jumbo prawns, uncooked (about 400 g/14 oz peeled)

150 ml (¼ pint) olive oil

400 g (14 oz) mushrooms, quartered or coarsely chopped

200 g (7 oz) serrano ham, diced

2 garlic cloves, chopped

6 tbsp dry Sherry or manzanilla

salt and pepper

chopped parsley

Peel the prawns and set aside. Heat the oil in a frying pan. Add the prawns, mushrooms, ham and garlic and toss them in the hot oil until the prawns have just turned pink. Immediately add the Sherry, cook for a few seconds longer, then remove from the heat. Add a very little salt and pepper and divide between 6 ramekins. Sprinkle with chopped parsley. Serve immediately.

SERVES 6

CLAMS WITH BEANS
ALMEJAS CON FAVES

Faves in Asturias are the same fat white beans used for *fabada* with sausages.

250 g (9 oz) small lima beans, soaked
    overnight

1 onion, quartered

2 garlic cloves

1 bay leaf

1 sprig of thyme or ½ tsp dried

sprig parsley

3 tbsp olive oil

1 tsp salt

1 kg (2 lb 3 oz) clams

¼ tsp saffron

1 tbsp breadcrumbs

salt and pepper

Drain the soaked beans and put them to cook in enough water to cover with the onion, 1 clove of garlic and the herbs. When beans are half-cooked, about 30 minutes, add the oil and salt. Meanwhile, scrub the clams and put them in a pan with a very little water. Cover and steam them open over a high heat, shaking the pan until the clam shells open. Remove from the heat immediately. Strain the liquid and reserve it. Shell the clams, discarding the shells and any clams that do not open. In a mortar, crush the saffron with the remaining clove of garlic and the breadcrumbs. Mix to a paste with a little of the liquid from the beans. Now add the shelled clams to the beans with the breadcrumb mixture. Season to taste. Simmer for 10 minutes, then allow to rest for a few minutes before serving.

SERVES 6

MARINATED OYSTERS
OSTRAS EN ESCABECHE

In bygone days, Galicia did a brisk trade shipping oysters to England. They were packed in a briny marinade and transported in barrels.

36 oysters

300 ml (½ pint) olive oil

10 garlic cloves, slivered

1 carrot, cut in julienne strips

1 onion, slivered

2 bay leaves

10 peppercorns

1 tbsp salt

200 ml (7 fl oz) vinegar, preferably Sherry vinegar

Shell the oysters, reserving their liquid but discarding the shells. In a frying pan, heat the oil and very gently fry the oysters for just a minute. Skim them out and pack in jars. Add the garlic, carrot and onion to the oil. Don't fry, but let them stew gently in the oil for a few minutes. Remove from the heat and add the bay leaves, peppercorns and salt, then the vinegar and oyster liquor. Boil for 5 minutes. Cool slightly, then pour over the oysters. Cover and marinate for at least 24 hours. Serve the oysters straight from the marinade as an appetizer, or dip them in a fritter batter and fry in hot oil.

SERVES 6

Squid in Ink Sauce
Chipirones en su Tinta

Dramatic in appearance – small white bundles in a pool of black sauce – this Basque dish is absolutely delicious. Innovative modern chefs have also paired stuffed red peppers (see recipe page 84) with the inky-black sauce. Serve as a starter or, with white rice, as a main course.

1 kg (2 lb 3 oz) small squid

30 g (1 oz) fine breadcrumbs

2 garlic cloves, finely chopped

3 tbsp olive oil

1 onion, finely chopped

1.5 kg (3 lb 5 oz) tomatoes, peeled and chopped

6 tbsp white wine

1 tbsp brandy

1 bay leaf

salt and pepper

pinch of cayenne

chopped parsley

triangles of fried bread

If you ask the fishmonger to clean the squid, ask for the ink sacs. To clean squid yourself, grasp the head, with the short tentacles attached in one hand, the body in the other, and pull gently. The head will come away from the body pouch, bringing the innards with it. The ink is enclosed in a tiny silver sac, like a dot of mercury, on the side of the innards. Cut it free with scissors. Save all the ink sacs in a cup with a little wine, and discard the rest of the innards. Still inside the pouch is the cartilage or quill, which looks like a strip of transparent plastic. Grasp the top of it and pull it out. Rinse out the pouch and pull off the purple-coloured membrane covering it. The wing flaps will come off too. Save them and the pouch. From the head, cut off the short tentacles just above the eyes. Save the tentacles, and discard the rest of the head.

Once the squid are cleaned, finely chop the wing flaps and tentacles and mix with the breadcrumbs and half the garlic. Stuff the squid with this mixture and close them with a cocktail stick. Heat the oil in a frying pan and gently sauté the squid. Transfer them to a *cazuela* or flameproof casserole. In the oil, sauté the onion and remaining garlic until soft. Add the tomatoes, 4 tablespoons of wine, brandy, bay leaf, salt, pepper and cayenne. Bring to the boil and simmer until reduced to a sauce. Purée in a blender or put through a sieve, then pour the sauce over the squid in the casserole. Cover and cook until the squid are very tender, about 25 minutes. Break the ink sacs with the back of a spoon and dilute with 2 tablespoons of wine. Stir the ink into the casserole and cook for another few minutes. Garnish with chopped parsley and serve with the fried bread.

FIRST COURSE SERVINGS 6

CUTTLEFISH WITH BROAD BEANS
CHOCOS CON HABAS

A spring-time dish when broad beans are in season, typical of Huelva. It can be served as a starter or main dish and is an unusual choice for a spread of tapa dishes.

1 kg (2 lb 3 oz) cuttlefish, cleaned

2 kg (4 lb 6 oz) broad beans (about 750 g/ 1 lb 10 oz, once shelled)

150 ml (¼ pint) olive oil

2 onions, chopped

8 garlic cloves, chopped

3 tbsp chopped parsley

1 tbsp paprika

6 tbsp white wine or water

salt

3 bay leaves

Cut the flesh of the cuttlefish into small cubes. Shell the broad beans. (If they are very small and freshly picked, they can be cooked unshelled: top and tail them, remove any strings from pods and cut crosswise into short sections.) Cook the beans in boiling water (use stainless, earthenware or enamelled cookware so the beans don't turn dark) for 5 minutes, drain and refresh the beans in cold water. In a *cazuela* or flameproof casserole, heat the oil and sauté the chopped onion and garlic until softened. Add the cuttlefish and continue to sauté a few minutes longer. Then add 2 tbsp of chopped parsley and the paprika. Stir in the wine or water, salt and bay leaves. Bring to a boil then reduce heat and simmer, covered, for 20 minutes. Add the broad beans and additional water if needed. Cook for a further 15 minutes until the cuttlefish is very tender and the beans are cooked. Sprinkle with additional chopped parsley and serve hot.

SERVES 4

Basque-Style Spider Crab
Txangurro

A single spider crab, *centollo*, yields only about 100 g (3½ oz) of meat, so this can be extended with bits of any flaky fish to make a quantity sufficient to fill the crab shells. Spider crabs are rarely eaten in the UK, but any fresh or tinned crab will work.

4 spider crabs or 1–2 crabs (cooked)
    (or 400 g, 14 oz tinned crab meat)

4 tbsp olive oil

1 onion, finely chopped

300 g (10½ oz) fish, cooked and flaked

100 ml (3½ fl oz) brandy

250 ml (8 fl oz) tomato sauce (see page 17)

150 ml (¼ pint) white wine

pinch of cayenne

salt and pepper

1 tbsp chopped parsley

4 tbsp fine breadcrumbs

1 tbsp butter

Put the live crabs into tepid, salted water. Bring them slowly to a boil and boil for 15 minutes. Drain and leave till cool enough to handle. Prise off the shells and reserve them, cleaned and oiled, for use as containers. From the crab, discard the spongy gills and stomach, but save any liquid from the shell. Scoop out the soft, dark meat and flaky white meat. Crack the legs with a mallet and extract the meat.

In a frying pan or *cazuela*, heat the oil and sauté the onion until softened. Add the crab meat and flaked, cooked fish to the pan. Heat the brandy in a soup ladle, ignite it and pour over the crab. When the flames die down, add the tomato sauce, white wine, cayenne, salt, pepper and parsley. Cook for 15 minutes, adding a little reserved liquid if needed to thin the sauce. Spoon the mixture into the crab shells or into 4–6 oiled earthenware ramekins. Sprinkle the tops with the breadcrumbs, dot them with butter and put under a hot grill or into a preheated hot oven until the tops are browned, about 5 minutes.

SERVES 4–6

SHELLFISH COCKTAIL
SALPICÓN DE MARISCOS

While this mélange of tomatoes and prawns is usually found at tapa bars, it makes a fine starter (an alternative to the ubiquitous prawn cocktail with pink mayonnaise) or a handsome dish on a buffet. Garnish the platter with sliced avocados sprinkled with lemon juice or quartered, cooked artichokes.

450 g (1 lb) raw prawns

450 g (1 lb) mussels

450 g (1 lb) large tomatoes, chopped

½ onion, chopped

1 green pepper (preferably a small, thin-skinned pepper), chopped

2 hard-boiled eggs, separated

1 garlic clove, crushed

6 tbsp olive oil

5 tbsp wine vinegar

3 tbsp chopped parsley

1 tsp salt

pinch of cayenne

lettuce to garnish

Unless using pre-cooked prawns, cook the prawns briefly in boiling, salted water. Drain and peel them. Scrub the mussels, steam them open, then remove and discard the shells and any mussels that do not open. (At a pinch, this dish can be made with frozen prawns and tinned mussels.) Mix together the tomatoes, onion, green pepper and egg whites, chopped, and combine them in a bowl. Mash the yolks with the crushed garlic. Whisk in the olive oil, then the vinegar, parsley, salt and cayenne. Add the prawns and mussels to the tomato mixture. Stir in the dressing and chill, covered, until serving time. Serve on a platter or in individual dishes, garnished with lettuce.

Variation: *ensaladilla de pulpo*, octopus salad. Substitute cooked octopus, diced with scissors, for the prawns and mussels.

SERVES 6

MUSSEL AND POTATO STEW
GUISO DE MEJILLONES Y PATATAS

2 kg (4 lb 6 oz) mussels

2 bay leaves

300 ml (½ pint) water

5 tbsp olive oil

1 kg (2 lb 3 oz) potatoes, peeled and thickly
   sliced

1 onion, chopped

125 g (4½ oz) green peppers, chopped

¼ tsp saffron, crushed

5 tbsp white wine

salt and pepper

pinch of thyme

chopped parsley

Preheat the oven to 180°C (350°F, gas 4).
Scrub the mussels and wash in running water.
Put them in a large pan with the bay leaves and
water. Cover and cook on a high heat, shaking
the pan, just until the mussel shells open. Strain
the liquid and reserve. Remove the mussels
from their shells. Discard the shells and any
mussels that do not open. Heat the oil in a
frying pan and fry the sliced potatoes, gently,
until they are partially cooked. Put them in an
ovenproof casserole with the mussels. In the
same oil, sauté the onion and peppers until
softened. Add to the casserole. Mix the crushed
saffron into the wine and add to the casserole
with a little salt (careful with salt as the mussel
liquid is salty), pepper and thyme. Add the
mussel liquid and put in the oven until the
potatoes are tender, about 45 minutes. Serve
sprinkled with chopped parsley.

SERVES 6

RIVER CRAYFISH
CANGREJOS DEL RIO

Hasta chupar los dedos – finger-licking good. It's the only way to enjoy this delicacy. They are fiddly to shell but have a fantastic flavour so when they turn up in *haute*-type menus, Spanish, French and Creole, they are usually shelled and stuffed. But there's no way better to enjoy them than 'hands on'.

Freshwater crayfish are popular throughout Castille-La Mancha and Cáceres in Extremadura. In Burgos, crayfish are cooked with lamb and partridge. This recipe comes from Cáceres, where crayfish are caught in traps in local rivers. Incidentally, folks in Cáceres also enjoy not only crayfish, but also frogs' legs and – now prohibited – lizards. Big lizards. They used to be sautéed with garlic and parsley.

To eat the crayfish: break off the head, split it open and suck out the liver and roe. Discard the head. Shell the tail and drop it into the sauce. Crack open the claws and pry out the tendril of meat. When finished, spoon up sauce and bits of tail meat.

1 kg (2 lb 3 oz) live crayfish

2 tbsp olive oil

1 onion, finely chopped

175 g (6 oz) green peppers, chopped

3 garlic cloves, chopped

chopped chilli pepper or red pepper flakes

175 g (6 oz) tomatoes, peeled and chopped

55 g (2 oz) *chorizo*, chopped

250 ml (8 fl oz) white wine

Wash the crayfish. De-vein them by twisting off the middle of the three tail flaps. In a *cazuela* or flameproof casserole, heat the oil and sauté the onion until softened. Add the peppers, garlic, chilli or red pepper flakes, tomatoes, and *chorizo*. Cook for 15 minutes until the tomatoes are reduced. Add the crayfish to the pan with the wine and cook over a high heat for a few minutes. Cover and simmer for 20 minutes.

SERVES 4

DRY SALT COD

Along with the processions, the drum rolls, the hooded penitents and flickering candles, another potent symbol of Holy Week in Spain is *bacalao*, salted and dried cod.

After the wild partying of Carnival, the end of meat-eating for the Lenten period, fish of all kinds and, in particular, salt cod are the food of *Cuaresma*, Lent, which lasts until Easter Sunday. And, while holidays become more secular and less religiously observed, customs and traditional foods go on and on. One of the most beloved during this season is *bacalao*. Cod thrives only in cold northern waters and, for centuries, Spanish fishing fleets have set off from home ports on the Bay of Biscay, often to be gone for many months, to fish the cod banks off Greenland and Newfoundland. The cod was cleaned, split and packed in salt aboard the boats.

In days before refrigeration and modern transport, inland villages throughout Spain rarely saw fresh seafood. It took several days by muleteer to transport fresh fish to the interior from the coasts. Only the rich could afford it and, even then, such was the deterioration that it required heavy dosing with lemon juice to mask the bad smell and taste. Salt cod, however, was a staple which kept for long periods of time. So, along with freshwater fish and crayfish, it became the most usual dish for those many days of abstinence from meat during Lent.

The rules say that only flesh from creatures which live and breathe in water may be eaten on days of abstinence. This led to various improprieties at some monasteries, such as putting chickens, pigs and even small cattle into pools until they drowned, then fishing them out for dinner with a clear conscience. Likewise, one priest's favourite Lenten dish was snails, which are not prohibited, though they live on land. But, unbeknownst to him, the cook prepared them in an especially rich chicken broth.

Because it is associated with Lenten meals, *bacalao* still gives off an odour of penitence. It's the preferred dish on *Viernes Santo*, Good Friday, even though, today, all sorts of fresh and frozen fish and shellfish easily could be substituted. Maybe it is the magic and mystery of *bacalao*'s transubstantiation from its ragged, smelly dry form into a soft, snowy-white fish that makes it appealing.

While once very cheap in all the little food shops in Spain, with the depletion of fishing grounds plus high-tech fishing industry, *bacalao* has become almost a luxury product. Interestingly, the higher the prices, the more trendy it has become. Every upmarket restaurant is likely to have several *bacalao* dishes, both traditional and innovative.

BUYING BACALAO

Bacalao traditionally comes in whole splits, which can weigh anywhere from 750 grams up to two or more kilos. In Spain, they hang from racks in market stalls, looking, unfortunately, like large grey bats; smaller cuts of *bacalao* are sold packaged in supermarkets. The best quality *bacalao* is grey, not yellow, and fairly flexible, not rigid, and with a thin skin that is easily sliced. You can buy *bacalao* in good fishmongers or delicatessens in the UK and they will cut off the weight you require.

PREPARING BACALAO

For most – but not all – *bacalao* dishes the fish is first de-salted. Trim off fins, spines and tail (frugal cooks would use the trimmings for a soup with potatoes or cauliflower). Cut the fish into squares or strips of about 7 cm (3 in) and put them into a bowl. Cover with lots of cold water. Soak the *bacalao* for 24–36 hours (very thick pieces should soak for up to 40 hours), changing the water four times. Each time you change the water, rinse the fish under running water and wash out the container. The last time you change the water, rub off any scales and squeeze the pieces of cod gently before putting to soak in fresh water. Then drain and place the pieces on a clean towel and cover with another to soak up excess water. Remove any remaining bones. For some dishes, such as *pil pil*, the slightly gelatinous skin of the fish is essential to bind the sauce.

For dishes where the flaky texture of the cod isn't so important (croquettes, fish balls and purées), instead of long soaking, you can put small pieces of cod into a pot with plenty of water, bring it just to a simmer and remove from heat. Let it soak for an hour. Drain and repeat the process twice more, for three soakings.

Toasting is another method of preparing *bacalao*, especially for salads and when small bits of the fish are used almost as a seasoning. Put chunks of *bacalao* directly over a gas flame, charcoal grill or under a grill. Toast it on both sides. Remove and rinse in running water, then cut it into small pieces and leave to soak in fresh water for up to an hour. With the fingers, remove any skin and bones. Squeeze out excess liquid and add the cod to the salad. No more cooking is needed.

Every region of Spain has dishes featuring salt cod, which is enjoyed year-round, not just during Lent. These dishes, in small portions, make excellent starters or they can be served as a main dish.

COD AND POTATO PURÉE
ATASCABURRAS

This is simple, country food but, made carefully with good quality cod and extra virgin olive oil, it makes a very sophisticated starter.

600 g (1 lb 5 oz) potatoes

400 g (14 oz) salt cod, soaked for 24–36 hours in several changes of water (see page 110)

3 garlic cloves, crushed

5 tbsp extra virgin olive oil

1 hard-boiled egg, cut into slices

walnuts

olives

lemon slices

Peel the potatoes and quarter them. Put to cook in water to cover. When they come to a boil, reduce the heat to a simmer and add the pieces of soaked salt cod. Simmer gently until the potatoes are tender. Drain, saving some of the liquid. Mash the potatoes, then combine with the crushed garlic. Flake the salt cod, removing all skin and bones. Add the fish flakes to the potatoes and stir in the olive oil, adding enough of the reserved liquid to make a thick purée. Serve at room temperature, garnished with the egg slices, walnuts, olives and lemon slices.

SERVES 8

BISCAY SALT COD
BACALAO A LA VIZCAINA

Te conozco bacalao, aunque vengas disfrazao.

I know you, codfish, even if you come in disguise.

This Basque dish, imitated everywhere in Spain, has great mystique, for every cook has a *secretillo* for its preparation. Though its ruddy sauce is frequently misinterpreted, using tomatoes, in Vizcaya it's made only with *choricero* peppers, dried sweet peppers which impart a dusky, smoky taste to the sauce. If you can't lay hands on real *choriceros* or the similar *ñoras*, use extra paprika and a red bell pepper or a spoonful of tomato sauce. Ham can be used although it would then not be strictly a Lenten dish.

6 *choricero* peppers (see above for alternatives; see also page 15)

200 ml (7 fl oz) olive oil

1 onion, chopped

1 leek, chopped

55 g (2 oz) minced serrano ham or fat

1 garlic clove, crushed

2 tbsp chopped parsley

150 ml (¼ pint) white wine

½ tsp strong paprika (or a little cayenne)

6 Marie biscuits (*galletas Marias*, see page 12)

250 ml (8 fl oz) water

500 g (1 lb 2 oz) salt cod, soaked for 24–36 hours in several changes of water (see page 110)

Remove the stems and seeds from the *choricero* peppers. Cover them with water and boil for 5 minutes. Leave them to soak. In a frying pan or *cazuela*, heat the olive oil and add the onion, leek, ham and garlic. Let this soften very slowly for 30 minutes. Then add the parsley, wine, paprika or cayenne, the peppers and the liquid in which they cooked, the biscuits and water. Cook for 30 minutes. Purée the sauce in a processor, then sieve it, pressing hard on the solids.

Cut the soaked cod into chunks, discarding all bones. Put it, skin side up, in a flameproof casserole and cover with the sauce. Simmer, covered, for 40 minutes, or bake in a moderate oven. This dish can be prepared a day in advance and reheated.

SERVES 4–6

GALICIAN-STYLE SALT COD AND CAULIFLOWER
BACALAO CON COLIFLOR A LA GALLEGA

1 kg (2 lb 3 oz) dry salt cod, soaked for 24
   hours in several changes of water
   (see page 110)

1 kg (2 lb 3 oz) potatoes

1 onion, quartered

1 kg (2 lb 3 oz) cauliflower, cut in florets

150 ml (¼ pint) olive oil

10 garlic cloves, coarsely chopped

1 tbsp paprika

pinch chilli (optional)

1 tbsp wine vinegar

salt to taste

Cut the soaked salt cod into small strips or squares, removing as much skin and bone as possible. Peel the potatoes and cut in quarters (though new potatoes can be left whole). Bring a large pan of water to a boil, add the potatoes and onion and cook 15 minutes. Add the cauliflower florets and cook for another 5 minutes. Add the pieces of cod and simmer gently until the potatoes and cauliflower are just cooked. Drain, saving some of the liquid, and place the cod, potatoes and cauliflower in a serving bowl and keep warm. Meanwhile, heat the oil in a frying pan and fry the garlic until very pale gold in colour. Remove from the heat and stir in the paprika, chilli and vinegar. Add enough of the reserved liquid to make a sauce and pour it over the cod. Taste for salt and add more if necessary.

SERVES 6–8

'LITTLE SOLDIERS' COD FRITTERS
SOLDADITOS DE PAVIA

The saffron in the batter turns these fritters yellow and they're sometimes wrapped in a strip of red pimiento, so the fritters are named, depending on which story you prefer, either for the colour of the uniforms worn by the Spanish Hussars who occupied the Italian city of Pavia in a famous battle of 1525, won by Emperor Charles V, or else for the troops of General Pavia, who wore red waistcoats, when in 1874 they stormed Parliament and forced its dissolution at bayonet point, ending Spain's first republic.

500 g (1 lb 2 oz) dry salt cod, soaked for
    24–36 hours in several changes of water
    (see page 110)
2 tbsp olive oil
1 tbsp lemon juice
¼ tsp strong paprika
5 g (1 tsp) fresh yeast
100 ml (3½ fl oz) warm water
pinch of saffron
100 g (3½ oz) plain flour
oil for frying

Drain the soaked salt cod and remove all the skin and bone. Cut it into 'fingers' about 6 cm (3¼ in) long and 3 cm (2½ in) wide. Squeeze out excess liquid in a clean towel. Add 1 tbsp of oil, the lemon juice and paprika to the strips of cod and let them marinate until ready to cook. Meanwhile, prepare the batter. Combine the fresh yeast with the warm water. Add the saffron, flour, and remaining 1 tbsp of oil. Beat for 1 minute, then let the batter set for at least 1 hour (or refrigerate overnight). Dip the strips of cod in the batter and fry them, a few at a time, in deep hot oil until they are browned.

Variation: instead of the yeast batter, you can substitute the batter as for *rebozadas*, page 242.

MAKES 12

SIZZLING COD
BACALAO AL PIL PIL

So called because the sizzling oil makes a 'pil pil' sort of sound. This dish, a Basque speciality, involves a certain amount of mystique, because the oil and liquid should emulsify to make a thick sauce in the casserole. The only trick to it is patience – about 30 minutes of cooking and swirling the dish. A teaspoon of flour mixed with a little water helps to bind the sauce.

630 g (1 lb 6 oz) dry salt cod, soaked for 24–36 hours in several changes of water (see page 110)

8 tbsp olive oil

6 garlic cloves

2 slices of chilli pepper (each about 1.5 cm/½ inch, wide)

about 3 tbsp water

In the last soaking of the fish, put into hot tap water. Drain and pat dry in a clean kitchen towel. Cut it into large pieces, removing any bones, but leave the skin intact.

In a *cazuela* or flameproof casserole large enough to hold the cod in one layer, put the oil. Heat it gently and put in the cod, skin-side down. Smash the garlic cloves with a mallet, but do not peel them. Add to the oil with the pieces of chilli. When the oil begins to sizzle, tip the casserole so the oil runs over the fish. Continue rocking and swirling the casserole while adding, a few drops at a time, about 3 tbsp of water. Cook for about 30 minutes. Serve very hot in the same casserole.

Variation: some people like to brown the coarsely chopped garlic in the oil, then skim it out before putting in the cod. When the dish is finished, the garlic bits are sprinkled on the top.

SERVES 4

COD FRITTERS WITH MOLASSES
TORTILLITAS DE BACALAO CON MIEL DE CAÑA

These crisp and tasty fritters, a tradition in Málaga, where sugar cane is harvested, are served with just a dribbling of dark molasses – an inspired combination of sweet and salty. These fritters are fine as an appetizer, or starter. If you must prepare the batter some time in advance, use the baking powder. Because flaked or shredded cod can be used, the fritters make a good follow-up to one of the cod dishes which require regular-sized pieces.

240 g (8½ oz) dry salt cod, soaked for 24–36 hours in several changes of water (see page 110)

2 tbsp parsley

2 garlic cloves

¼ tsp saffron

1 tbsp brandy or Sherry

2 eggs, separated

200 g (7 oz) plain flour

2 tsp baking powder (optional)

olive oil for frying

3 tbsp molasses

Put the soaked salt cod in a pan with water to cover and bring just to a simmer, then remove from the heat. Drain and save the liquid. When the cod is cool enough to handle, remove any bones and skin. The fish should be in thick flakes. In a processor, mince the parsley and garlic with the crushed saffron dissolved in brandy or Sherry. Add the 2 egg yolks. Beat in 300 ml (½ pint) of the reserved liquid, then the flour. The batter should be the consistency of pancake batter. Add the pieces of cod. Allow to rest for 2 hours. Beat the egg whites until stiff, then fold them into the batter. (Add baking powder if the batter has to wait.) Heat oil (a depth of two fingers) in a deep frying pan. Fry a tablespoonful of batter, turning to brown it on both sides. Drain on absorbent paper. Serve hot with molasses.

APPETIZER SERVINGS 10

CODFISH BALLS
ALBÓNDIGAS DE BACALAO

This is a Catalan dish, sauced with a typical *picada*, a mixture of ground nuts and garlic.

225 g (8 oz) dry salt cod, soaked for
    24–36 hours in several changes of water
    (see page 110)

1 bay leaf

60 g (2 oz) stale bread, sliced

5 tbsp milk

1 egg, beaten

¼ tsp pepper

¼ tsp cinnamon

1 tbsp chopped parsley

salt

55 g (2 oz) plain flour

250 ml (8 fl oz) olive oil

¼ tsp saffron

3 garlic cloves

12 hazelnuts, skinned and toasted

6 tbsp white wine

250 ml (8 fl oz) water

Put the soaked salt cod in fresh water to cover, add the bay leaf. Bring it just to a simmer and cook for 5 minutes. Drain and remove all skin and bones. Squeeze out gently and chop the fish in a processor. Soak half of the bread in the milk until spongey. Squeeze out and add to the fish with the egg, pepper, cinnamon, parsley and salt, if needed (taste the mixture). Add just enough flour to make a mixture stiff enough to shape into small balls. Heat half the oil in a frying pan. First fry the remaining slices of bread until golden, then remove. Then fry the codfish balls until browned and remove. In a mortar or processor, grind the saffron, garlic and hazelnuts with the fried bread. Dissolve in the wine. Put the remaining oil in a *cazuela* or frying pan and add the hazelnut paste. Fry it for 1 minute, then add the water and stir until smooth. Cover and cook 15 minutes. Then put in the codfish balls and cook for a further 15 minutes, adding a little additional wine or water if the sauce is too thick.

SERVES 6

Meat Starters

Garlic Paté
Ajo Pringue

This is a smooth and savoury spread made with liver and pork fat, well seasoned with garlic. Typical of sections of La Mancha (central and eastern Spain), it is one of the dishes made during the *matanza*, or winter pig butchering. The liver, cooked up with fat and packed in a clay pot, could be preserved for weeks in cold weather. A very similar dish is *morteruelo*, typical of Cuenca, which contains, in addition to pig liver, pieces of hare and partridge.

Although the fat gives this spread a tasty, creamy consistency, in this day of refrigeration it's no longer necessary in order to preserve the meat. If preferred, increase the quantity of liver and drain off melted fat.

300 g (10½ oz) stale bread, crusts removed

300 g (10½ oz) fresh or salted belly fat (*tocino fresco*), or substitute unsmoked fatty bacon, finely diced

300 g (10½ oz) pig's liver, cubed

10 garlic cloves

1 tbsp paprika

1 tsp cinnamon

1 tsp ground black pepper

1 tsp oregano

pinch of ground cloves

600 ml (1 pint) hot water

salt, if necessary

55 g (2 oz) toasted pine nuts

chopped parsley

Cut the bread into chunks. Crumb it in a processor or cut into small dice. Place it in a bowl. In a *cazuela* or heavy pan, fry the pieces of pork fat very slowly, until most of fat is rendered out. Skim out the bits and reserve. Add the pieces of liver to the fat with the garlic and fry for 3 minutes. Skim out the liver and garlic. (At this point, if desired, the fat can be poured off and discarded.) Mash or grind the liver and garlic cloves in a mortar, processor or mincer. Return it to the pan with the breadcrumbs, bits of fried pork fat, paprika, cinnamon, pepper, oregano and cloves. Stir in the water. Bring the mixture to the boil, stir well, salt to taste then partially cover and simmer very gently for 1 hour, stirring occasionally, until very thick. (A heat diffusor helps to keep the bottom from scorching.) Transfer it to a bowl. Serve hot or cold with a garnish of toasted pine nuts and chopped parsley. Use bread sticks or toast strips for dipping or serve, reheated, as a side dish with fried eggs.

SERVES 6

PORK ROLLS
FLAMENQUINES

thinly sliced pork loin

thinly sliced serrano ham

strips of cheese

flour

beaten egg

breadcrumbs

olive oil for frying

Place sliced pork between two layers of cling film and pound thin with a mallet. Top each slice with a slice of ham and a strip of cheese. Roll up into a cylinder and secure with cocktail sticks if necessary. Dip in flour, then beaten egg, then breadcrumbs. Fry in oil until browned on all sides. Drain and serve hot.

Allow 1 roll per person.

MAIN DISHES

RICE

Valencia, tierra de Dios, ayer trigo y hoy arroz.

_____

Valencia, God's country, yesterday wheat and today rice.

Rice is the traditional food of the Albufera, a large, marshy, inland lake region near Valencia on the east coast. The Arabs introduced rice cultivation here – the first in Europe – when they occupied Spain in the eighth century. In the Albufera they found the perfect conditions for the grain. The Spanish word for rice, *arroz*, derives from the Arabic, *aruz*.

The Moorish settlers in Spain set up intricate systems of canals, dykes and terraced paddies which continued in use for hundreds of years in the Albufera and in Murcia's Calasparra region. The water tribunal in Valencia, dating from Moorish times, still meets every Thursday outside the Cathedral. Festivals are still held to honour the patron saints of rice, Abdon and Senen.

By the time of Valencia's Reconquest, in 1238, rice plantations were fairly widespread where water was abundant. After the expulsion of the Moors, with their irrigation know-how, rice growing went into decline and at times was even banned because it was believed to be a cause of the dread disease malaria. By the end of the

19th century, after these bans were lifted, rice cultivation picked up. Important new plantations were made in the Ebro Delta in Tarragona and in the Marismas of the Guadalquivir in Seville.

Paella, the best-known rice dish today, didn't emerge until relatively recent times, though its antecedents can be found in older dishes. In medieval times rice was ground into flour for bread or gruel, or the cracked grains used in sweetened puddings – not unlike the rice pudding still enjoyed throughout Spain. Saffron, introduced by the Moors, flavoured rice. The people who planted and harvested rice used the grain in simple dishes, with the addition of frogs, snails and eels, which abound in the wetlands; of wild rabbit, duck or partridge; or fish and shellfish from the nearby sea.

Rice farming overlapped with market gardening, so, naturally, and depending on what was in season, broad beans, peas and artichokes and, after the discovery of New World vegetables, red and green peppers, tomatoes and beans, were added too.

PAELLA

Where I live in southern Spain, many village folk spend Sundays at their small farms in the country, tending their gardens and cooking up lunch from what's available in the *huerta*, fields. One of the best paellas I've ever eaten was at a friend's *finca*, small farm. It was spring-time and we picked *habas*, broad beans, to add to the rice with chicken, pork and a few prawns to garnish the top. So simple and so delicious.

Villagers seize any excuse for an outing to the country – a Sunday, a festival, *romería*, a pilgrimage to a country shrine. Favourite fare for such outings is a paella, cooked over a wood fire. On hunting trips, men make a paella with their catch – rabbit or partridge.

Paella is always eaten at midday, never for supper. It's said to be too 'heavy' to eat at night. What is certainly true is that such a sunny dish deserves to be enjoyed in the sunshine.

Paella is a rice dish that contains only titbits of meat, poultry or fish. For that reason, it is often served – just as the Italians serve pasta – as a first course, to be followed by a main dish. However, as the festive centrepiece of a holiday meal or Sunday lunch, paella would be the main course, preceded by a selection of *entremeses*: ham, sausage, prawns, stuffed eggs, salads.

Paella comes in as many versions as there are cooks to make it and, at any gathering, there's always plenty of good-natured arguing about the best way. A typical Valencian version would likely contain *ferraura*, flat green beans, and *garrafóns*, white butter beans, and possibly snails in addition to the chicken. In traditional cookery, wild duck would have been used instead of today's chicken. In Seville and Cádiz big prawns from the mouth of the Guadalquivir, *langostinos de Sanlúcar*, and even lobster go into the rice. The Costa del Sol version substitutes peas or broad beans for the green beans and mussels for the snails, and garnishes the rice with bright strips of red pimiento.

Paella, named for the pan in which it is cooked and served – a shallow, two-handled metal pan (from the Latin *patella*, a shallow metal plate) – is a 'dry' rice, meaning all the liquid is absorbed during cooking. Rice cooked in an earthenware casserole, *cazuela de arroz*, can be dry or *meloso*, of a thick and syrupy consistency. (*Meloso*, by the way, is the consistency of Italy's *risotto milanese*, a saffron-flavoured rice dish of Spanish ancestry.) Cooked in a soup pot, *caldero*, rice is *caldoso*, soupy. Calasparra rice, from the Murcia region of the Segura valley, is much esteemed for *caldoso* rice because it doesn't overcook and become mushy.

An authentic metal paella pan, made from rolled steel, does rust. Wash it immediately after use and dry it thoroughly. Don't oil it though, unless you use it regularly, for if stored, the oil makes a sticky coating which must be scoured off.

PAELLA INGREDIENTS

Rice. Spanish rice, paella rice, is always a round, medium-short grain variety (5.2–6 mm). This medium-grain rice has a marvellous capacity for soaking up the flavours in which it cooks: the chicken, seafood, saffron, oil, vegetables. If you can't get real Spanish paella rice, use Italian *arborio* rice (risotto rice) for paella-making. Long-grain pilaf-style rice does not work, nor does short-grain/pudding rice.

When making paella or any other Spanish rice, don't wash the rice. **Do not wash Spanish rice.** Unlike pilaf rice and Oriental steamed rice, which are usually washed in several changes of water, medium-grain rice cooked in the Spanish style needs that outer coating of starch to keep its shape.

It's easy to overcook rice to a sticky mass. The trick is to remove the paella from the heat when the rice is tender, but with a little kernel of resistance in the centre. The only way to be sure is to taste it. Then let it stand for at least 5 minutes after you remove it from the heat to finish cooking. The cooked rice grains should cling together but not be sticky. Rice cooked in earthenware *cazuelas* will continue to cook after being removed from the heat source, as the earthenware holds the heat.

Saffron. The queen of spices – it takes the stigmas of 75,000 crocuses to make 450 g (1 lb) of the spice – flavours and colours the finest of paellas. But it's not indispensable and, in fact, many village cooks don't use it because of the expense. Instead they use powdered artificial yellow colouring. If real saffron is not available, use artificial yellow colouring, or paprika, which is widely used in paellas, both for colour and flavour, but not yellow turmeric, which has a very distinctive flavour of its own.

To use saffron, crush it to a powder in a mortar. If properly stored, the threads should be dry and easy to crumble. If not, toast them lightly for a few seconds in a dry pan. Dissolve the saffron powder in a little liquid before incorporating in the paella.

Oil. Olive oil always flavours paella, although when it is made with fatty meats such as duck or pork, less is needed.

Vegetables. While peppers, tomatoes, beans, peas or artichokes are usual, paella made with other vegetables is perfectly acceptable.

Liquid. Normally, just water is used for paella. However, you can add flavour by using stock from cooking fish, shellfish shells, chicken and vegetables. You will need double the volume of liquid to rice, plus enough additional liquid at the beginning to cook the meat.

Procedure, quantity and timing. Allow about 80 g (2¾ oz) of dry rice per person. Use a 40 cm (16 inch) paella pan for a paella for six, using 500 g (1 lb 2 oz) of rice. If you have no paella pan, use a very large frying pan or a flat-bottomed wok.

A fast-burning wood fire, made with grape prunings, is perfect for paella. Nowadays, special gas rings are used for oversized, outdoor paellas. In the kitchen, limit paella to a four-person quantity that fits on one burner or, more difficult, rotate a larger pan on two burners for six to eight people.

Add rice to boiling liquid. Typically, chicken or rabbit and fish, if used, are browned in oil with a *sofrito* of onion, peppers and tomato. Then liquid is added and brought to a boil before adding the rice. Some cooks recommend sautéing the rice first – the coating of oil keeps the rice from expanding. If using this method, add boiling liquid to the rice.

Once the rice is added, stir it around to distribute the rice. Cook the paella on a high heat for the first 5–10 minutes. Then reduce the heat and don't stir it again, though you can shake the pan. Once the rice is added, the paella should take about 18 minutes to cook, so be sure the chicken and other ingredients are almost cooked when the rice is added. If more liquid is needed, add it boiling hot and without stirring.

Take the rice off the heat when it's still slightly undercooked – tender but with a chewy centre. Let it stand for at least 5 minutes before serving. The rice will absorb the remaining liquid and continue cooking.

VALENCIA PAELLA RICE
PAELLA VALENCIANA

If snails are not used, a sprig of fresh rosemary gives a hint of wild flavour. As the two white beans, *tabella* and *garrafon,* are unlikely to be available freshly podded, use dried beans, soaked overnight and then partially cooked.

6 tbsp olive oil

1 kg (2 lb 3 oz) chicken and/or rabbit, cut in small joints

salt

200 g (7 oz) green peppers, cut in squares

300 g (10½ oz) green beans (preferably the wide, flat ones), cut in short lengths

2 garlic cloves, chopped

200 g (7 oz) tomatoes, peeled and finely chopped

200 g (7 oz) cooked white beans and/or small butter beans (*tabella, garrafon*)

24 cooked snails

2 litres (3½ pints) water, approximately

2 tsp paprika

½ tsp saffron, crushed, and/or yellow colouring

500 g (1 lb 2 oz) medium-grain rice

Heat the oil in a paella pan (40–45 cm, 16–18 inches for this quantity) and slowly brown the pieces of chicken and/or rabbit. Sprinkle them with salt. Add the peppers and green beans and fry for 2 minutes, then add the garlic, tomatoes, cooked white beans and snails. Add all but 1 cup of the water, and cook until the chicken is nearly done, about 15 minutes. Combine the paprika and saffron, dilute in some of the remaining water and add to the paella with 1 tsp of salt. Raise the heat so the liquid boils and stir in the rice, distributing it evenly. Cook for 5 minutes, then lower the heat and cook until the rice is nearly tender, another 12–15 minutes. Remove from the heat and leave to stand for 5 minutes.

SERVES 6

PAELLA WITH SEAFOOD
ARROZ EN PAELLA A LA MARINERA

This is more typical of the southern coast of Spain, where it usually contains shellfish as well as chicken.

12 mussels

500 g (1 lb 2 oz) large prawns, preferably raw

6 tbsp olive oil

2 garlic cloves

1 bay leaf

1 kg (2 lb 3 oz) chicken or rabbit, cut in small joints

150 g (5¼ oz) pork, cubed

150 g (5¼ oz) green peppers, cut in strips

300 g (10½ oz) squid, cleaned and cut in rings (see recipe for Squid in Ink Sauce, page 125, for instructions)

450 g (1 lb) tomatoes, peeled, seeded and chopped

100 g (3½ oz) shelled peas, broad beans or green beans

1.5 litres (2½ pints) water or stock

500 g (1 lb 2 oz) medium-grain rice

½ tsp saffron

10 peppercorns

½ tsp paprika

2 tsp salt

3 tbsp white wine or water

1 tinned red pimiento, cut in strips

1 lemon, cut in wedges

Scrub the mussels. Place in a large pan with a cup of water, cover and cook for 2 minutes to steam them open. Discard the empty half-shells and any mussels that do not open. Strain and reserve the mussels and their liquid. Peel most of the prawns. (If desired, boil the shells to make a stock.) Cook a few unpeeled ones (if necessary) to garnish the paella. Drain and save the liquid.

Heat the oil in a paella pan (40 cm, 16 inches) and fry the garlic and bay leaf until lightly browned, then remove from the pan and reserve. In the oil, slowly brown the pieces of chicken or rabbit and pork. Add the green pepper and squid, then the tomatoes and peas or beans. Measure 1.5 litres (2½ pints) of reserved prawn or mussel broth, stock or water. Add it to the pan and bring to the boil. Stir in the rice with the peeled prawns. In a mortar, crush the saffron, peppercorns, paprika, fried garlic and bay leaf and salt. Mix it into the wine or water. Add to the pan. Cook briskly for 10 minutes, then reduce the heat. Garnish the rice with cooked mussels and prawns, and top with strips of red pimiento. Cook for a further 8–10 minutes, then allow to stand for 5 minutes. Serve with lemon wedges.

SERVES 6

NOODLE PAELLA
FIDEUÁ

Cooked in the same pan as a rice paella and with similar ingredients, this dish, typical of the Levante, is elsewhere called *cazuela de fideos*, noodle casserole, in which case, it's usually cooked in a clay *cazuela*. *Fideos* are round soup noodles, like vermicelli, about the thickness of spaghetti, but cut in short lengths.

1 kg (2 lb 3 oz) solid-fleshed fish such as monkfish, bream or sea bass

450 g (1 lb) large prawns or small Dublin Bay prawns, preferably raw

6 tbsp olive oil

1 small squid (300 g/10½ oz), cleaned and cut in rings (see recipe for Squid in Ink Sauce, page 102, for instructions)

1 small onion, chopped

100 g (3½ oz) green peppers, chopped

450 g (1 lb) large tomatoes, peeled and chopped

100 g (3½ oz) shelled peas or broad beans

250 g (9 oz) clams, scrubbed

¼ tsp saffron, crushed

½ tsp paprika

pinch of cayenne or chilli

salt and pepper

400 g (14 oz) *fideos* or spaghetti

sprigs of mint

Clean and fillet the fish and cut the flesh into chunks. Use the head, bones and trimmings and 2 litres (3½ pints) of water to make a stock. (The prawns can be peeled, if desired, and the shells added to the stock.) Strain the stock and reserve.

Heat the oil in a paella pan (40 cm/16 inches) or a *cazuela*, fry the pieces of fish quickly, then remove them. Sauté the prawns, then remove them. Then fry the rings of squid. Add the onion and peppers to the squid and cook for 2 minutes, then add the tomatoes, peas or beans and clams. Add 1 litre (1¾ pints) of the reserved stock. Bring to a boil. Dissolve the saffron, paprika, cayenne or chilli, salt and pepper in a little stock and add to the pan. When the liquid boils, add the *fideos*. Lower the heat to a bubble and add the fried fish and prawns. Cook until the *fideos* are nearly done and clam shells opened. Remove from heat, cover the pan and allow to stand for 5 minutes. This dish should be juicy, but not soupy. Garnish with sprigs of mint.

SERVES 6

MURCIA RICE AND FISH POT
CALDERO MURCIANO

This simple dish is prepared aboard fishing boats or in the homes of fishermen. It's almost identical to *arroz abanda* from further up the east coast. The fish is cooked with *ñoras*, small round dried peppers, to produce a *caldo*, broth, in which the rice is cooked. Use one or more firm-fleshed fish such as monkfish, skate, gilthead or grouper, and rockfish such as gurnard and scorpion fish. Shellfish such as prawns and mussels can be added, too.

1.5 kg (3 lb 5 oz) whole fish

salt

5 tbsp olive oil

10 garlic cloves

1 large tomato, quartered (200 g/7 oz)

1 onion, quartered

2 litres (3½ pints) water

1 tbsp salt

1 tbsp paprika

½ tsp saffron

400 g (14 oz) medium-grain rice

FOR THE AJO-ACEITE SAUCE

1 slice bread, crusts removed

4 garlic cloves

200 ml (7 fl oz) olive oil

½ tsp salt

juice of 1 lemon

chopped parsley

Clean and scale the fish. Cut off the heads and reserve. Cut the fish into thick slices, salt them and set aside. Heat the 5 tbsp of oil in a pan or flameproof casserole. Fry the garlic until they are just golden, then skim them out. Add the fish heads to the oil with the tomato and onion and fry for a few minutes. Add the water and bring to a boil. In a mortar (or blender) crush the fried garlic cloves with the salt, paprika and saffron. Dissolve it in some of the liquid from the pan and stir into the fish heads. Cover and simmer for 30 minutes.

Strain the broth into a bowl, pressing on the solids to extract all the juices. Return 2 litres (3½ pints) of the broth to the casserole, bring it to the boil and add the sliced fish. Cook until the fish just flakes, about 10 minutes, then skim the fish out on to a serving dish, cover and keep it warm. (If using shellfish, cook them briefly, too.) Bring the broth back to the boil and stir in the rice. Cook over a high heat for a few minutes, then simmer until rice is just tender, about 18 minutes. The rice should be 'wet'.

Meanwhile, make the *ajo-aceite* sauce. Soak the slice of bread in any remaining broth, then squeeze it out. Pound the garlic in a mortar (or blender) with the softened bread. Whisk in the olive oil, drop by drop, until the sauce is emulsified. Stir in the salt and lemon juice. (Alternatively, add the crushed garlic to ready-made mayonnaise with a dash of lemon juice.)

Spoon a little of the broth over the fish and sprinkle with parsley. Serve the rice in its casserole. Serve the garlic sauce separately.

Serves 4

SEVILLE-STYLE RICE WITH PRAWNS AND LOBSTER
CAZUELA DE ARROZ CON CIGALAS Y LANGOSTA, A LA SEVILLANA

400 g (14 oz) lobster or crayfish

400 g (14 oz) Dublin Bay prawns or king
   prawns, preferably raw

150 ml (¼ pint) olive oil

½ onion, chopped

1 green pepper, chopped

1 tomato, peeled and chopped

300 g (10½ oz) medium-grain rice

grating of nutmeg

salt and pepper

1 bay leaf

½ tsp saffron

1 tbsp white wine

1 litre (1¾ pints) fish or chicken stock

Any combination of prawns, crayfish and lobster can be used. Don't shell the crustaceans, for the shells flavour the rice. The lobster is cut into crosswise slices, with shell. Heat the oil in a flameproof casserole and quickly sauté the shellfish, then remove. Fry the onion, pepper and tomato. Add the rice, nutmeg, salt and pepper and bay leaf. Crush the saffron, dissolve in a little white wine and add to the casserole with the stock. Cook briskly for a few minutes, then add the shellfish. Reduce the heat and cook until the rice is just tender, about 10 minutes more. Allow to stand for 5 minutes (the rice will still be soupy). Serve from the casserole. As the shellfish must be peeled at table, provide fingerbowls or hand towels.

Serves 2–3

Valencian Rice and Lamb Casserole
Arroz Rosetxat

In the traditional Valencian kitchen, this dish would be made with the leftover meat and broth from the *cocido* (see page 133). The top of the rice was browned by covering it with a heavy lid and heaping hot coals on top.

3 litres (5¼ pints) water

400 g (14 oz) boneless lamb

1 carrot, cut into chunks

1 turnip, cut into chunks

1 stalk celery, cut into chunks

150 g (5¼ oz) chickpeas, soaked overnight

2 tsp salt

150 g (5¼ oz) *butifarra* (white sausage)

150 g (5¼ oz) *butifarra negra* with onions (black pudding)

55 g (2oz) salt pork

2 slices toasted bread

200 g (7 oz) minced pork or veal

1 egg, beaten

salt and pepper

pinch of cinnamon

1 tbsp chopped parsley

5 tbsp olive oil

2 garlic cloves, chopped

400 g (14 oz) medium-grain rice

½ tsp saffron

Put the water and the lamb (bones can be added) in a large pan to heat. When the water comes to the boil, add the vegetables with the drained chickpeas. Skim the froth and simmer until everything is half-cooked, about 1 hour. Add the salt, sausages and salt pork and continue cooking. Meanwhile, make the *pelota* or big meatball: crumb the bread in a processor or grate it, add the minced pork or veal, beaten egg, salt and pepper, cinnamon and chopped parsley. Form it into a ball and add to the pan. Cook until everything is tender, about another 1 hour. Strain out the broth and reserve. Preheat the oven to 180°C (350°F, gas 4). Heat the oil in a flameproof casserole and sauté the chopped garlic. Stir in the rice and let it fry briefly in the oil. Crush the saffron, dissolve in a little broth and add to the rice with the meat, chickpeas and vegetables and approximately 750 ml (1½ pints) of the hot broth. Cook over a high heat for a few minutes, then slice the meatball and place it on top of the rice. Put in the oven to finish cooking, about 20 minutes.

Serves 6

'COBBLESTONES' — RICE WITH BEANS
EMPEDRADO

This could be made with leftover cooked lentils or beans.

200 g (7 oz) lentils or red beans,
    soaked overnight

100 g (3½ oz) salt pork or bacon

1 bay leaf

200 g (7 oz) shelled peas

3 tbsp olive oil

1 onion, chopped

3 garlic cloves, chopped

400 g (14 oz) medium-grain rice

1 litre (1¾ pints) water or bean liquid

2 tsp paprika

salt and pepper

Cook the lentils or beans with the salt pork or bacon and bay leaf in ample water to cover for about 30 minutes. Add the peas and cook until done, 10–15 minutes. Drain, reserving the liquid. In a *cazuela* or flameproof casserole, heat the oil and sauté the onion and garlic until softened. Add the rice and stir until the grains are translucent, then add the water or bean liquid, the paprika, salt and pepper. Bring to a boil, then stir in the beans and peas. Cook, covered, until the rice is nearly done, 15 minutes. Remove from the heat and allow to stand for 5 minutes.

SERVES 6

BLACK RICE
ARROZ NEGRE

This Catalan dish needs the ink from squid or cuttlefish to colour it. You can buy tiny sachets of ink at fishmongers or delicatessens. The cut-up fish can be added to the rice if desired. The quantities given here are for a side dish or starter course.

100 ml (3½ fl oz) olive oil

1 onion, chopped

1 green pepper, chopped

3 garlic cloves, chopped

375 g (13 oz) tomatoes, peeled and chopped

900 ml (1½ pints) water or stock

1 tsp salt

4 sachets ink (or 4 tsp)

2 tbsp dry white wine or stock

400 g (14 oz) medium-grain rice

prawns and mussels for garnish, if desired

In a *cazuela* or flameproof casserole heat the oil and sauté the onion, pepper and garlic until softened. Add the tomatoes and continue to cook for 10 minutes. Add the water or stock, salt and the ink thinned with a little wine or stock. Bring to a boil and add the rice. Cover and simmer on a low heat until rice is cooked and liquid absorbed, about 15 minutes. Remove from the heat and allow to stand for 5 minutes. If desired, garnish the rice with cooked prawns and mussels.

SERVES 6

STURDY ONE-POT DISHES

The *olla*, a tall, pot-bellied cooking pot, is certainly the emblem of Spanish cooking. In it is cooked the daily meal, a *cocido, puchero, escudella, pote*, all versions of a meal-in-a-pot, a boiled dinner consisting of soup followed by meat and vegetables. Most of the *cocidos* contain pulses, making them sturdy, filling meals. *Potajes*, too, fit in this category. They are more than soups, not quite stews, but different from the *cocido* in that the broth is not separated out to make a soup. *Cocido* and its relatives are cooked in the morning, served at midday. They're considered too 'heavy' to eat at night, though the broth might be saved for a light supper. The mother of all *cocidos* is the *olla podrida*, 'rotten pot', probably so called because of the rather 'high' smell of old ham bone and beef jerky, and because it was cooked gently for a long time, until the meat was literally falling off the bones. As gluttonous Sancho Panza says in the book *Don Quixote*, *'que mientras más podridas son, mejor huelen'*, the more rotten the pot, the better it smells! The *olla podrida* was originally an aristocratic dish (King Alfonso XII requested it for his birthday), chock full of the best beef, mutton, ham, fowl and game, but by the 19th century, it had become a bourgeois meal. Gone were the mutton and partridge and in were potatoes and cabbage.

While the bustle of big city life has tended to phase out the slow-cooked *cocido*, except for holidays, in villages it is still the mainstay of everyday meals.

MEAL-IN-A-POT
COCIDO ESPAÑOL

La olla y la mujer, reposadas han de ser.

———————

Both stewpots and women have to settle.

This recipe provides a soup first course, then a main course of vegetables, assorted meats and meatballs, accompanied by a tomato sauce. Boiling fowl tend not to be found in supermarkets in the UK, though the Spanish housewife will often buy a quarter or half of a large hen for this dish. Try to use a flavoursome chicken.

FOR THE MAIN POT

3 litres (5¼ pints) water

400 g (14 oz) stewing beef

1 beef shin bone

90 g (3 oz) salt pork

1 meaty ham bone

300 g (10½ oz) chickpeas, soaked overnight

boiling fowl (approx. 1–2 kg, 2–4 lb in weight)

2 carrots

1 turnip

2 leeks

1 stalk celery

1 onion

2 cloves

1 tbsp salt

FOR THE RELLENOS, MEATBALLS

55 g (2 oz) bread, soaked in water or milk

100 g (3½ oz) minced beef and/or pork

1 garlic clove, crushed

1 tbsp chopped parsley

salt and pepper

grating of nutmeg

1 egg, beaten

FOR THE SECOND POT

6 medium potatoes, peeled and cut in chunks

1 small cabbage, cut in wedges or coarsely chopped

160 g (5½ oz) *morcilla*

160 g (5½ oz) *chorizo*

150 g (5¼ oz) fine soup noodles, rice or bread

chopped parsley or mint

tomato sauce to serve (optional) (see page 17)

Put the water in a large soup pan and add the stewing beef, shin bone, salt pork and ham bone. Bring to a boil and skim. Drain the soaked chickpeas and add to the pot with the boiling fowl, carrots, turnip, leeks, celery and the onion stuck with the cloves. Keep skimming off the froth as the liquid boils, then reduce to a simmer. Cover and cook for 1 hour. Add the salt and continue cooking. Meanwhile, squeeze out the bread and mix with the minced meat. Season with the garlic, chopped parsley, salt, pepper and nutmeg. Add the beaten egg and mix well. Form into small balls or one big ball – the *relleno* – and brown them in a little oil in a frying pan. Set aside. The balls will be added to the *cocido* for its last 20 minutes of cooking.

In a second pan, using some of the broth from the *cocido* or with additional water, cook the potatoes, cabbage, *morcilla* and *chorizo*, until the potatoes are tender, about 30 minutes. (These are cooked separately so the *chorizo* doesn't colour the broth.)

Strain some of the broth from the first pan into a third pan. Liquid from the cabbage can be added, if desired. (At this stage, put the meatballs into the first pan.) Bring it to a boil and cook in it the fine noodles or rice. (If using bread instead, remove the crusts, cut into strips and place in soup plates.) Ladle the broth and noodles or rice into the plates and garnish with chopped parsley or mint. Serve as the meal's first course.

For the main course, serve one platter with the drained chickpeas, carrots, turnip, leeks, potatoes, and cabbage. Cut the beef, chicken, sausages, fat pork and ham into pieces and serve them on a second platter with the meat dumplings. Accompany with the tomato sauce.

Leftover broth can be used for *sopa de picadillo* (see recipe page 45). Leftover meat can be used for *ropa vieja* (see recipe page 227). Cooked chickpeas, drained, are good in salads.

Variations: in Burgos, this type of dish is served in three courses, known as *sota, caballo y rey*, (the card-game equivalent of Jack, Queen, King). Likewise in Valencia, where it might include lamb instead of beef, with the addition of par-boiled artichokes. The Catalan *escudella* for Christmas has huge pasta elbows added to the soup. The Basque *cocido*, cooked in three pots, is made with red beans in addition to the chickpeas. The Galician version contains *grelos*, turnip greens. In Andalusia, green beans, pumpkin and even pears are added in some places, while in the Canary Islands, New World ingredients such as maize and sweet potatoes go in the pot.

SERVES 6–8

'ALTOGETHER' POT
TOJUNTO

All of the ingredients for this dish are put to cook together. This dish is typical of La Mancha. It's said the women of Almagro invented it so they could get on with their lace-making and not have to watch the pot. It can be made with lamb, pork, chicken or rabbit in place of the beef.

Leftover boiled beef can be used in the recipe for *ropa vieja*, 'old clothes', see page 227.

6 tbsp olive oil

1 kg (2 lb 3 oz) stewing beef, cut in
    4–6 pieces

100 g (3½ oz) green peppers

1 onion, quartered

3 garlic cloves, chopped

¼ tsp ground pepper

pinch of ground cloves

1 bay leaf

¼ tsp saffron, crushed

1 kg (2 lb 3 oz) potatoes, peeled and diced

120 ml (4 fl oz) white wine

1 tbsp salt

water to cover

Put the oil in the bottom of a deep cooking pot. Add all the remaining ingredients and water just to cover them. Put over a high heat and bring to a boil. Reduce the heat, cover, and simmer until meat is completely tender, about 1½ hours. Serve the meat, potatoes and broth ladled into soup plates over sliced bread.

SERVES 4

PORK SHOULDER WITH GREENS
LACÓN CON GRELOS

This is the 'national' dish of Galicia, in Spain's northwest corner, eaten from the time of the first pig butchering in November, through Christmas, until *Martes Lardero*, the Carnival celebrated before the beginning of Lent. *Lacón* is cured pork shoulder, which is soaked for 24 hours to de-salt it. Fresh pork, with skin and fat, can be used instead. *Grelos* are the stems and leaves of turnips. Cabbage, chard or other greens could be substituted. It produces a soup, to be eaten first, then a platter with sliced meat, greens, *chorizo* and potatoes. Leftover meat can be boned out and weighted to press it. Refrigerate and serve as cold cuts.

1 cured pork hock or 2 kg (4 lb 6 oz) fresh unboned pork hock, with skin

salt (if using fresh pork)

1.5 kg (3 lb 5 oz) *grelos*, cut in pieces, or other greens

400 g (14 oz) *chorizo*

1 kg (2 lb 3 oz) potatoes

150 g (5¼ oz) any soup pasta

If cured *lacón* is used, soak it for 24–48 hours, depending how long the meat was cured. Put the whole piece of meat to cook in ample water to cover. Add salt if using fresh pork. Bring to a boil, skim, then let it simmer for 2½ hours (or calculate 30 minutes for every 450 g/1 lb) of weight). Then add the *grelos* or other greens. After 30 minutes, add the *chorizo* and peeled potatoes. Cook until the potatoes are tender, another 25 minutes. Separate some of the broth and cook the pasta in it. First serve the soup, then the platter of meats and vegetables.

SERVES 6–8

ANDALUSIAN VEGETABLE POT
BERZA

Dias y ollas levantan catedrales

It takes time and food to build cathedrals

While this is best known in the Cádiz area, some version of it is served throughout Andalusia. Although the dictionary says *berza* means cabbage, this dish seldom contains cabbage; Andalusians use the word to mean any green vegetable. It is usually made with chard in the winter and green beans in the summer. Just about any other vegetable to hand can be thrown in as well. Unlike the *cocidos*, no soup is separated out of the *berza*. Leftover meat and fat, called *pringá*, is chopped and served in a bread roll, a favourite tapa in Seville.

200 g (7 oz) chickpeas, soaked overnight

100 g (3½ oz) salt pork or bacon

225 g (8 oz) pork

2 litres (3½ pints) water

200 g (7 oz) white beans or black-eyed peas, soaked overnight

500 g (1 lb 2 oz) chard or green beans, chopped

160 g (5½ oz) *chorizo*

160 g (5½ oz) *morcilla*

2 cloves

8 peppercorns

3 garlic cloves

2 tsp salt

2 tsp paprika

500 g (1 lb 2 oz) potatoes, peeled and cut into large chunks (4 cm/1½ inches)

225 g (8 oz) pumpkin, peeled and cut into large chunks

If using both the chickpeas and beans, drain and put the chickpeas to cook first with the salt pork or bacon, fresh pork and water. Bring to a boil, skim, then simmer for 30 minutes. Then add the drained beans. Let all simmer for about 1 hour, then add the chard or green beans, and the *chorizo* and *morcilla*. In a mortar crush the cloves and peppercorns with the garlic, salt and paprika and add to the pan. When the meat and chickpeas are nearly tender, add the potatoes and pumpkin. Cook for another 30 minutes. Cut the pork and sausages into small pieces and serve into soup bowls.

SERVES 6

ASTURIAN BEANS
FABADA

When winter comes to Asturias, in the north of Spain, this lusty bean casserole really hits the spot. The big white beans, called *fabes*, have taken the place of dried broad (fava) beans, used before the haricot bean came from the New World. In Asturias, *chorizo* and *morcilla* sausages are hung to smoke in big chimneys, adding another taste. If not available, use a chunk of smoked bacon instead of the salt pork. The cured pork shoulder or ham should preferably be raw, and soaked overnight before use (if using cooked ham, no soaking is required).

450 g (1 lb) dried lima beans
400 g (14 oz) cured pork shoulder or ham
100 g (3½ oz) streaky salt pork
400 g (14 oz) smoked *chorizo*
400 g (14 oz) smoked *morcilla*
½ tsp saffron, crushed
1 bay leaf

The day before, put the beans to soak in water. Separately, soak the cured pork or ham and salt pork in warm water. The next day, drain the beans and put in a *cazuela* or pan with water to a depth of two fingers over the beans. Quickly bring to a boil and skim off the froth. Add the cured pork or ham and salt pork to the beans, pushing them to the bottom of the beans. Cover and cook 10 minutes and skim again. Now add the *chorizo* and *morcilla*, cook for 5 minutes more and skim. Moisten the saffron in a little water and add to the beans with the bay leaf. Cook very gently for about 2 hours. Add a little cold water occasionally so the beans are always just covered. When the beans are tender, allow them to stand for 10 minutes. If too much liquid remains, purée some of the cooked beans in the blender and add them to the beans to thicken. Shake, don't stir, the *cazuela* or pan. Cut the meat and sausages into pieces to serve.

SERVES 4–6

FISH

Spain is a country with over 4,800 kilometres of coastline. Most of the coast is dotted with villages whose populations have traditionally earned their living from the sea – fishing, boat-building, canning and preserving. Although, before refrigeration, inland people might go a lifetime and never taste fresh seafood, nearer the sea fish made up a large part of the diet, resulting in many fine ways to prepare it.

Some of the best are the simplest – frying in olive oil, grilling over coals or on a hot *plancha*, an iron griddle – incredibly good when the fish is fresh. Others take advantage of local produce, combined with the fish in tasty ways.

It's a moonless night on the Mediterranean coast. Out on the dark sea, a line of lights twinkles, like fallen stars. They are the *traina*, fishing boats, each carrying bright lanterns to attract the fish. The nets are hauled in at dawn and the boats pulled up on the beach.

In former times, barefoot runners awaited the glistening catch – mainly small anchovies and sardines – to carry it to inland markets at fantastic speeds, attested to by the bulging leg muscles. Then, later from the shade of the morning streets of the pueblos came the hoarse, drawn-out cries of the fish vendors: '*que fresco, que bueno*', 'so fresh, so good', calling housewives to buy the fresh catch.

In modern times, fishing has gone global and high-tech. Enormous demand for food from the world's oceans has led to over-fishing and high prices at the fish market. The good news is that new ventures in fish farming on Spain's coasts are sending glistening fresh sea bass, bream, turbot and prawns to market at very reasonable prices.

MIXED FISH FRY
PESCA'ITO FRITO

On the Málaga and Cádiz coasts, this is fantastically good. The Andalusians have an ingenious way of preparing small fish for frying: first toss the fish lightly in a bowl of flour, then remove them to a flat-bottomed sieve, and shake the sieve hard to remove all excess flour. Even the tiniest fish are evenly coated with flour and there is no flour residue to burn in the oil. For best results, use olive oil. On no account should you combine two different oils for frying, because they have different smoking temperatures.

Allow per person a very small sole or any fish fillet; a slice of fresh hake or a tiny one (*pescadilla*), usually fried with its tail caught between its teeth; a dozen fresh anchovies (*boquerones*), a few rings of squid and, if desired, a few whole prawns. Flour and fry each kind of fish separately, then serve them hot on a platter with wedges of lemon.

GRILLED FISH WITH GARLIC DRESSING
PESCADO A LA PLANCHA

A *plancha* is an iron griddle. Use any whole fish, steaks or fillets. Fish to be grilled needn't be scaled. Very thick fish will cook faster if slashed through the thickest part of the flesh. Brush the griddle with oil and sprinkle it with coarse salt. Heat it until a drop of water sizzles when sprinkled on the griddle. Lay the fish on the griddle and cook on one side, turn and grill the other side. Fish, if prodded, should just pull away from the centre spine. Serve with the following dressing.

FOR THE DRESSING
- **3 garlic cloves, chopped**
- **3 tbsp chopped parsley**
- **½ tsp salt**
- **3 tbsp olive oil**
- **2 tbsp lemon juice**

Combine all the ingredients in a bowl. Spoon over grilled fish.

SEAFOOD GRILL WITH CATALAN PEPPER SAUCE
PARRILLADA DE PESCADOS Y MARISCOS CON ROMESCO

For a mixed seafood grill, *parrillada de pescados y mariscos*, cook several fish and shellfish on the griddle and serve with this sauce.

Besides fish and shellfish, this sauce, which comes from Tarragona, is served with any grilled meat, with vegetables, or as a salad dressing.

FOR THE DRESSING (MAKES ABOUT 300 ML/½ PINT)

250 ml (8 fl oz) extra virgin olive oil

2 dried red peppers or use more paprika

1 small chilli pepper or red pepper flakes

24 hazelnuts or almonds, blanched
   and skinned

1 slice bread (30 g/1 oz)

3 garlic cloves

½ tsp paprika

1 tsp salt

¼ tsp pepper

1 tbsp red or white wine

1 tbsp wine vinegar

Heat 6 tbsp of the oil in a heavy pan. Add the red peppers and chilli and fry until crisped but not brown, then remove. Add the nuts to the oil, brown them, then remove. Finally fry the bread until crisp, then remove. Grind the peppers, nuts, bread and garlic in a mortar, blender or processor, making a smooth paste. Add the paprika, salt, pepper, wine and vinegar, and blend until smooth. Whisk or blend in the remaining oil in a slow stream until the sauce is the consistency of thick cream. For a perfectly smooth sauce, pass it through a sieve. Cover and allow to stand for several hours before serving. Thin, if needed, with water or additional wine.

BASQUE-STYLE HAKE
MERLUZA A LA VASCA

En los meses sin erre, ni pescado ni mujeres.

In months with no 'R', neither fish nor women.

Such a great dish, so simple and full of flavour, when prepared with fresh, fresh fish, preferably that caught on a long line (*de anzuela*, found in the markets still hooked on a line). In spring-time, when asparagus is in season, use the fresh vegetable in this dish. Otherwise, garnish with tinned asparagus or a few cooked frozen peas. While hake is Spain's favourite flaky-white fish, cod or haddock could be used in its place.

1 kg (2 lb 3 oz) thick slices or medallions of hake

salt

1 tbsp plain flour plus more flour for coating fish

6 tbsp olive oil

6 garlic cloves, chopped

150 ml (¼ pint) white wine

12 asparagus tips, cooked, or 2 tbsp peas, cooked

salt and pepper

3 tbsp chopped parsley

2 hard-boiled eggs, chopped

Lightly salt the fish slices and let them stand for 30 minutes. Dredge them in flour. Heat the olive oil in an earthenware casserole or heavy frying pan. Add the pieces of fish and cook on a high heat, without letting them brown (earthenware prevents 'frying', but if you're using a metal pan, regulate the heat so the fish doesn't colour). Add the garlic when the fish is turned, then sprinkle with the spoonful of flour. Add the wine. Tilt the casserole or frying pan back and forth to combine the flour and wine, adding a little additional liquid if necessary to make a sauce the consistency of cream. Top with the cooked asparagus or peas, the chopped parsley and the chopped eggs. Serve in the same cooking pan.

SERVES 6

FRIED HAKE IN WINE MARINADE
MERLUZA FRITA AL VINO

As described in the previous recipe, there is nothing better than absolutely fresh hake, even for simple 'fish and chips'. In today's world, fish is likely to be frozen, available anywhere and of excellent quality. Frozen, thawed fish is always somewhat drier than fresh and just a little more bland. Therefore, this marinade preparation – fantastic with fresh fish – works well with frozen fish fillets. Thaw them slowly in the refrigerator.

700 g (1 lb 8½ oz) fillets of hake, cod or
  haddock

salt (only for fresh fish)

250 ml (8 fl oz) white wine

juice of 1 lemon

1 tbsp chopped parsley

1 garlic clove, minced

80 g (2¾ oz) plain flour

1 egg, beaten with a little water

80 g (2¾ oz) breadcrumbs

olive oil for frying

lemon wedges

Defrost frozen fish fillets for 1 hour. Place them in a shallow bowl in a single layer. If using fresh fish, salt well. Pour over the wine, lemon juice, chopped parsley and garlic. Let the fish marinate for 1 hour. Drain off the marinade (which can be used for a cooked soup). Dip the pieces of fish in flour, then beaten egg, then breadcrumbs. Fry them in hot oil in a frying pan, turning to brown both sides. Serve with lemon wedges.

SERVES 4

CHICLANA-STYLE HAKE
MERLUZA A LA CHICLANERA

The Basques don't have a monopoly on great fish dishes. In Andalusia, several recipes are outstanding. This is one, from the Bay of Cádiz area.

1–2 whole hake, or 750 g (1 lb 10 oz) fillets
salt
30 g (1 oz) plain flour
3 tbsp olive oil
150 g (5¼ oz) green peppers, chopped
150 g (5¼ oz) mushrooms, chopped
1 onion, chopped
2 garlic cloves, chopped
800 g (1 lb 12 oz) tomatoes, peeled and
    chopped
200 ml (7 fl oz) white wine

If using fresh fish, sprinkle with salt and allow to stand for 30 minutes. Coat the pieces of fish in flour and fry them briefly in hot oil. They do not need to brown. Transfer the fish to a *cazuela* or flameproof casserole. In the remaining oil, sauté the peppers, mushrooms, onion and garlic until the onion is softened. Then add the tomatoes and wine. Season with about ½ tsp salt, bring to a boil and simmer for 10 minutes. Pour over the fish and simmer gently until the fish flakes easily, about 15 minutes.

SERVES 4

FISH IN YELLOW SAUCE
PESCADO EN AMARILLO

Don't use a delicate, flaky fish for this dish. Good choices are grey mullet, conger eel, dogfish, bass, monkfish or cuttlefish. Although swordfish is cooked *en amarillo*, I find it dries that fish out too much.

800 g (1 lb 12 oz) fish fillets or steaks

salt

4 tbsp olive oil

2 slices bread, crusts removed (55 g, 2 oz)

3 garlic cloves

800 g (1 lb 12 oz) potatoes, peeled and cut in chunks

1 small onion, chopped

1 small green pepper, chopped

200 ml (7 fl oz) water

1 tsp salt

½ tsp saffron, crushed (or yellow colouring)

5 tbsp white wine

2 tbsp cooked peas (optional)

Salt the fish lightly and allow to stand for 30 minutes. Heat the oil in a *cazuela* or heavy frying pan. Fry the bread and 2 of the cloves of garlic until golden, then remove them. Add the potatoes, onion and pepper to the oil and sauté for a few minutes. Then add the water and salt, and simmer until the potatoes are almost tender, about 15 minutes. In a mortar, blender or processor grind together the fried bread and garlic cloves with the remaining clove of garlic and the crushed saffron. Thin with the wine. Stir this paste into the potatoes and add the pieces of fish. Cook, covered, until the fish is tender, about 10 minutes, adding a little extra water if the sauce is too thick. Add the cooked peas at the last minute, if desired.

SERVES 6

BREAM WITH WHITE WINE
BESUGO AL TXACOLÍ

The Basque country produces a white wine with an acidic bite, *txacolí*, which complements fresh fish admirably. Basque men-only 'cooking clubs' are famed for their interpretations of local favourites. This is one.

4 medium bream (about 375 g/13 oz each) or 800 g (1 lb 12 oz) fish fillets (John Dory is one good choice, sea bass would work well)

salt

40 g (1½ oz) plain flour

4 tbsp olive oil

50 g (1¾ oz) pine nuts or skinned almonds

2 garlic cloves

1 onion, finely chopped

2 tbsp chopped parsley

400 ml (14 fl oz) white wine

2 tbsp lemon juice

Clean the bream and cut into slices (or use fillets). Salt lightly and allow to stand for 30 minutes. Drain. Flour the pieces of fish and fry quickly in oil – the fish doesn't need to brown. Remove the pieces to a *cazuela* or heavy frying pan.

In the remaining oil, fry the pine nuts or almonds and garlic cloves, then remove. Add the onion to the oil and sauté until soft, 10 minutes. In a mortar, processor or blender, first grind the parsley, then add the cooked pine nuts, garlic and onion. Add the white wine. Pour the mixture over the fish. Add the lemon juice and 1 tsp of salt. Cook for 15 minutes or until the fish flakes easily and the sauce is reduced.

SERVES 4

BAKED FISH

PESCADO AL HORNO

This easy-to-prepare fish dish, a speciality of the Málaga and Cádiz coasts, is wonderful. Typically, a very large bream would be used.

1 whole fish (about 2 kg/4 lb 6 oz)

salt

5 tbsp olive oil

1 kg (2 lb 3 oz) potatoes, thinly sliced

5 garlic cloves, chopped

3 tbsp chopped parsley

110 g (4 oz) green peppers, chopped

salt and pepper

1 onion, sliced

375 g (13 oz) tomatoes, sliced

1 bay leaf

120 ml (4 fl oz) white wine

Preheat the oven to 190°C (375°F, gas 5). Gut and scale the fish. Rub it inside and out with salt and leave for 15 minutes. Pour the oil into the bottom of a large flameproof oven dish and add a layer of half the potatoes. Sprinkle half the garlic, half the parsley and half the peppers over them and sprinkle with salt and pepper. Add a layer of all the sliced onion and most of the tomato. Add the remaining potatoes, garlic, parsley and peppers. Sprinkle with salt and pepper. Place the fish on top of the potatoes and top with the remaining slices of tomato. Put pieces of bay leaf around it. Pour the wine over and put on low heat until liquid begins to simmer. Then cover with foil and cook in the oven until the potatoes and fish are done, about 40 minutes. Remove the foil during the last 15 minutes.

SERVES 6

BREAM GRILLED 'ON ITS BACK'
BESUGO A LA ESPALDA

Mentir y comer pescado quiere cuidado.

———————

Lying and eating fish both require care.

Traditionally grilled *a la brasa*, over oak charcoals, this is a speciality of San Sebastian in the Basque Country. Here I suggest cooking under an ordinary grill. If you want to try grilling on the barbecue, use a hinged fish rack which allows you to turn the whole fish easily, t hen remove the bones after cooking. Allow a whole fish of at least 750 g (1 lb 10 oz) for two people.

3 whole bream

salt

olive oil

6 garlic cloves, sliced

4 tbsp chopped parsley

approx 2 tsp tiny chilli peppers or red pepper flakes (or to taste)

juice of 1 lemon

salt

Butterfly the fish by slitting open along the belly. Lay the fish open, skin side down, and salt lightly. Leave briefly. Brush with oil. Put the fish on a preheated and oiled grill pan and put under a hot grill. Grill until the fish is done and flakes easily, 8–10 minutes. Do not turn the fish. While the fish are grilling, gently heat 120 ml (4 fl oz) of oil with the garlic, parsley and chilli or red pepper flakes. Remove from heat and add the lemon juice and salt. Slide the grilled fish on to serving dishes and spoon some of the oil and garlic over them.

SERVES 6

MADRID-STYLE BREAM
BESUGO A LA MADRILEÑA

All roads lead to Madrid, carrying the freshest seafood from ports on the Bay of Biscay, Atlantic and Mediterranean to the capital in the centre of the plains.

1 whole fish (about 1.5 kg/ 3 lb 5 oz)

salt

1 lemon (one half sliced, the other juiced)

3 tbsp olive oil

6 garlic cloves, chopped

4 tbsp chopped parsley

20 g (¾ oz) fine breadcrumbs

1 tsp paprika

1 bay leaf

120 ml (4 fl oz) white wine

Preheat the oven to 180°C (350°F, gas 4). Gut and scale the fish, salt it and leave to stand for 15 minutes. Cut 4 or 5 slits in the skin and insert a lemon slice into each. Put the oil in the bottom of an ovenproof pan large enough to hold the fish and place the fish on top. Combine the garlic, parsley, breadcrumbs, paprika and 1 tbsp of lemon juice and pour the mixture over the fish. Place pieces of bay leaf around the fish. Pour the wine into the pan around the fish. Cook in the oven, basting the fish with liquid in the pan frequently, until fish is done and flakes easily, about 25 minutes, depending on thickness. Best served from the same pan.

SERVES 4

SEA BASS COOKED WITH CIDER
LUBINA CON SIDRA

Asturias, in the north of Spain, is almost the only region which produces no wine. Apple cider fills the gap nicely, both in taverns and as a cooking medium. If Asturian cider isn't available, use any dry cider. The bubbles aren't important for cooking, but the cider should have a 'fresh' taste. Hake, bream or grey mullet can be used instead of bass.

1 whole sea bass (about 2 kg/4 lb 6 oz) or 800 g (1 lb 12 oz) fillets

salt

70 g (2½ oz) plain flour

120 ml (4 fl oz) olive oil

200 g (7 oz) onions, chopped

3 garlic cloves, chopped

600 g (1 lb 5 oz) tomatoes, peeled and chopped

2 tbsp chopped parsley

1 tsp paprika

600 ml (1 pint) dry cider

1 tsp salt

350 g (12¼ oz) unshelled clams (optional)

Clean and scale the whole fish and cut either into fillets or steaks. Salt the fish and leave to stand for 30 minutes. Flour the pieces lightly, patting off excess. Heat the oil in a frying pan and quickly fry the pieces of fish, 1 minute on each side. They do not need to brown. Transfer the fish to a *cazuela* or flameproof casserole. In the same oil, sauté the onions until softened. Add the garlic, then the tomatoes, parsley, paprika, cider and salt. Cook the sauce for 15 minutes until the vegetables are soft. Either press through a sieve or purée in a processor. Pour over the fish. Add the clams, if desired. Put the *cazuela* on a medium to high heat until the sauce begins to bubble. Reduce the heat and continue to cook, shaking the *cazuela* occasionally, until the clam shells open and the fish is cooked, about 10 minutes (or longer for thick cuts of fish).

SERVES 4

FISHERMAN'S-STYLE SWORDFISH
PEZ ESPADA A LA MARINERA

Make this with any whole fish or large fish steak with a firm flesh. Fish cooked this way is often served as a tapa, scooped up by the spoonful for individual servings.

1 kg (2 lb 3 oz) swordfish steak

salt

3 tbsp olive oil

1 onion, chopped

150 g (5¼ oz) green peppers, chopped

4 garlic cloves, chopped

375 g (13 oz) tomatoes, peeled and chopped

a few small clams (optional)

a few peeled prawns (optional)

1 bay leaf

2 cloves

10 peppercorns

120 ml (4 fl oz) white wine

1 tbsp chopped parsley

Sprinkle the fish with salt and leave to stand for 15 minutes. In a *cazuela* or flameproof casserole large enough to hold the fish, heat the oil and add the onion and peppers. Let them fry for 4 or 5 minutes, then add the garlic and tomatoes. When the tomatoes are sizzling, add the fish, clams and prawns, if desired, bay leaf, cloves and peppercorns and cook on a medium heat for a few minutes. Add the wine, bring to a bubble, then let everything simmer, spooning the sauce over the fish as it cooks. By the time the tomatoes and wine are reduced to a sauce, the fish should be cooked and the clam shells open, about 15 minutes. Serve garnished with parsley.

SERVES 5–6

MONKFISH WITH ALMOND SAUCE IN CASSEROLE
CAZUELA DE RAPE CON ALMENDRAS

The monkfish or angler fish is an ugly specimen with a huge head, but the solid flesh of the tail is sweet in flavour. Often, only the tails will be on sale in the UK, but if you can buy the head, you can use it to make a flavourful fish stock, the basis for an excellent soup.

1 kg (2 lb 3 oz) monkfish, sliced

salt

flour

4 tbsp olive oil

20 almonds, blanched and skinned

2 garlic cloves

1 sprig of parsley

1 slice bread, crusts removed

½ tsp saffron

3 tbsp white wine

1 onion, chopped

175 g (6 oz) tomatoes, peeled and chopped

120 ml (4 fl oz) fish stock or water

salt and pepper

Preheat the oven to 180°C (350°F, gas 4). Salt the fish slices and let them stand for 15 minutes. Then dust them with flour. Heat the oil in a frying pan and fry the fish quickly on both sides. Remove it to a *cazuela* or ovenproof casserole. In the same oil, fry the almonds, garlic, parsley and bread until the bread is crisped, then skim out. In a mortar, blender or processor grind the saffron with the almonds, garlic, parsley, bread and wine to make a paste. In the remaining oil, fry the onion until softened. Add the tomatoes and fry for several minutes. Stir in the almond paste and fish stock or water and simmer for 2 minutes. Season with salt and pepper and pour over the fish. Bake in the oven until the fish flakes easily, about 20 minutes.

SERVES 6

MULE DRIVER'S-STYLE CONGER EEL

CONGRIO AL AJO ARRIERO

This dish is a favourite in León, Aragon and the Rioja. Avoid the tail section of conger eel, which is bony. You can substitute monkfish or salt cod, soaked for 24–36 hours (see page 110), in this recipe.

1 litre (1¾ pints) water

2 tsp salt

3 tbsp wine vinegar

1 kg (2 lb 3 oz) conger eel, cleaned and cut
    in crosswise slices

4 tbsp olive oil

80 g (2¾ oz) bread, diced

4 garlic cloves, coarsely chopped

40 g (1½ oz) plain flour

1 tbsp paprika

dash of cayenne (optional)

2 hard-boiled eggs, chopped

1 tbsp chopped parsley

Bring the water to a boil with the salt and 2 tbsp of the vinegar. Put in the sliced fish and cook for 5 minutes. Drain, saving the liquid. When cool enough to handle the fish, cut away the centre bone and pick out any fine bones. Heat 2 tbsp of the oil in a *cazuela* or frying pan and fry the bread and garlic until crisp. Remove and set aside. Add the remaining oil to the pan. Flour the pieces of conger and add to the pan, turning to brown them quickly. Add the paprika, cayenne, the remaining vinegar and 200 ml (7 fl oz) of the reserved liquid, cover and cook 15 minutes. Add the fried bread cubes and garlic bits to the pan. Add the chopped eggs and a sprinkling of chopped parsley.

SERVES 4

CUTTLEFISH WITH PEAS
SEPIA AMB PESOLS

Versions of this dish are made on all of Spain's coasts. This one is from Catalonia.

1.5 kg (3 lb 5 oz) cuttlefish (cleaned, about 800 g/1 lb 12 oz)

5 tbsp olive oil

10 garlic cloves

50 g (1¾ oz) sliced bread

30 g (1 oz) almonds, blanched and skinned

1 sprig of parsley

1 onion, finely chopped

375 g (13 oz) tomatoes, peeled, seeded and chopped

150 ml (¼ pint) white wine

500 g (1 lb 2 oz) fresh peas, shelled (or 200 g/7 oz frozen)

¼ tsp saffron

10 peppercorns

a few red pepper flakes (optional)

1 tsp salt

a few sprigs of fennel and mint

Cut the cleaned cuttlefish into bite-size squares. Heat the oil in a *cazuela* or heavy frying pan and fry the garlic, bread, almonds and parsley until browned. Skim out and reserve. In the same oil, fry the onion until softened. Add the tomatoes, the pieces of cuttlefish, the wine and peas. Reserve a few almonds for garnish, then in a mortar, processor or blender, grind the fried garlic, bread, remaining almonds, parsley, saffron, peppercorns and red pepper flakes, if using, with the salt. Thin with a little water and add to the cuttlefish with the sprigs of fennel and mint. Cook, covered, until the cuttlefish is very tender, about 1 hour. Serve topped with a few of the reserved toasted almonds.

SERVES 4

Larded and Pot Roasted Tuna
Atún Mechado

Off the Cádiz coast in the Straits of Gibraltar, not far from the beach of Bolonia where excavations have uncovered the Roman town of Baelo Claudia, a centre of the making of *garum*, the tuna fishing fleet still pulls in tons of the big fish by the same methods that were used 2000 years ago. The *almadraba* nets, forming long chambers, are anchored to the bottom. Blue-fin tuna swimming through on their migration to spawn in the Mediterranean are trapped in the nets. Fishermen in boats pull the nets into a tightening circle, until the huge fish are trapped in the middle. The men gaff them and haul them on board. Freezing the serrano ham makes it easier to handle.

1 red pepper

1.2 kg (2 lb 10 oz) fresh tuna, in one piece (leave skin on, to help keep the flesh together)

100 g (3½ oz) serrano ham or lean bacon, cut into thin strips interleaved with greaseproof paper and placed in the freezer for several hours

10 olives (anchovy-stuffed, if possible), sliced

50 g (1¾ oz) plain flour

5 tbsp olive oil

10 garlic cloves

1 onion, quartered and sliced

450 g (1 lb) tomatoes, peeled and chopped

250 ml (8 fl oz) white wine

Preheat the oven to 180°C (350°F, gas 4). Cut the pepper into long, thin strips. With a thin, sharp knife, make deep slits crosswise in the tuna. Using the tip of a knife, push into each slit a strip of ham, a strip of red pepper and a slice of olive. When the tuna is criss-crossed with these lardings of ham, pepper and olives, trim off excess. Dredge the piece of tuna in flour. Heat the oil in a roasting pan and brown the tuna on all sides. Leave it skin-side down in the pan and add the garlic, onion, tomatoes and wine. Bring to a boil, then bake the tuna in the oven, basting with the pan juices, for 1 hour. Remove and allow to rest for 10 minutes before slicing the tuna. The vegetables and pan juices can be puréed or served as they are.

Serves 6

TUNA AND POTATO STEW
MARMITAKO

A Basque fisherman's stew, this is named after the *marmita*, the earthenware pot in which it cooks. In northern Spain, the albacore, a light-fleshed tuna, is called *bonito*.

1 kg (2 lb 3 oz) fresh tuna or bonito, without bones

3 tbsp olive oil

1 onion, chopped

4 garlic cloves, chopped

2 red or green peppers, cut in strips

500 g (1 lb 2 oz) tomatoes, peeled and chopped

2 tsp paprika

salt and pepper

a few chilli pepper or red pepper flakes, to taste

1 kg (2 lb 3 oz) potatoes, peeled and cut in chunks

200 ml (7 fl oz) white wine

120 ml (4 fl oz) water

Cut the tuna into chunks. Heat the oil in a deep cooking pan and sauté the onion, garlic and peppers until soft. Add the tomatoes, paprika, salt and pepper and chilli and cook until the tomatoes are somewhat reduced. Add the potatoes, stir for a few minutes, then add the wine and water. Cover the pan and cook on a high heat until the potatoes are nearly tender, about 15 minutes. Add the fish to the casserole, cover and cook for another 5–10 minutes or until the fish flakes easily. Let the stew rest, covered, for 5–10 minutes before serving.

SERVES 6

TUNA CONSERVE
ATÚN EN CONSERVA

The tuna canning industry has thrived on Spanish coasts since the beginning of the 19th century but, where tuna was brought in, fishermen's wives often preserved their own, as follows: for every 1 kg (2 lb 3 oz) of fresh tuna, use 1 litre (1¾ pints) of water and 100 g (3½ oz) of salt. Simmer the tuna in this brine for 3 hours. Drain and pat dry on a clean towel. Remove any skin and dark meat. Cover and leave to stand overnight. Pack the tuna in jars and completely cover with either olive oil or sunflower oil. Leave the tuna for at least 1 week. (For safety, tuna for long-term keeping should be further processed by cooking the sealed jars on a rack in boiling water for 1 hour.)

500 g (1 lb 2 oz) tuna, conserved as described, or tinned tuna (packed in oil), drained

250 g (9 oz) potatoes, boiled, peeled and sliced

2 hard-boiled eggs, chopped

2 tbsp finely chopped onion

1 tbsp chopped parsley

1 tbsp chopped capers (or *cornichons*, chopped)

2 tbsp juice from the capers or *cornichons*

lemon juice or wine vinegar

lettuce and tomatoes for garnish

Arrange chunks of tuna on a serving dish, and surround it with sliced potatoes. Mix the eggs with the onion, parsley, capers and juice plus lemon or vinegar to taste and a little of the oil from the drained tuna. Pour this dressing over the tuna and potatoes and garnish with lettuce and tomatoes.

FIRST COURSE SERVINGS 6

STUFFED MACKEREL
CABALLAS RELLENAS

6 medium mackerel

300 g (10½ oz) boneless white fish
    (hake, monkfish, sole)

50 g (1¾ oz) breadcrumbs

2 egg yolks

salt and pepper

½ onion, minced

1 tbsp chopped parsley

grating of fresh nutmeg

1 tbsp raisins, chopped

1 tbsp pine nuts

2 tinned anchovy fillets, minced

3 tbsp white wine vinegar

2 tbsp olive oil

2 tbsp dry white wine

Preheat the oven to 180°C (350°F, gas 4). Have the fishmonger bone the fish, leaving head and tail intact. (To do this yourself: slit the fish along the belly from tail to head. Gut the fish and wash them. Starting at the tail, ease the knife along the backbone, freeing the flesh of the upper fillet all the way to the head. Turn the fish over and repeat the operation. Now cut the backbone free at the tail and head and remove it.)

For the filling, finely mince the boneless white fish (can be done in processor). Mix it with the breadcrumbs, egg yolks, salt and pepper, onion, parsley, nutmeg, raisins, pine nuts, anchovies and vinegar. Stuff the mackerel with this mixture. Sew up the cavity openings with needle and thread. Pour the oil into an ovenproof dish and place the fish in it. Bake in the oven (adding a little wine after 10 minutes) for about 35 minutes, until the fish flakes easily and the stuffing is thoroughly cooked.

SERVES 6

MACKEREL AND NOODLE CASSEROLE
CABALLA CON FIDEOS

There are dozens of variations on this theme (see also noodles with pork chops, page 189). This is a very economical dish.

4 medium mackerel, filleted and sliced

salt

4 tbsp olive oil

1 onion, chopped

5 garlic cloves, chopped

250 g (9 oz) potatoes, peeled and diced

1 bay leaf

1 litre (1¾ pints) water

350 g (12 oz) spaghetti or thick vermicelli, broken into short lengths

¼ tsp saffron

4 peppercorns

6 tbsp white wine

2 tbsp chopped parsley

Sprinkle the mackerel fillets with salt and leave to stand for 30 minutes. Heat the oil in a *cazuela* or flameproof casserole and sauté the onion, garlic and potatoes until the onion is softened. Add the bay leaf, 1 tsp salt and the water. Bring to a boil, then reduce to a simmer and add the pieces of fish and the spaghetti or vermicelli. Crush the saffron and peppercorns and dissolve in the wine. Stir into the fish and pasta. Cook until the pasta is tender, about 15 minutes. The dish should be juicy, but not soupy. Serve sprinkled with chopped parsley.

SERVES 8

CASSEROLED ANCHOVIES
CAZUELA DE BOCARTES

A speciality of Santander, made with large, fresh anchovies. If these are not available, use instead small mackerel.

1 kg (2 lb 3 oz) fresh anchovies or mackerel

salt and pepper

3 tbsp olive oil

1 onion, chopped

3 garlic cloves, chopped

flour

½ tsp paprika

6 tbsp white wine

4 tbsp water

2 tsp wine vinegar

1 bay leaf

2 tbsp chopped parsley

Clean the fish and remove the heads. Sprinkle with salt and pepper and leave to stand for 30 minutes. Heat the oil in a *cazuela* or flameproof casserole large enough to hold the fish. Sauté the onion and garlic until softened. Stir in 2 tsp of flour and the paprika, then add the wine, water, vinegar and bay leaf. Cook, stirring, for a few minutes. Lightly flour the fish, then place them in the *cazuela*, spooning some of the sauce over them. Cook for 10–15 minutes, rocking the casserole to keep the sauce distributed. Sprinkle with chopped parsley and remove from the heat. Allow to rest for a few minutes before serving.

SERVES 6

GALICIAN FISH STEW
CALDEIRADA

This stew is real fisherman's fare, made aboard Galician and Basque fishing trawlers. Typically the potatoes would be boiled in sea water, then chunks of the day's catch of fish added, the whole to be served with a ruddy sauce of garlic and paprika. A similar dish from Valencia, *suc de llobarro*, is made with sea bass. Since much of today's fishing fleet specializes in the capture of fish to be frozen at sea, I have adapted the traditional recipe to use frozen fish.

750 g (1 lb 10 oz) frozen fish fillets such as monkfish or haddock

800 g (1 lb 12 oz) potatoes, peeled and quartered

1 litre (1¾ pints) water

1 onion, quartered

2 bay leaves

1 tbsp salt

5 tbsp olive oil

5 garlic cloves, slivered or coarsely chopped

1 tbsp paprika

2 tbsp wine vinegar

Remove the fish fillets from the deep freeze 1 hour before starting the dish. Put the potatoes in a deep cooking pan with the water, onion, bay leaves and salt. Bring to a boil and simmer for 10 minutes. Place the still-frozen slab of fish on top of the potatoes and keep the liquid at a bubble.

Meanwhile, in a separate frying pan, heat the oil and fry the bits of garlic until they are just barely golden. Remove the pan from the heat and stir in the paprika and the vinegar. Reserve.

When the potatoes are tender and the fish just flakes (15–20 minutes more), pour off the liquid and reserve it. Put the fish and potatoes in a serving bowl. Add 200 ml (7 fl oz) of the reserved liquid to the garlic–paprika sauce. Bring quickly to a boil, stirring, then pour it over the fish and potatoes.

SERVES 4

NAVARRE-STYLE TROUT
TRUCHAS A LA NAVARRA

Truchas y mentiras, poco valen si son chicas.

———————

Trout and lies, small ones aren't worth it.

Not only Navarre, but many mountainous regions of Spain have cold-water streams running with trout. Nowadays, trout farms provide a regular supply of this freshwater fish to markets.

4 trout (about 350 g/12 oz each)

salt

100 g (3½ oz) serrano ham or bacon, thinly sliced

55 g (2 oz) plain flour

olive oil for frying

1 lemon, cut into wedges

Gut the fish but leave them whole. Rub with salt inside and out and leave to stand for 30 minutes. Wrap each fish with a thin slice of ham and secure it with a cocktail stick. Dredge the fish in flour, patting off excess, then fry them gently in oil, over medium heat, for about 4–5 minutes on each side (until the fish flakes). Serve with lemon.

SERVES 4

ASTURIAS-STYLE SALMON
SALMON A LA RIBEREÑA

Wild salmon is taken in the rivers of northern Spain. Because the flavour of wild salmon is so fine, it is usually simply grilled, roasted or poached. Here is a slightly more elaborate preparation, excellent with farmed salmon.

4 salmon steaks

salt

plain flour

4 tbsp butter

2 tbsp olive oil

100 g (3½ oz) serrano ham, diced

6 tbsp cider or white wine

salt and pepper

Salt the fish and leave to stand for 30 minutes, then flour it lightly. Heat the butter and oil in a frying pan and put in the fish, moderating the heat so the fish cooks through in the time it takes to brown both sides, about 10 minutes. Remove the steaks to a platter and keep warm. In the same fat, sauté the ham. Stir in 1 tsp of flour, then add the cider or wine, salt and pepper. Simmer, stirring, until the sauce is thickened slightly. Pour over the salmon.

SERVES 4

POULTRY AND SMALL GAME

Before battery-raised chickens became widely available, chicken for dinner was not an everyday event. Though *pueblo* housewives might buy a quarter of a stewing hen, or less, to give depth of flavour to the *cocido*, the meat to be divided between a family of six or eight, a whole chicken in the pot was cause for celebration.

Small game – rabbit, hare, partridge, woodcock, turtledove – was, and is, abundant and there are hundreds of recipes for their preparation.

Farmed rabbit, hare, partridge and other game are now widely available, although you can easily substitute chicken and turkey if you prefer.

ROAST CHICKEN
POLLO ASADO

Tribulacion, hermanos — tres pollos entre cuatro.

Hard times, brothers – three chickens between four.

Country folk in Spain have always kept a few chickens, mainly for eggs, but for feast days a tender fowl, simply roasted, would make the occasion special. Because free-range chicken, *pollo del corral*, is leaner than battery-raised chicken, the basting with lard both keeps the meat moist and adds to the rich flavour.

1 roasting chicken, 2.5 kg (5½ lb)
brandy, Sherry or white wine
salt and pepper
slice of onion
sprigs of rosemary, thyme and parsley
bay leaf
3 tbsp lard or olive oil

Preheat the oven to 180°C (350°F, gas 4). Remove the giblets and wash and dry the chicken. Rub the chicken inside and out with brandy, Sherry or wine and salt and pepper.

Into the cavity place the slice of onion and the herbs. Rub the outside of the chicken with softened lard or olive oil. Roast in the oven, basting frequently, until golden and tender, about 2 hours.

Variation: Put 70 g (2½ oz) of *chorizo* sausage in the chicken's cavity and do not use the lard. Put in a roasting pan with diced potatoes. As the chicken roasts, baste it with the red drippings. Turn the potatoes to brown.

SERVES 6

STUFFED CHICKEN, CAPON OR TURKEY
POLLO, CAPÓN O PAVO RELLENO

For the feast of feasts, Christmas, when all the family gathers for a meal, this would be its centrepiece. In many parts of Spain, the feast takes place on *Noche Buena*, Christmas Eve, with the midday meal on Christmas Day being more informal. The quantities of fruits can be varied, with chopped apples substituting for some of the dried fruits. A lovely side dish, typical in Galicia, is puréed chestnuts with cream. If you cannot buy Málaga raisins, use the best quality seeded raisins. Roasted and peeled chestnuts are also available tinned or frozen.

1 roasting fowl, 3–4 kg (6½ lb–8¾ lb)

salt and pepper

lemon juice

50 g (1¾ oz) lard

200 g (7 oz) serrano ham, chopped

6 fresh pork sausages, skinned and chopped

50 g (1¾ oz) prunes, soaked, stoned and chopped

50 g (1¾ oz) dried apricots, soaked, stoned and chopped

30 g (1 oz) Málaga raisins, seeded

2 apples, peeled, cored and diced

½ onion, finely chopped

30 g (1 oz) pine nuts or walnuts

10 chestnuts, roasted, peeled and chopped

½ tsp cinnamon

salt and pepper

6 tbsp Sherry or medium-dry white wine

100 g (3½ oz) breadcrumbs

pork fat, thinly sliced

herb bouquet of thyme, oregano, bay, rosemary, parsley

120 ml (4 fl oz) wine or brandy, mixed with a little water, for basting

Preheat the oven to 200°C (400°F, gas 6). Clean the fowl, wash it and pat dry. Make a note of the weight. Rub the fowl inside and out with salt and pepper and lemon juice. Prepare the stuffing: heat the lard and sauté the ham and sausages until lightly browned, then remove and place in a large bowl. Add the prunes, apricots, raisins, apples, onion, pine nuts or walnuts, chestnuts, cinnamon, salt and pepper. Stir in the Sherry or wine and add breadcrumbs. Mix well. Stuff the bird with this mixture, and sew up the openings. Cover the breast with sliced pork fat and truss the bird with string, tying the legs and wings close to the body. Put the bird in a roasting pan with the herb bouquet. Put in the hot oven for 10 minutes, then reduce the heat to 180°C (350°F, gas 4) and roast the bird, basting frequently, for 1 hour. Add a little wine and continue roasting and basting, adding wine as it is cooked away. Remove the fat towards end of cooking time so skin browns. Allow about 20 minutes per 450 g (1 lb) of bird (weight dressed but before stuffed). Remove to a serving platter. Remove excess fat from the pan drippings and serve the sauce with the turkey.

Serves 12

CHICKEN IN ALMOND SAUCE
POLLO EN PEPITORIA

Con gallina en pepitoria bien se puede ganar la gloria.

With chicken in almond sauce, you're on the way to heaven.

Legend has it that a Moorish prince of Al-Andalus wed a blonde beauty and brought her to live in his southern realm. But, come winter, the lady grew sad and pined for the white snows which blanketed her own country. To make her happy, the prince had the hills surrounding the palace planted with thousands of almond trees, which bloomed in the bright winter days and covered the ground with their snowy blossoms.

Almond trees, which bloom white and palest pink in January and early February, still cover the hillsides of southern and eastern Spain, an early promise of spring. The nuts are harvested in autumn and are an ingredient in many of Spain's best-loved sweets, such as *turrón*, nougat, as well as many savoury dishes such as this one, in which they thicken and flavour a saffron-tinged sauce.

On the flip-side of the melting pot: one of the most famous dishes of Mexico, turkey in *mole poblano*, was created in the 16th century by Spanish nuns for the visit of a Spanish viceroy. That dish is, basically, chicken in *pepitoria* – a dish with full Moorish credentials – to which were added those New World ingredients turkey, chilli pepper and, a sumptuous discovery, chocolate.

Coming round full circle (perhaps when those nuns returned to Spain), chocolate from the New World was added to some savoury dishes (see recipe for *pollo a la Catalana*, Catalan chicken page 173). Some Catalan recipes use chocolate with rabbit and with lobster.

Pepitoria is a feast-day dish, especially enjoyed at Christmas. The reserved hard-boiled egg whites may be stuffed with tuna mayonnaise for a first-course dish.

1 large chicken or small turkey, 2.5–3 kg
    (5½–6½ lb)

salt and pepper

plain flour

5 tbsp lard or olive oil

25 almonds, blanched and skinned

6 garlic cloves

1 thick slice bread, crusts removed

1 onion, chopped

1 tbsp chopped parsley

¼ tsp ground cinnamon

grating of fresh nutmeg

pinch of ground cloves

10 peppercorns or ground black pepper

½ tsp saffron

120 ml (4 fl oz) dry Sherry or white wine

250 ml (8 fl oz) chicken stock

1 bay leaf

2 hard-boiled eggs, yolks only

1 tbsp sesame seeds, toasted

Joint the chicken or turkey. Rub the pieces with salt and pepper, then dredge with flour. Heat the lard or oil in a large frying pan and brown the pieces on both sides. Remove them to a flameproof casserole or large pan.

In the same fat, fry the almonds, garlic and slice of bread until golden. Remove them. Add the onion to the fat and sauté slowly. Grind the almonds, garlic cloves and bread in a mortar or food processor with the parsley, cinnamon, nutmeg, cloves, peppercorns and saffron. Mix in the Sherry or wine. Stir the spice mixture into the onion and pour it over the chicken pieces. Add enough stock to partially cover the chicken. Put in the bay leaf. Bring to a simmer, cover, and cook until chicken is very tender, about 1 hour. Shortly before serving, mash the egg yolks and stir into the sauce to thicken it slightly. (Alternatively, beaten eggs can be used.) Serve sprinkled with toasted sesame seeds.

Serves 6 or more, depending on size of the fowl.

Serves 6

CHICKEN WITH OLIVES
POLLO CON ACEITUNAS

A dish of Al-Andalus, Moorish Spain, which is made in a similar way in nearby Morocco. In Andalusia, the olives used would be split home-cured ones, slightly bitter and redolent of thyme, fennel and garlic. If these are not available, use pitted Seville olives and add herbs and garlic. An interesting variation is made with anchovy-stuffed olives. Wild duck is prepared in the same way as this chicken dish.

4 tbsp olive oil

1 chicken, 1.8 kg (4 lb), jointed

1 onion, chopped

200 g (7oz) tomatoes, peeled and chopped

3 tbsp brandy

175 ml (6 fl oz) dry Sherry or Montilla

salt and pepper

1 garlic clove, peeled

½ tsp dried thyme

½ tsp dried fennel

100 g (3½ oz) stoned olives

Heat the oil in a large pan and slowly brown the chicken pieces. Add the chopped onion while chicken is browning. Then add the tomatoes and fry briefly on a high heat. Add the brandy, Sherry or Montilla, salt and pepper and herbs. Cover and simmer the chicken until very tender, about 1 hour. (If desired, the sauce can be sieved and returned to the pan.) Add the olives and cook, uncovered, for a further 15 minutes.

SERVES 6

CHICKEN WITH SWEET PEPPERS
POLLO AL CHILINDRÓN

This dish is typical of Navarre and Aragón, where the sweetest peppers are grown. The same preparation is used with lamb, cut into pieces.

1 chicken, jointed, or 1.5 kg (3¼ lb) legs and breasts

salt and pepper

4 red peppers

3 tbsp olive oil

4 garlic cloves, cut in slivers

200 g (7 oz) serrano ham, in thin strips

1 onion, finely chopped

1 kg (2 lb 3 oz) tomatoes, peeled and chopped

Rub the chicken pieces with salt and pepper. Roast the peppers under the grill or over a gas flame, turning them until blistered and charred. Remove and let them sit, covered. Then peel them and cut the flesh into wide strips. Heat the oil in a *cazuela* or flameproof casserole and brown the chicken pieces, a few at a time. Add the garlic, ham and onion and fry for several minutes. Add the strips of pepper and the tomatoes. Cook the chicken, partially covered, until quite tender, about 45 minutes. The sauce should be reduced and thickened.

SERVES 4–6

CATALAN CHICKEN WITH VEGETABLES
POLLO EN SAMFAINA A LA CATALANA

You can also use this *samfaina* vegetable mixture with rabbit, salt cod or pig's trotters. The vegetables cook up into a thick sauce. If you prefer them crisper, cook the chicken with the onions, tomatoes and wine, but sauté the aubergine, peppers and courgette separately and add them to the chicken at the end of the cooking time.

1 chicken, 2 kg (4½ lb), jointed

salt and pepper

6 tbsp olive oil or lard

1 large aubergine (400 g/14 oz), peeled and diced

2 green or red peppers, cut in large pieces

400 g (14 oz) courgette, diced

2 onions, thinly sliced

3 garlic cloves, chopped

400 g (14 oz) tomatoes, peeled and finely chopped

5 tbsp white wine

1 bay leaf

sprig of thyme

sprig of parsley

Rub the chicken pieces with salt and pepper. In a *cazuela* or frying pan heat half the oil or lard and brown the chicken pieces, then remove them. Add the remaining fat and fry the aubergine until soft. Add the peppers and then the courgette, onions and garlic and fry for a few minutes. Add the tomatoes, then the wine, more salt and pepper, the bay leaf, thyme and parsley. Return the chicken pieces to the sauce, cover and cook until chicken is tender, about 50 minutes.

SERVES 4–6

CATALAN-STYLE CHICKEN
POLLO A LA CATALANA

This is one of several dishes which include just a touch of chocolate in the sauce, giving a rich taste. Use either grated plain chocolate or unsweetened cocoa powder. Choose a good quality chocolate with 70 per cent cocoa. If you add sliced lobster to this preparation, you have the delicious Catalan invention *mar i terra*, 'surf and turf'. Rabbit is also prepared with this sauce and *perdices a la navarra*, partridge, Navarre style, is similar.

1 chicken, 1.8 kg (4 lb), jointed

salt and pepper

2 tbsp lard or olive oil

3 cm (1¼ inch) piece of cinnamon stick

2 garlic cloves, chopped

1 onion, chopped

6 tbsp brandy or rum

150 ml (¼ pint) white wine

herb bouquet consisting of a bay leaf, sprig of thyme and parsley and a strip of lemon zest

¼ tsp saffron, crushed

30 g (1 oz) almonds and/or hazelnuts, blanched, skinned and toasted

30 g (1 oz) dark chocolate, grated or 15 g (½ oz) unsweetened cocoa powder

Rub the chicken pieces with salt and pepper. Heat the lard or oil in a *cazuela* or frying pan and brown the chicken slowly, covered, with the cinnamon stick and garlic, turning frequently. Add the onion and fry a few minutes more. Then add the brandy or rum, the wine and the herb bouquet. Cover and bring to a simmer. In a mortar or processor grind together the saffron, nuts and chocolate. Thin with a little water and add to the chicken. Season with salt and pepper and cook until chicken is very tender, about 40 minutes. Remove the cinnamon stick and herb bouquet before serving.

SERVES 4–6

GALICIAN-STYLE DUCK
PATO A LA GALLEGA

Domesticated ducks are raised in many parts of northern Spain, from Gerona in Catalonia to La Coruña in Galicia. In Galicia, turnips and chestnuts, always to hand, braise with the fowl, making an admirable cold-weather dish.

2 ducks, each weighing 1.8–2 kg (4 lb–4½ lb)

salt

2 tbsp lard

1 onion, sliced

250 g (9 oz) shelled chestnuts (fresh, dried or tinned)

4 carrots

8 turnips

250 ml (8 fl oz) white wine

4 tbsp anise brandy

600 ml (1 pint) stock

1 bay leaf

sprig of thyme

sprig of parsley

salt and pepper

Preheat the oven to 180°C (350°F, gas 4). Clean the ducks, removing excess fat from body cavities. Salt them and prick the skins with a skewer. Rub each with lard. Place the onion in a roasting pan, place the ducks on top and roast in the oven while you prepare the vegetables, about 30–40 minutes. If available, use the necks, wing tips and gizzards to make a stock.

If using dried chestnuts, soak them in warm water until soft, then drain.

While the ducks are roasting, peel the carrots and cut each in half crosswise. Peel the turnips and cut in half. Parboil the vegetables for 10 minutes, then drain. Drain the fat from the roasting pan and put the carrots and turnips around the ducks. Continue roasting until the ducks are nearly done, about a further 1 hour. Cut the ducks into quarters and place the pieces in a pan or deep flameproof casserole with the carrots, turnips and chestnuts. Pour off any remaining fat from the roasting pan. Add the wine to the roasting pan and deglaze the drippings. Add the anise brandy and stock. Bring to a boil. (If desired, the stock and ducks can be refrigerated overnight, allowing excess fat to solidify so it can be removed.) Then strain the liquid on to the ducks. Add the herbs and the salt and pepper. Bring to a boil, cover and simmer until the duck and vegetables are very tender, about 60 minutes, or return to the oven to finish cooking.

SERVES 8

PASTA WITH HARE STEW
ANDRAJOS CON LIEBRE

This dish from Jaén is much too good to be skipped over just because hare is not readily available. Make it instead with chicken, rabbit or the dark meat of turkey. The pasta (*andrajos* literally means 'rags' or 'scraps') can be simply made with flour and water, or substitute squares of lasagne.

FOR THE PASTA

- 125 g (4½ oz) flour (preferably hardwheat pasta flour)
- ½ tsp salt
- 1 tbsp olive oil
- 5 tbsp water

FOR THE STEW

- 1.5 kg (3¼ lb) chicken, hare or rabbit, jointed
- 2 litres (3½ pints) water
- ½ onion
- sprig of parsley
- sprig of mint
- sprig of thyme
- salt and pepper
- 5 tbsp olive oil
- 1 green pepper, chopped
- 1 onion, chopped
- 4 garlic cloves, chopped
- 100 g (3½ oz) wild mushrooms (optional), chopped (if using dried, use about 20 g/ ¾ oz)
- 400 g (14 oz) tomatoes, peeled, seeded and chopped
- ½ tsp ground cumin
- 1 tbsp paprika
- salt and pepper
- 1 tbsp chopped parsley or fresh mint

Combine the flour and salt in a bowl or on a pastry board. Make a well in the centre and add the oil and water. Mix the flour into the liquid until combined. Turn out on a lightly floured board and knead the dough until smooth. Cover and let it rest for 1 hour. To shape, roll the dough out as thinly as possible and cut into pieces approximately 6 cm (2½ inches) square. Let them dry or use immediately.

Put the chicken, hare or rabbit in a deep cooking pan with the water, onion, parsley, mint, thyme and salt and pepper. Bring to a boil, then cover and simmer until the meat is tender, about 45 minutes. Strain and reserve the broth. (Chicken broth can be chilled and the fat skimmed off.) When the meat is cool enough to handle, remove and discard the skin and bones. In a *cazuela* or flameproof casserole heat the oil and fry the pepper, onion, garlic and wild mushrooms, if using, until the onion is soft. Add the tomatoes and cook until reduced, about 8 minutes. Stir in the cumin, paprika and salt and pepper. Add about 1 litre (1¾ pints) of the reserved broth and the boned meat. When the liquid is nearly boiling, add the squares of pasta. Cook until they are tender, about 8 minutes (slightly longer if dried pasta is used). Serve from the *cazuela*, garnished with chopped parsley or mint.

SERVES 4

PASTA WITH RABBIT
GURULLOS CON CONEJO

As with the previous dish, this Almería stew works admirably with chicken instead of rabbit. For the pasta, use the pasta recipe from page 175. After resting the dough, roll it out into long thin cords. Let them dry then break into short (4-mm, ³/₁₆-inch) bits. Tiny soup macaroni could be substituted.

200 g (7 oz) white beans, soaked overnight

4 tbsp olive oil

4 garlic cloves

1 dried sweet pepper, stem and seeds removed, or 2 tsp paprika

1 rabbit, quartered, or 1 kg/2¼ lb chicken, jointed

1 onion, chopped

1 red pepper, chopped

300 g (10½ oz) tomatoes, peeled, seeded and chopped

120 ml (4 fl oz) dry Sherry

300 ml (½ pint) water or liquid from beans

salt and pepper

125 g (4½ oz) pasta (see above)

sprig of fresh thyme or fennel, chopped

Drain the soaked beans, add water to cover and cook them only until just tender, about 35 minutes. While the beans are cooking, heat the oil in a *cazuela* or flameproof casserole and fry the garlic and dried pepper until golden, then remove them. In the same oil, brown the pieces of rabbit, adding the onion and pepper. Then add the tomatoes, Sherry, water, 1 tsp salt and pepper. Grind the fried garlic cloves and dried pepper together and add to the rabbit. Cover and cook until the meat is tender, about 40 minutes. Add the pasta and cook until it is tender, about 5 minutes. Add the cooked beans and serve with a sprinkling of thyme or fennel.

SERVES 4–6

COUNTRY-STYLE RABBIT
CONEJO A LA CAMPERA

De las gallinas, el suelo; de los conejos, el techo.

The best of the chicken is the 'floor' (breast); the best of the rabbit, the 'roof' (saddle).

This is the sort of simple dish hunters might cook up after a day's shooting.

3 garlic cloves

3 tbsp olive oil

10 peppercorns

1 rabbit, cut into pieces

100 g (3½ oz) wild mushrooms, if available
(if using dried, use about 20 g/¾ oz)

1 onion, sliced

1 green pepper, chopped

1 tomato, chopped

1 litre (1¾ pints) water or stock

2 tbsp brandy or Sherry (optional)

2 sprigs of thyme or 1 tsp dried thyme

2 bay leaves

4 medium potatoes, peeled and quartered

1 tsp salt

Fry the garlic cloves in the oil until golden, then remove them. Crush them with the peppercorns. Fry the rabbit in the same oil until browned, then add the wild mushrooms, if available, the onion, pepper and tomato. Fry for another few minutes, then pour in the water or stock (leftover broth from the *cocido* would be used), brandy or Sherry if using, thyme, bay leaves, potatoes and salt. Cook until the rabbit is tender, about 35 minutes. Serve in soup bowls over thinly sliced bread.

SERVES 4

Mallorca-Style Rabbit
Conejo a la Mallorquina

A delicious dish, also made with hare or chicken.

1 rabbit, cut into pieces

2 tbsp lard

2 onions, sliced

140 g (5 oz) *sobrasada* (soft Mallorcan sausage) or *chorizo*

pinch of cayenne

ground cinnamon

Brown the rabbit pieces very slowly in the lard. Add the onions, sausage and cayenne. Continue cooking very slowly until the rabbit is tender, about 35 minutes. If necessary, add a little water to keep the rabbit just simmering. Serve with a sprinkling of cinnamon.

Serves 4

La Mancha-Style Shepherds' Stew
Galianos de Pastor de la Mancha

This old dish, made by shepherds living with their flocks far from towns, contains wild game killed in the uplands and *arroyos*. It used to be eaten from the heavy cooking pot, with *torta*, unleavened bread, serving as plate and spoon. Also called *gazpachos*, it's related to Andalusian gazpacho because it is thickened with bread. Use water biscuits or Hebrew matzo for the *torta*. Wild rabbit, pheasant, venison or turkey could be substituted for the hare and partridge.

1 hare or rabbit (1·5kg, 3 lb 5 oz skinned and dressed out), cut into 6–8 pieces

3 litres (5¼ pints) water

1–2 partridges, jointed

½ boiling fowl or large chicken (1.25 kg, 2 lb 12 oz), jointed

50 g (1¾ oz) salt pork or ham fat (optional)

3 bay leaves

sprigs of thyme and rosemary or 1 tsp dried herbs

3 dried sweet peppers, if available, or 1 red pepper

1 onion, quartered

2 tsp salt

6 tbsp olive oil

4 garlic cloves

1 onion, chopped

400 g (14 oz) tomatoes, peeled and chopped

2 tsp paprika

½ tsp saffron

10 peppercorns

6 tbsp red or white wine

125 g (4½ oz) water biscuits

Place the hare pieces in a large cooking pan with the water. Bring to a boil and simmer, partially covered, for 1 hour. Add the cleaned partridges and boiling fowl and the salt pork. Add the herbs, dried sweet peppers, onion and salt. Continue cooking gently until the meats are very tender, about 2 hours. Meanwhile, heat the oil in a frying pan and fry the cloves of garlic until golden, then remove. In the same oil, sauté the onion until softened, then add the tomatoes. In a mortar or blender crush the fried garlic cloves with the paprika, saffron and peppercorns. Thin this paste with the wine and stir it into the mixture in the frying pan. Pour the broth through a colander into a big bowl, draining the meat. When the meats are cool enough to handle, skin and bone them and cut into chunks. Return to the cleaned pan with about 2 litres (3½ pints) of the strained broth. Stir in the mixture from the frying pan. About 20 minutes before serving, break the water biscuits into pieces and add to the simmering broth. Serve into deep plates, with meat, broth and biscuits.

SERVES 8–10

PARTRIDGE WITH CABBAGE
PERDICES CON COLES

Pájaro que vuela es para la cazuela.

———————

Any bird that flies is for the stew pot.

Cabbage becomes wonderfully flavourful cooked in this way. A slightly more complicated version, from Catalonia, calls for stuffed cabbage rolls to be added to the braised partridge.

2 partridges or 1 chicken (about 1.6 kg/ 3½ lb)

3 tbsp olive oil or lard

1 onion, chopped

1 garlic clove, slivered

50 g (1¾ oz) ham or bacon, diced

1 tbsp plain flour

120 ml (4 fl oz) white wine or cider

300 ml (½ pint) water or stock

1 tbsp wine vinegar

½ tsp thyme

strip of orange zest

2 bay leaves

1 tsp salt

1 small cabbage (1 kg/2 lb 3 oz)

1 tbsp chopped parsley

If using chicken, cut it in half. Truss and tie the partridges or chicken halves. Brown them slowly in a pan with the oil or lard. Add the onion, garlic and ham or bacon. When the birds are nicely browned, sprinkle with the flour. Add the wine or cider, water or stock, vinegar, thyme, orange peel, bay leaves and salt. Cover and cook slowly until tender, about 1 hour. Meanwhile, chop the cabbage and blanch it in boiling salted water for 10 minutes. Drain. Add the cabbage to the pot about 20 minutes before the partridge is done. To serve, skim out the cabbage on to a serving dish. Split the partridges or chicken halves and arrange on top. Sprinkle with chopped parsley. Boil the remaining liquid to reduce, strain and serve the sauce separately.

SERVES 4

PARTRIDGE STEWED WITH BEANS
PERDIZ ESTOFADO CON ALUBIAS

Made with partridge or wild hare this is a delicious country dish, but it works very nicely with turkey drumsticks substituted for the small game.

400 g (14 oz) white beans, soaked overnight

1 onion, quartered

2 bay leaves

sprig of thyme

salt

3 partridges or 3 turkey legs (each weighing about 400 g/14 oz)

400 g (14 oz) tomatoes, quartered

1 carrot, sliced

3 tbsp olive oil

1 head roasted garlic (see page 13)

ground black pepper

¼ tsp chopped thyme or rosemary

1 tbsp brandy (optional)

Drain the soaked beans and put them to cook in ample water with a quarter of the onion, the bay leaves and sprig of thyme. Simmer for 20 minutes, then add a dash of cold water and 1 tsp of salt. Simmer for another 15 minutes until the beans are tender, but not mushy. Drain them, reserving 300 ml (½ pint) of the liquid.

In a *cazuela* or deep pan, place the partridges or turkey legs, tomatoes, carrot, oil, cloves of roasted garlic, remaining onion, 1 tsp salt, some pepper and thyme or rosemary. Pour in the bean liquid. Bring to a boil and simmer until the partridge or turkey is very tender, about 1¼ hours. Skim out the meat and allow to cool. Press the liquid and solids through a sieve and return the sauce to the pan. Add the cooked beans. When the meat is cool enough to handle, strip off and discard the skin and bones. Cut the meat into bite-size pieces and add to the pan. Add the brandy, if desired. Simmer the stew for another 35 minutes.

FIRST COURSE SERVINGS 6; MAIN DISH SERVINGS 4

Toledo-Style Marinated Partridge
Perdiz en Escabeche a la Toledana

Y vivieron felices, comieron perdices y a mí no me dieron.

And they ate partridge, and lived happily ever after.

Toledo, in the centre of Spain, is famous for its red-legged partridge, once taken in such quantity that the birds were conserved in a strong, vinegar-based marinade. Placed in clay pots and topped with oil, they would keep for long periods of time. Today, with refrigeration, less vinegar is needed. Quail can be prepared in the same manner.

4 partridges

5 tbsp olive oil

4 onions, quartered

4 garlic cloves, slivered

1 carrot, quartered

4 bay leaves

1 tsp chopped thyme

sprig of parsley

10 peppercorns

2 cloves

120 ml (4 fl oz) wine vinegar

120 ml (4 fl oz) white wine

2 tsp salt

water

Clean the partridges and tie them with string so they keep their shape. In a *cazuela* or deep flameproof casserole, brown them slowly in the oil then remove. Pour off most of the oil. Return the partridges to the pan with the onions, garlic, carrot, bay leaves, thyme, parsley, peppercorns and cloves. Turn them in the oil for a few minutes, then add the vinegar, wine and salt. Cook for 10 minutes, covered, then add enough water to cover the birds completely. Cover and simmer until they are very tender, about 1 hour, adding more water as needed so that the partridges stay nearly covered. Remove from the heat and let the birds cool in the liquid. Remove the string from the partridges and put them in a glass or ceramic pot. Strain the liquid over them and cover tightly. Refrigerate for at least 2 days. Serve the partridges at room temperature with garnishes of lettuce, tomato, hard-boiled eggs. (Or strip it from the bones and use in any of the stewed partridge dishes or in a salad, see recipe page 34).

First course servings 8–10
Main dish servings 4

PORK

It's said that juicy, delicious pork made more converts to Christianity than all the rigours of the Inquisition. The flesh of the pig, of course, was forbidden to both Muslims and Jews, but many, faced with forced conversion or expulsion, ate it to prove their adherence to the new faith. Unlike cattle, which require good grazing land, pigs are not particular what they eat, so they can be raised just about anywhere, including a back patio, where they grow fat on table scraps. Also, because of the animal's fat density, pork, more than other meats, lends itself to preserving by salting, smoking or curing, a boon in those bygone days before refrigeration.

The winter *matanza*, pig butchering, is a tradition throughout Spain. The whole village participates in the butchering and preparation of sausages and hams, taking it in turns, from house to house, to help one another. Early every morning the women start preparing great pots of food to feed all the helpers.

The work goes on for two or three days. Usually, a skilled butcher is called in for the slaughtering. The blood is drained into tubs, later to be made into black sausage. The intestines and stomach, to be used as sausage casings, are cleaned and put to soak. Liver and kidneys are cooked immediately. On the second day, the pig is cut up – hams, shoulders, head, fat back, belly fat, loins, ribs, ears, tail – nothing is wasted. Hams, bacon, even ribs and ears are packed in salt. Meat is ground for sausages, seasoned with garlic and spices. After kneading, it's left to stand for two days. Then some is fried up, to taste if the seasonings are right. Fatty skin, slowly rendered down, yields lard (which is packed in crocks to last a whole year) and *chicharrones*, crisp-fried crackling, a real treat. Especially prized is the loin, either cooked and preserved in lard or put in *adobo*, a type of conserve with vinegar.

Each region makes its particular sausages – a version of *chorizo*, the ruddy-coloured paprika sausage, and *morcilla*, blood sausage, which might contain pine nuts, rice, raisins, onions, cinnamon, sugar or honey, potatoes or pumpkin! But there are dozens more types. Spicy fresh pork sausage is meant to be cooked immediately, but most of the others are cured. Only in the north are sausages likely to be smoked.

In spite of all the work, such get-togethers are always festive occasions, a chance for neighbours or country folk to meet, to gossip, flirt, sing and dance.

In former days, when people worked extremely hard to scratch a living from the earth and hauled firewood to warm themselves through bitter winters, the extra calories in lard, salt pork and sausages were vital to survival.

Today, of course, they are bad news to the health conscious! Though the flavours of fatty foods are still enticing, village housewives cook with less pork now, using more beef, lamb and chicken than in former times.

MARINATED PORK LOIN
LOMO EN ADOBO

This is the most luxurious by-product of the pig butchering – the whole loin is boned and preserved in a marinade which keeps the pork conserved for several weeks in cold weather. Typically, a few pieces at a time would be sliced off and fried, as required. With refrigeration, the preserving isn't essential, but the flavours are still appreciated. Roasted whole with herbs, the loin makes a showy buffet presentation. If desired, roast it on top of potatoes prepared as for *patatas a lo pobre* (see recipe on page 89). The meat is marinated for 48 hours before cooking.

1.5 kg (3 lb 5 oz) boned pork loin

4 garlic cloves

1 tsp oregano

pinch of thyme

pinch of rosemary

¼ tsp saffron, crushed

10 peppercorns

1 tsp salt

1 tsp paprika

2 tbsp olive oil

200 ml Sherry or wine vinegar

Put the pork loin into a deep bowl. Crush the garlic with the oregano, thyme, rosemary, saffron, peppercorns, salt and paprika. Combine with the oil and vinegar. Pour over the pork. Cover and marinate, refrigerated, for about 48 hours, turning the meat twice a day.

Preheat the oven to 200°C (400°F, gas 6). Drain the piece of meat and pat it dry. Place it in an oiled roasting pan and put in the oven for 5 minutes. (If available, fresh sprigs of rosemary, thyme and bay can be placed in the bottom of the roasting pan.) Reduce the oven temperature to 180°C (350°F, gas 4) and roast until the pork is done, about 1½ hours. Allow the meat to rest for 10 minutes before slicing.

SERVES 8–10

PORK LOIN STUFFED WITH PINE NUTS
LOMO DE CERDO RELLENO CON PIÑONES

This is a dish for festive occasions, such as an *almuerzo*, luncheon, following a christening, wedding or first communion. Pine nuts, with their subtle, resinous flavour, are free for the picking in sierras for those patient enough to extract the tiny nuts from the shells. Walnuts could be substituted in this recipe. Your butcher will need to prepare the meat, as described below.

1 piece of boneless pork loin
    (about 1.4 kg/ 3 lb)

salt and pepper

200 g (7 oz) pine nuts

1 tsp olive oil

1 head garlic

200 g (7 oz) minced beef

200 g (7 oz) minced pork

1 egg, beaten

1 tsp salt

¼ tsp pepper

grating of fresh nutmeg

2 tbsp chopped parsley

pinch of chopped thyme

175 ml (6 fl oz) medium Sherry (*oloroso*
    or *amontillado*)

100 g (3½ oz) serrano ham, cut in strips

4 tbsp olive oil or lard

1 onion, sliced

4 bay leaves

200 ml (7 fl oz) water

Have the butcher open the pork loin like this: first cut lengthwise through the centre, without cutting through, and open the loin like a book. Then, from the centre, slice through the meat towards the outer edge, without cutting through, and open up that flap of meat. Repeat on the other side. You should now have a rectangular slab of meat of more or less equal thickness. Sprinkle the meat with salt and pepper.

To make the filling, fry the pine nuts in the teaspoon of oil until they are golden, then remove. In a mortar or processor, grind half the nuts with 2 cloves of the garlic. Combine with the minced meats, egg, salt, pepper, nutmeg, parsley and thyme. Mix well. Add 2 tbsp of the Sherry. Spread half the filling over the two centre sections of the opened-out slab of meat. Top with half of the strips of ham and half of the remaining pine nuts. Fold in the outer flaps. Spread with remaining stuffing, ham and pine nuts. Bring the edges together and sew together with needle and heavy thread. Secure the meat with twine.

Heat the oil or lard in a deep, heavy cooking pan. Slowly brown the meat on all sides. Add the onion to brown when meat is nearly browned. Add to the pan the remaining cloves of garlic, the bay leaves, the remaining Sherry and the water. Bring to a boil, then cover and simmer, turning the meat occasionally, until it is tender, about 1½ hours. Lift the meat from the pan on to a cutting board, and let it rest at least 10 minutes. Meanwhile, reduce the sauce, skim off any fat and strain the sauce. Remove the thread and string from the meat before carving into slices. The meat can be served hot or cold.

SERVES 8–10

ROAST FRESH HAM OR PORK SHOULDER
JAMÓN O LACÓN ASADO

This recipe requires the meat to be marinated for 12–24 hours. Quantities for the marinade are for 2 kg (4 lb 6 oz) meat, and need to be increased for higher weights.

2–4 kg (4½ lb – 8¾ lb) fresh ham on the bone or pork shoulder

2 tbsp chopped parsley

1 tsp chopped rosemary or ¼ tsp dried

1 tsp chopped thyme or ¼ tsp dried

2 bay leaves, crushed

½ tsp coarsely ground black pepper

1 tbsp oregano

2 tbsp paprika

6 garlic cloves

4 tbsp olive oil

1 tsp salt

150 ml (¼ pint) dry Sherry, brandy, white wine or cider

potatoes or chestnuts, for roasting (optional)

If you like crackling and can tolerate the extra fat, buy meat with the skin on. Otherwise, trim the ham or pork shoulder of all extra fat.

The day before: combine the parsley, rosemary, thyme, bay leaves, pepper, oregano and paprika. Crush the cloves of garlic in a mortar or blender with the olive oil and salt, then mix with the herbs to make a paste.

Prick the meat all over and rub it on all sides with this paste. Cover and marinate for 12–24 hours. Bring to room temperature before roasting.

To cook: preheat the oven to 230°C (450°F, gas 8) and place the meat in a roasting pan. Roast in the oven for 20 minutes. Reduce the oven temperature to 180°C (350°F, gas 4) and roast the meat, allowing about 25 minutes per 450 g (1 lb). Prick it several times while roasting. Forty minutes before the meat is done, pour over the Sherry, brandy, wine or cider. Add peeled and quartered potatoes, if desired. Chestnuts, slit, can also be roasted with the meat.

SERVES 8

PORK FILLET WITH ORANGE
SOLOMILLO DE CERDO A LA NARANJA

Pork fillet is for special occasions, perhaps a gala dinner for New Year's Eve, when the orange season is at its peak. Peeled chestnuts can be roasted with the meat.

3–4 pork fillets (750 g/1 lb 10 oz)
3 garlic cloves
salt and pepper
pinch of rosemary
300 ml (½ pint) fresh orange juice
30 g (1 oz) sugar
fresh rosemary (optional)

Rub the fillets with crushed garlic, salt, pepper and rosemary and allow them to marinate for several hours, covered and refrigerated. Put them in a pan, add the orange juice and sugar and simmer the fillets until cooked through, about 25 minutes, turning them once. Remove them to a serving platter and keep warm. Raise the heat and boil the juice until thickened. Slice the meat and spoon over the sauce. Garnish, if desired, with sprigs of fresh rosemary.

SERVES 4–5

PORK FILLET WITH POMEGRANATE SAUCE
SOLOMILLO CON SALSA DE GRANADAS

A Mallorcan dish flavoured with the ruby seeds of pomegranates. If fresh pomegranates are not available, use a little grenadine syrup, but balance the sweetness with lemon juice. Accompany with thickly sliced potatoes fried gently in lard.

1–2 pomegranates

50 g (1¾ oz) lard

4 pork fillets (about 800 g/1 lb 12 oz)

1 onion, chopped

100 ml (3½ fl oz) dry Sherry

100 ml (3½ fl oz) meat stock

salt and pepper

Cut the pomegranates in quarters and with a knife loosen the seeds from the membrane. Reserve a handful for garnish. Heat the lard in a pan and brown the fillets with the chopped onion. Add the pomegranate seeds to the meat with the Sherry, stock, salt and pepper. Cover and simmer for 20 minutes. Remove the meat and keep warm. Cook the sauce for another 15 minutes to reduce. Sieve the sauce and serve it over the meat. Garnish with the reserved pomegranate seeds.

SERVES 4–5

NOODLES WITH PORK CHOPS
FIDEOS CON CERDO

Fideos are essentially soup noodles, ranging from the fine 'angel's hair' to thick vermicelli. Spaghetti can be substituted in this dish, but break it into short (5 cm/2 inch) lengths before cooking. Pieces of chicken or fish can be cooked with noodles in the same manner.

3 tbsp olive oil or lard

10 almonds or hazelnuts, blanched
  and skinned

 garlic cloves

4 pork loin chops

1 onion, chopped

300 g (10½ oz) tomatoes, peeled
  and chopped

21 litre (1¾ pints) boiling water

1 tsp salt

400 g (14 oz) spaghetti or thick vermicelli

150 g (5¼ oz) shelled peas (can use frozen)

¼ tsp saffron, crushed

¼ tsp ground black pepper

1 tbsp chopped parsley

2 plain Marie biscuits (*galleta Maria*)

150 ml (¼ pint) white wine

Heat the oil or lard in a *cazuela* or flameproof casserole and fry the almonds and garlic until golden. Remove them. Brown the pork chops in the fat and remove. Add the onion and continue frying until softened, then add the tomatoes and reduce for a few minutes. Add the boiling water and salt. Return the pork chops to the *cazuela* and add the spaghetti or vermicelli and the peas. When the water returns to a boil, turn it down to a slow bubble. In a mortar, processor or blender grind together the toasted nuts and garlic with the saffron, pepper, parsley and biscuits. Thin with the wine and add to the *cazuela*. Cook until the noodles are tender, about 25 minutes.

SERVES 4

RED SAUSAGE
CHORIZO

This is Spain's most characteristic sausage, flavoured with garlic and the pulp of dry red *choricero* peppers which give the meat a sweet, dusky flavour. Actually, two different sausages are called *chorizo*, because they are flavoured similarly. One is a hard, cured sausage, sliced and served as a cold cut. The other, air-dried, sometimes smoked, is soft, usually tied off in short links and is always cooked. It can be fried – wonderful with eggs – or stewed with beans and vegetables, an indispensable ingredient for typical casseroles and stews.

If you enjoy the challenge of sausage-making, find out where to buy sausage casings, get out your mincer and have a go. But, even if not, you can enjoy the unique flavour of *chorizo* without the bother of stuffing. Either shape it into patties for frying or, for simmering, roll it in cheesecloth or muslin and tie tightly. To cook on the barbecue, encase it in foil.

2 dried sweet *choricero* peppers, if available (or 1 tbsp paprika)

3 tbsp white wine (optional)

1 kg (2 lb 3 oz) pork, lean and fat, put through the mincer twice

5 garlic cloves, crushed

1 tbsp salt

3 tbsp paprika

1 tsp cayenne

½ tsp ground black pepper

If using the dried peppers, remove the stems and seeds and cook them in enough water to cover for 30 minutes. Cool, saving the liquid, and scrape out the pulp, discarding the skins. Mash the pulp and blend with the white wine or a little of the liquid. In a bowl, combine the minced meat with the garlic, salt, paprika, cayenne, pepper and the pepper pulp. Knead it very well with the hands. Cover tightly and refrigerate for 24 hours. Take a little of the meat, fry it until thoroughly cooked and taste it (*la prueba de chorizo*) for seasoning. If necessary, add more salt, paprika or cayenne or garlic. Let the meat season for another 24 hours. At this point, it can be stuffed into casings, tied off at 10 cm (4 inch) lengths, and hung to dry for a week, then stored in a cold place for a month. To serve, fry, grill or simmer the sausages.

MAKES 1 KG (2 LB 3 OZ)

ANDALUSIAN HASH
PICADILLOS A LA ANDALUZA

Make this with pork or pork liver or with chopped beef.

100 g (3½ oz) pine nuts or almonds,
    toasted

2 tbsp olive oil

500 g (1 lb 2 oz) pork, cut into small dice
    or shredded

125 g (4½ oz) salt pork or bacon, diced

1 onion, finely chopped

400 g (14 oz) tomatoes, peeled and chopped

½ tsp ground cinnamon

grating of fresh nutmeg

¼ tsp saffron, crushed

½ tsp ground black pepper

1 tsp salt

6 tbsp white wine

6 tbsp water

2 hard-boiled eggs, sliced

1 tbsp chopped parsley

triangles of fried bread

Fry the pine nuts or almonds in the oil until golden, then set them aside. In the same oil, fry the diced pork and salt pork or bacon. Add the onion. When the meat is browned, add the tomatoes and fry for a few minutes. Then add the cinnamon, nutmeg, saffron, pepper, salt, wine and water. Cover and cook until meat is tender and the liquid absorbed, about 30 minutes. Garnish with the fried pine nuts, eggs, chopped parsley and triangles of fried bread.

SERVES 4

ROAST SUCKLING PIG
COCHINILLO ASADO

The ancient kingdoms of Old Castille and León occupy Spain's high plains, where much of the country's grain is grown. Dry scrubland supports huge flocks of sheep and cold uplands are renowned for the quality of their *chacinería*, cured pork sausages. Where pigs are raised, frequently one or more of a litter is taken from a sow to give the remaining a better start on the road to becoming sausages. Hence, roast suckling pig. The best piglets are said to be 'family-reared,' preferably by a miller's wife who feeds them with wheat, corn and bran mash. Traditionally the piglet was roasted in a domed bread oven, heated with aromatic burning herbs, wild oak, vine prunings. The piglet should be no more than three weeks old and weigh from 3.5 to 4 kg (7¾–8¾ lb 12 oz). It is split in half and opened out for roasting. However, for a home oven, it may be more convenient to quarter the piglet.

1 suckling pig, 3.5–4 kg (7¾–8¾ lb)

100 g (3½ oz) lard

4 garlic cloves, crushed

2 bay leaves, crushed

sprig of thyme

sprig of rosemary

1 tbsp salt

1 tbsp wine vinegar

3 tbsp water

Have the butcher open the piglet lengthwise without cutting through or else cut it into quarters. Preheat oven to 200°C (400°F, gas 6). Wrap foil around the ears and feet to keep them from browning too fast. Beat the lard until softened and add the garlic. Place the pig, skin side down, in a roasting pan and spread the meat with half the lard. Sprinkle with a little bay, thyme and rosemary (the pig can also be placed on top of branches of bay stripped of their leaves). Add enough hot water to cover the bottom of the roasting pan. Place the pig in the preheated oven and immediately turn down the heat to 160°C (325°F, gas 3). Roast the pig for 1 hour, adding additional water if needed to keep skin from sticking to the pan. Remove from oven and carefully turn the meat skin side up. With a fork or knitting needle, prick the skin all over and brush with the remaining lard. Return to the oven for 15 minutes. Then mix the salt, vinegar and water and baste the meat with it. Roast, basting once again, until the skin is crackly and meat is very tender, about 30 minutes more (raise oven temperature, if necessary, to brown).

SERVES 6–8

LAMB

From as far back as the 13th century, when the shepherds' guild, *La Mesta*, was established, Spain has been a sheepraising country. By the 15th century, the trade in fine merino wool with Bruges and Antwerp was at its height. Thousands of sheep would be moved across the central plains of Castille and La Mancha into Extremadura in a seasonal transhumance; the movement still occurs, though now stock is sometimes moved by train and lorry.

Shepherds' food – simple stews, flour, porridge with sheep's milk, cheese and sausage, with the occasional rabbit or partridge – makes up a large body of traditional fare.

Where sheep are kept for milk, it is customary to remove newborn male animals after a few weeks so the ewes' milk can be consumed by humans or made into cheese (Spain's best-known cheese, Manchego, is a sheep's milk cheese). So these tiny suckling animals wind up in the stew pot or, in Castille, in the roasting ovens. Supposedly, the best lamb comes from ewes which have grazed the herb-covered highlands. The meat is said to be infused with herbs from the mother's milk. Baby lamb should be milk-fed, between four and seven weeks old, and weigh, dressed, from 5–7 kg (11–15½ lb). Spring lamb, which has already begun to graze, is usually slaughtered at four or five months.

In many parts of Spain, where dairy cattle could never survive, herds of goats graze steep hillsides and provide milk, cheese and meat. Baby kid is enjoyed as much as lamb. It can be used in place of lamb in any of the following recipes.

Castillian-Style Roast Baby Lamb
Lechazo Asado al Castellano

A leg of spring lamb can be roasted in the same manner.

1 baby lamb, about 5 kg (11 lb)

salt and pepper

3 garlic cloves

1 tbsp chopped parsley

1 tsp chopped thyme

1 pinch of rosemary

1 tsp wine vinegar

1 tbsp olive oil

1 tsp paprika

50 g (1¾ oz) lard

250 ml (8 fl oz) white wine

Have the butcher split open the lamb lengthwise, without cutting through, or else quarter it, and remove the head (which is usually braised separately). Rub the meat inside and out with salt and pepper. In a mortar crush the garlic, parsley, thyme and rosemary and mix with the vinegar, oil and paprika. Rub the lamb with this mixture and let it stand for 2 hours. Preheat the oven to 200°C (400°F, gas 6). Place the lamb in an earthenware roasting dish, skin side up. Spread it with the lard and place in the oven. Immediately reduce the heat to 160°C (325°F, gas 3). Roast for 30 minutes, then pour over the wine. Continue roasting, basting with the pan drippings occasionally, until the meat is very tender, about 2½ hours. If the meat is browning too fast, cover it with foil.

Serves 8

LAMB IN PEPPER SAUCE
COCHIFRITO DE CORDERO

700 g (1 lb 8½ oz) boned lamb
  (shoulder or leg)

1 red pepper (or 125 g/4½ oz tinned
  pimientos

3 tbsp olive oil or lard

3 garlic cloves

2 slices bread

1 bay leaf

½ tsp chopped thyme

¼ tsp freshly ground black pepper

pinch of ground cloves

cayenne or red pepper flakes (optional)

200 ml (7 fl oz) water

1 tbsp wine vinegar

2 tbsp chopped parsley

1 tsp salt

Cut the lamb into pieces as for stew. If using the fresh pepper, roast it over a gas flame or under the grill until charred on all sides. Cover with a cloth until cool, then peel off all the charred skin. Discard the stem and seeds. Heat 2 tbsp of the oil or lard in a pan and fry 2 cloves of the garlic and the slices of bread until golden, then remove. Add the remaining oil and brown the pieces of meat. Add the bay leaf, thyme, pepper, cloves, cayenne, a little of the water and the vinegar. Cover and bring to a simmer. In a mortar, blender or processor, grind together the roasted pepper or tinned pimientos, fried garlic and bread and the remaining clove of garlic with the parsley, the salt and the remaining water. Add this mixture to the lamb and cook until meat is tender, about 45 minutes total, adding additional water if necessary.

SERVES 4–5

Lamb Stew
Caldereta de Cordero

A real shepherd's dish, this would be cooked in a big iron cauldron set over a wood fire. It's delicious when made with tiny baby lamb or kid, but a leg of spring lamb or even lamb chops can be used. (Baby lamb can be cut in small joints or hacked into pieces. Spring lamb can be cut off the bone into large pieces. Lamb chops should be trimmed of excess fat.) The liver both thickens the sauce and gives it a rich flavour. If lamb's liver is not available, substitute chicken livers.

200 ml (7 fl oz) olive oil

200 g (7 oz) lamb's liver, quartered, or chicken livers

2 slices bread

8 garlic cloves

1.5 kg (3 lb 5 oz) lamb on-the-bone, jointed or cut in large chunks

250 ml (8 fl oz) white wine

2 bay leaves

1 tsp salt

1 tsp chopped thyme

10 peppercorns

250 ml (8 fl oz) water

4 medium potatoes, peeled and cut in pieces

chopped fresh mint or parsley

Heat half the oil in a deep pan. Fry the liver with the bread and garlic cloves until they are all browned. Remove. Add remaining oil to the pan. On a high heat, brown the pieces of lamb on all sides. Pour off any excess fat. Add the wine to the lamb with the bay leaves, salt, thyme and peppercorns. Bring to a boil, cover and simmer. In a processor or blender, mince the fried liver, bread and garlic cloves, adding enough of the water to make a paste. Add this to the lamb with remaining water. Cook the lamb about 45 minutes, adding the potatoes about half way through. Serve the stew with chopped fresh mint or parsley.

Serves 6

LAMB WITH HONEY
CORDERO A LA MIEL

A direct descendant from Spain's Moorish past.

1 leg of lamb (about 1.8 kg/4 lb), boned

5 tbsp olive oil

1 large onion, thinly sliced

175 g (6 oz) green peppers, shredded

2 garlic cloves, chopped

1 slice lemon

3 tbsp brandy

120 ml (4 fl oz) white wine

½ tsp saffron, crushed

1 tbsp paprika

¼ tsp ground pepper

pinch of cinnamon

1 tsp salt

3 tbsp wine vinegar

90 g (3 oz) honey

Cut the lamb into thick pieces. Heat the oil in a pan and sauté the onion, the peppers and the garlic. Add the pieces of lamb and brown them. Cut the lemon, peel and all, into shreds and add to the lamb with the brandy and wine. Dissolve the saffron in a little liquid and add to the meat with the paprika, pepper, cinnamon and salt. Cook, covered, until the meat is very tender, about 1 hour. When the meat is done, add the vinegar and honey and cook for 10 minutes more.

SERVES 6

NAVARRE-STYLE LAMB CHOPS
CHULETAS DE CORDERO A LA NAVARRESA

16 baby lamb chops (or 8 regular chops)

2 tbsp olive oil

2 tbsp lard

550 kg (1 lb 3 oz) tomatoes, peeled
   and chopped

salt and pepper

250 g (9 oz) *chorizo*, skin removed
   and sliced

Preheat the oven to 180°C (350°F, gas 4).
Brown the chops in a frying pan in the oil and
lard. Remove them to a *cazuela* or casserole.
Fry the tomatoes in the fat, season with salt and
pepper and cook for 10 minutes until reduced.
Pour the tomatoes over the lamb chops and put
them in the oven until tender, 20 minutes. Top
them with the sliced *chorizo* and return to the
oven for 10 minutes.

SERVES 4

BARBECUED LAMB CHOPS WITH ALIOLI SAUCE
CHULETAS DE CORDERO A LA BRASA

These marinated chops are best cooked over a wood fire, but charcoal will do. They are served with the following alioli sauce.

1 kg (2 lb 3 oz) lamb chops

1 tsp salt

3 tbsp chopped parsley

1 tsp chopped oregano

1 tsp chopped thyme

1 bay leaf, crushed

freshly ground pepper

juice of 1 lemon

3 tbsp olive oil

FOR THE ALIOLI SAUCE

1 egg

3–4 garlic cloves

175 ml (6 fl oz) olive oil

2 tbsp wine vinegar or lemon juice

½ tsp salt

Place the chops in a glass or ceramic dish in one layer. Sprinkle them with the salt, parsley, oregano, thyme, bay leaf, pepper, lemon juice and oil. Marinate for at least 4 hours or overnight, refrigerated. Barbecue the chops over hot coals, basting with any remaining marinade, until they are browned, about 8 minutes per side.

Place the egg and peeled garlic into a blender and process until the garlic is smooth. Add the oil in a slow stream, with the motor running, until the sauce is thick and emulsified. Add the vinegar or lemon juice and salt.

SERVES 4

WEDDING STEW
CAZUELA DE BODA

Throughout the famous book *Don Quixote*, Cervantes tells much about life and food in the late 16th century (*Don Quixote* was published in 1604). The most memorable meal is certainly that of the *bodas de Camacho*, the wedding feast of a rich man named Camacho (who doesn't, by the way, get the girl). Don Quixote and his sidekick, Sancho Panza, one who unabashedly relishes his food, encounter some 50 cooks at work preparing the meal. A whole young bullock stuffed with a dozen suckling pigs is roasting on a huge spit. Lamb, hare and chickens are stewing in enormous earthenware pots. Loaves of bread are piled into a mountain and whole cheeses, stacked like bricks, form a wall. A treasure chest of spices is at hand. Cooks are frying sweet pastries in great cauldrons of oil, then dipping them into boiling honey syrup.

Sancho Panza cannot contain himself. He begs permission to dip a crust of bread into one of the cookpots and is bidden to skim off what he likes – and take the ladle too! Happy, he scores three hens and a couple of geese for breakfast.

This is almost such a dish, traditional for country wedding feasts. At its most sumptuous, it contains two or more lambs or kids, cut into pieces, plus rabbit, partridge, chicken. It would be cooked in a wood-fired bread oven.

2 kg (4 lb 6 oz) baby lamb or lamb chops
   and/or jointed chicken

150 ml (¼ pint) olive oil

8 medium potatoes, peeled and sliced

1.2 kg (2 lb 10 oz) medium tomatoes, sliced

2 large onions, sliced

3 small green peppers, cut in strips

2 tbsp chopped parsley

1 head garlic, roasted (see page 13)

4 bay leaves

2 tsp salt

2 garlic cloves

10 peppercorns

4 cloves

1 tsp ground cinnamon

1 tsp saffron

500 ml (16 fl oz) white wine

Preheat the oven to 230°C (450°F, gas 8). If using baby lamb, have it cut into even-sized pieces. Pour the oil into the bottom of a very large roasting pan, cooking pot or deep casserole. Put a layer of half the sliced potatoes on the bottom, then a layer of half the sliced tomatoes and half the onions. Then put in the meat. Cover with strips of green pepper, parsley, the cloves of roasted garlic, bay leaves and another layer each of the remaining sliced potatoes, tomatoes and onion. In a mortar or blender crush the salt, 2 cloves of garlic, peppercorns, cloves, cinnamon and saffron. Mix in a little of the white wine and add to the pot with the rest of the wine. Put the casserole into the very hot oven for 10 minutes, then reduce the oven temperature to 180°C (350°F, gas 4) and cook, without stirring, until the meat and potatoes are very tender, about 2 hours. Or, simmer the stew, tightly covered, on the hob, adding water from time to time so the bottom layer does not scorch.

SERVES 8

MALLORCAN-STYLE LAMB'S LIVER
FRITO MALLORQUÍN

Traditionally, this would be made with liver, lungs, heart, sweetbreads and the solidified blood. It's very good with just liver.

3 garlic cloves

4 tbsp olive oil

600 g (1 lb 5 oz) lamb's liver, cubed

1 red pepper, cut in squares

5 spring onions, sliced

100 g (3½ oz) wild or cultivated
    mushrooms, chopped

¼ tsp red pepper flakes

2 bay leaves

salt and pepper

pinch of cinnamon

pinch of cloves

450 g (1 lb) potatoes, peeled

oil for frying

150 g (5¼ oz) cooked peas and/or broad
    beans (can be frozen)

1 tbsp chopped fennel leaves or ¼ tsp
    fennel seeds

Smash the garlic cloves with a mallet and peel them. Heat the oil in a *cazuela* or frying pan. Put in the garlic, then the liver and pepper. Fry over a high heat for a few minutes. Add the onions and mushrooms and continue frying. Add the red pepper flakes, bay leaves, salt and pepper, cinnamon and cloves. Reduce the heat, cover the pan, and cook for 20 minutes until the liver is very tender. Meanwhile, cut the potatoes into cubes. Using a separate pan, fry the potatoes in oil until golden and tender. Cook the peas or broad beans. When the meat is cooked, add the fried potatoes and cooked peas and broad beans to the *cazuela*. Cook a few minutes more and serve sprinkled with the fennel.

SERVES 4

BEEF AND VEAL

Vaca y carnero, olla de caballero.

Beef and mutton, gentleman's food.

Although *ternera* translates as 'veal', in fact, almost everywhere in Spanish markets, *ternera* is actually young beef. Pink, milk-fed veal is called *ternera lechal* or *ternera de Avila* (both a place and a breed). Real beef with a big beef flavour (slaughtered at 3–5 years) is called *buey*. In Galicia and Asturias, where dairy cattle are husbanded, *carne de vaca*, meat from well-fed cows, is much appreciated.

ONION-BRAISED BEEF
ENCEBOLLADO DE TERNERA

3 tbsp olive oil

8–10 small onions

1 kg (2 lb 3 oz) boneless beef roast (such as brisket, rump or sirloin)

1 green pepper, cut in pieces

450 g (1 lb) tomatoes, peeled and cut in pieces

2 bay leaves

1 head garlic, roasted (see page 13)

3 carrots

750 ml (1¼ pints) water or stock

¼ tsp saffron

10 peppercorns

2 cloves

½ tsp paprika

1 tsp salt

750 g (1 lb 10 oz) potatoes, peeled and quartered

1 tbsp wine vinegar

Heat the oil in a heavy braising pan and slowly brown the whole, peeled onions. Add the piece of meat and brown on all sides, then add the pepper and tomatoes, bay leaves, cloves of roasted garlic and whole carrots. Add the water or stock, bring to a boil and simmer, covered. In a mortar, crush the saffron, peppercorns, cloves, paprika and salt. Mix in a little liquid from the pan and stir into the broth. Cook the meat for 1 hour, then add the pieces of potato. Cook for another hour until meat is fork-tender. Immediately before serving, add the vinegar to the pot.

SERVES 4–5

VEAL ROLLS
ROLLITOS DE TERNERA

500 g (1 lb 2 oz) veal, cut in 4 thin cutlets

1 onion, very finely chopped

½ tbsp olive oil

1 garlic clove, chopped

1 tbsp chopped parsley

1 tbsp fine breadcrumbs

1 tsp wine vinegar

1 hard-boiled egg, chopped

salt and pepper

¼ tsp chopped thyme

100 g (3½ oz) serrano ham, thinly sliced

30 g (1 oz) plain flour

3 tbsp oil

2 bay leaves

175 ml (6 fl oz) white wine

½ tsp ground cinnamon

Pound the cutlets thin and set aside. In a frying pan, sauté 3 tbsp of the onion in the oil with the garlic, until softened. Remove from the heat and stir in the parsley, breadcrumbs, vinegar, egg, salt, pepper and thyme.

Spread out the veal cutlets and cover them with the ham. Spread a spoonful of the onion-garlic-bread mixture over each. Roll up, starting with the wide end, and secure each roll with a cocktail stick. Dredge the rolls in flour, pat them to remove any excess, then, in a frying pan, brown them slowly in hot oil, turning to brown all sides. Remove the rolls and place in a *cazuela* or flameproof casserole, with the bay leaves. Add the remaining chopped onion to the oil in the frying pan and sauté until it is softened. Add the wine and cinnamon, scraping up the browned bits. Pour the liquid over the meat rolls. Cover and cook for 1 hour, turning the rolls after 30 minutes. Remove and allow to rest for 5 minutes. Slice the meat crosswise into 3 or 4 pieces and serve hot or cold. If desired, the sauce can be strained.

SERVES 4

BIG BEEF CHOP
CHULETÓN DE BUEY

8 rib or entrecôte steaks, cut very thickly
olive oil
lemon juice

FOR THE FRIED PEPPERS
1.25 kg (2 lb 12 oz) green peppers,
    preferably small
salt
olive oil for frying

Rub the steaks with oil and lemon juice. Roast over charcoal, basting with oil, until done to medium. Remove and salt them. Serve with a heap of *pimientos fritos*, fried green peppers.

This is usually made with small, thin-skinned peppers. If they are not available, use strips of large green peppers.

If using small peppers, cut a slit in the bottom of each pepper and rub a pinch of salt inside. Leave the peppers whole, stems and all. If using green peppers, cut them into strips. Fry them slowly in hot oil until limp and soft, but not browned. Remove and drain. Serve hot as a side dish with meat and poultry.

SERVES 8

BREADED VEAL CUTLETS
FILETES DE TERNERA EMPANADAS

4 thin frying steaks or veal cutlets (about
    600 g/1 lb 5 oz)
120 ml (4 fl oz) white wine
1 tbsp chopped parsley
pinch of saffron, crushed
1 tsp salt
¼ tsp ground black pepper
1 egg, beaten
55 g (2 oz) fine breadcrumbs
olive oil for frying
1 lemon, sliced

Place the steaks or cutlets, one at a time, between two sheets of cling film and pound them thin with a mallet. Place in a glass or ceramic dish in one layer and add the wine, parsley, saffron, salt and pepper. Let them marinate at room temperature for 1 hour. Dip them in beaten egg, then breadcrumbs and fry slowly in oil, turning to brown both sides. Serve with lemon slices.

SERVES 4

ANDALUSIAN-STYLE LARDED POT ROAST

TERNERA MECHADA A LA ANDALUZA

¼ tsp ground pepper

pinch of cloves

¼ tsp grated nutmeg

2 tbsp chopped parsley

2 garlic cloves, crushed

1 hard-boiled egg, mashed

1 tbsp olive oil

1.5 kg (3 lb 5 oz) boneless beef roast

55 g (2 oz) salt pork or serrano ham, cut in thin strips

55 g (2 oz) pork fat, cut in thin strips (optional)

4 tbsp olive oil or lard

1 onion, quartered

3 carrots, halved

2 tomatoes, quartered

1 head garlic, roasted (see page 13)

1 bay leaf

120 ml (4 fl oz) dry Sherry

120 ml (4 fl oz) water or stock

Combine the pepper, cloves, nutmeg, parsley, garlic, egg and oil to make a paste. Using a sharp knife, cut deep gashes into the piece of meat, spacing the gashes regularly on the meat's surface, and with the knife blade insert some of the paste and a strip of salt pork or serrano ham into each slit. Tie the meat with string to give it a good shape and help keep the larding in place. If desired, meat can be covered with strips of pork fat. Heat the oil or lard in a pan big enough to hold the piece of meat and brown the meat, very slowly, on all sides. Add the quartered onion, carrots, tomatoes and roasted garlic cloves. Put in the bay leaf, Sherry and water or stock and cook the meat very slowly until fork-tender, about 2 hours, adding more stock as needed. Remove the meat to a serving platter and let it rest for 10 minutes. Discard the string and slice. Sieve the sauce, pressing on the solids, and spoon it over the meat.

SERVES 8

MEAT AND TOMATOES
CARNE ENTOMATADA

5 tbsp olive oil

750 g (1 lb 10 oz) thin frying steaks

750 g (1 lb 10 oz) tomatoes, sliced

1 tbsp fresh thyme or 1 tsp dried

salt and pepper

Put the oil in the bottom of a *cazuela* or flameproof casserole. Layer the slices of meat and sliced tomatoes, sprinkling with thyme and salt and pepper. Heat until simmering, then cover and cook until meat is tender, about 45 minutes.

SERVES 4

BEEF STEW
ESTOFADO DE CARNE

Either add potatoes to cook with the stew or serve it with *patatas fritas*, chips, added to the gravy. Regional variations are made with the addition of peas, artichokes, broad beans or turnips.

1 kg (2 lb 3 oz) stewing beef

1 green pepper, cut in strips

1 large tomato, peeled and quartered

2 onions, sliced

2 carrots, halved lengthwise

½ tsp saffron, crushed (optional)

½ tsp ground black pepper

pinch of cloves

¼ tsp ground cinnamon

5 tbsp water

1 head garlic, roasted (see page 13)

3 tbsp olive oil

2 bay leaves

sprig of parsley

2 tsp salt

250 ml (8 fl oz) white wine

Cut the meat into 3 cm (1¼ inch) cubes. Place in a large pan with the pepper, tomato, onions and carrots. Combine the saffron, pepper, cloves and cinnamon and mix in the water. Add to the pan with the cloves of roasted garlic, the oil, bay leaves, parsley, salt and wine. Cover and cook for about 1 hour, adding additional liquid if needed. If desired, the meat can be skimmed out and the gravy strained before serving.

SERVES 6

BRAISED OXTAIL
RABO DE TORO

This is the tail of the bull, as in *toro bravo*, fighting bull. However, ordinary butchers' oxtails work fine. This dish is a speciality in Córdoba and Seville.

1 oxtail, about 1.25 kg (2 lb 12 oz)

3 tbsp olive oil

1 onion, chopped

1 leek, chopped

3 carrots, chopped

2 garlic cloves, chopped

55 g (2 oz) serrano ham, diced

5 tbsp brandy

120 ml (4 fl oz) dry Sherry or Montilla

1 bay leaf

sprig of parsley

sprig of thyme

salt and pepper

pinch of ground cloves

1 piece chilli pepper or a few red
    pepper flakes

1 tomato, peeled and chopped

Have the butcher cut the oxtail into segments of about 7 cm (3 inches). Wash well, then blanch them in boiling water and drain. In a large pan, heat the oil and add the onion, leek, carrots, garlic and ham and sauté until softened. Add the pieces of oxtail and brown on a high heat. Add the brandy, set it alight, and stir with a long-handled spoon until the flames subside. Then add the Sherry or Montilla, herbs, salt and pepper, cloves, chilli and chopped tomato. Simmer until the meat is very tender, about 2 hours, adding stock or water as needed. When cooked, the sauce should be fairly thick from reduction. It can be thickened with a little flour mixed with water, if desired.

SERVES 4

CALVES' LIVER IN VINEGAR SAUCE
HÍGADO DE TERNERA EN ADOBO

This can also be made with pigs' liver, in which case let the liver simmer in the sauce for 20 minutes.

1 kg (2 lb 3 oz) calves' liver, sliced and cut in strips

3 tbsp olive oil

3 garlic cloves

pinch of chopped chilli pepper or a few red pepper flakes

3 tbsp Sherry or wine vinegar

5 tbsp water

½ tsp salt

1 tsp paprika

½ tsp pepper

1 tsp chopped oregano

Sauté the liver in the oil until browned on both sides, then remove from the pan. In a mortar or blender, grind together the garlic, chilli, vinegar, water, salt, paprika, pepper and oregano. Pour this into the pan and cook until the liquid is reduced to a thick sauce. Return the liver to the pan and reheat.

SERVES 6

BRAISED BEEF TONGUE
LENGUA DE TERNERA GUISADA

1 ox tongue (about 1.25 kg/2 lb 12 oz),
    trimmed

3 tbsp olive oil or lard

1 carrot, chopped

1 onion, chopped

100 g (3½ oz) salt pork or bacon, diced

1 stalk celery, chopped

2 garlic cloves, slivered

10 peppercorns

2 cloves

120 ml (4 fl oz) white wine or dry Sherry

400 g (14 oz) tomatoes, peeled and
    quartered

herb bouquet with bay leaves, thyme
    and rosemary

2 tsp salt

water or meat stock

Scrub the tongue in running water, then let it soak for 1 hour in salted water to which a little vinegar has been added. Rinse. Blanch the tongue in boiling water for 15 minutes, then drain. When cool enough to handle, remove the outer skin. Heat the oil or lard in a large pan and sauté the carrot, onion, salt pork or bacon, celery and garlic for a few minutes. Put the tongue into the pan with the peppercorns, cloves, wine or Sherry, tomatoes, herbs and salt. Add water or meat stock to half the depth of the meat. Cover and simmer until the tongue is very tender, about 2 hours. Remove the tongue to a platter. Remove the herb bouquet and sieve the sauce, pressing hard on the solids. It can be thickened, if desired, with bread, flour, ground almonds or walnuts. Slice the tongue and spoon the sauce over.

SERVES 6

3

LUNCH, TEA AND SUPPER

Lunch, Tea and Supper

Mas vale un buen dia con huevo que un mal mes con un cerdo.

Better a good day with only an egg than a bad month with a pig.

At six o'clock in the afternoon, throughout the village mothers can be heard calling their children: '*Paqui, Antoñito, Mari, ven a merendar.*' It's the hour of the *merienda*, tea-time, snack time. A bite to eat to tide a body over until the later supper, *cena*.

The merienda may be simply a sandwich or pastry, with milk, coffee, tea or juice, though men coming home from heavy labour might take something more substantial – eggs fried with sausages, a slice of thick omelette, a bread roll toasted and filled with pork loin and spicy red lard, a bowl of gazpacho.

Most of these dishes could equally well be served at supper, the last meal of the day, or for *almuerzo*, a light lunch or mid-morning snack.

Eggs

While rarely consumed for breakfast, eggs, in dozens of different preparations, are served frequently for supper. Besides the dishes given here, several more are to be found with the recipes for vegetable dishes, some of which are finished off with eggs.

Before the days of battery hens, eggs were such an important source of income that poor families who kept chickens sometimes never ate an egg all year, for all were carried to town to sell.

Omelettes
Tortillas

A tortilla is more than an omelette, it's really an egg cake filled with any number of savoury ingredients. The potato tortilla is the best known (see recipe on page 232), but everything from spinach to peppers, broad beans to lambs' brains, can be incorporated in the eggs, which are turned out in a thick, round cake.

Don't use a heavy iron frying pan for tortilla making, because the technique requires you to turn the pan upside down. In former days, long-handled frying pans of thin pressed steel were used. Today's non-stick pans are absolutely perfect.

MADRID-STYLE OMELETTE WITH PICKLED FISH
TORTILLA DE ESCABECHE A LA MADRILEÑA

This omelette, made with tinned *bonito* or tuna in *escabeche*, a vinegar marinade, is typical for a family *merienda* or a summer *verbena*, a fiesta day outing.

4 tbsp olive oil

450 g (1 lb) potatoes, peeled and thinly sliced

1 onion, finely chopped

6 eggs

1 tbsp chopped parsley

½ tsp salt

200 g (7 oz) tinned tuna or *bonito* in vinegar, drained

Heat 3 tbsp of the oil in a non-stick frying pan and very slowly fry the potatoes. When they are partially cooked, 15 minutes, add the onion and continue frying until the potatoes are tender, another 15 minutes (they should not brown).

In a bowl, beat the eggs with the parsley and salt. Flake the fish and add to the eggs. Stir in the cooked potatoes and combine. Add the remaining oil to the pan and pour in the egg and potato mixture. Let it cook until set on the bottom – the omelette should be a little golden, not browned – then turn it out on to a plate and slip it back into the pan to cook on the reverse side. Shake the pan to keep the omelette from sticking. Slide out on to a plate when done. Serve hot or cold.

SERVES 4–6

MURCIA OMELETTE
TORTILLA MURCIANA

Murcia is the Levante province with fabulous market farms, rich with peppers, aubergines and other fresh vegetables.

3 tbsp olive oil

3 tomatoes, peeled, seeded and chopped

4 red peppers, cut in strips

1 small aubergine, peeled and diced

6 eggs

½ tsp salt

Heat 2 tbsp of the oil in a frying pan and fry the tomatoes, peppers and aubergine together until most of the liquid has evaporated, about 15 minutes. Beat the eggs and salt in a bowl. Mix the fried aubergine mixture into the eggs.

Heat the remaining oil in the pan and pour in the egg mixture. Let the omelette set on the bottom, then turn out on to a plate and slide back in to cook the reverse side.

SERVES 4–6

SACROMONTE OMELETTE
TORTILLA SACROMONTE

Sacromonte is the gypsy cave district of Granada, high on a hill overlooking the city. The omelette was supposedly invented at the abbey on the hill.

1 lamb's kidney

4 tbsp milk

1 set lamb's brains (optional)

4 tbsp olive oil

100 g (3½ oz) serrano ham, chopped

3 tbsp finely chopped onion

80 g (2¾ oz) cooked peas

4–6 eggs

½ tsp salt

Remove any fat and membrane from the kidney and soak in the milk (or in water with vinegar) for 20 minutes. Poach it in simmering water for 5 minutes. Wash the brains and poach them for 5 minutes. Drain. Dice the kidney and brains. Heat the oil in a non-stick frying pan and sauté the kidney and brains very gently with the ham and onion, until the onion is softened. Add the peas. Beat the eggs with the salt and pour into the pan, stirring once to combine. Let the omelette set on the bottom, then turn out on to a plate and slide back in to cook the reverse side.

SERVES 4

GREEN BEAN OMELETTE
TORTILLA DE JUDÍAS VERDES

Make this with any combination of cooked vegetables. Broad beans are good – when sliced, the tortilla reveals nuggets of pale green embedded in the yellow egg.

340 g (12 oz) green beans

3 tbsp olive oil

2 tbsp chopped onion

30 g (1 oz) serrano ham, chopped

4 eggs

½ tsp salt

Top and tail the beans, remove any strings and snap them into short pieces. Cook in boiling salted water until tender. In a small non-stick frying pan, heat half the oil and sauté the beans with the onion and ham until the onion is softened. Beat the eggs in a bowl with salt. Stir in the beans and ham. Heat the remaining oil in the pan and pour in the eggs and beans. Let the omelette set on the bottom, turn out on to a plate, then slide back in to cook the reverse side.

Variation: *tortilla de esparragos trigueros*, omelette with wild asparagus. Substitute wild or cultivated green asparagus for the beans in the above recipe.

SERVES 2–4

BREAD CAKE
TORTILLA DE PAN

Simple, yes, but filling. Children love it.

225 g (8 oz) stale bread

4 tbsp lard or olive oil

chopped serrano ham or bacon (optional)

2 garlic cloves, chopped

4 eggs

1 tsp salt

Soak the bread in sufficient water to cover for 30 minutes. Squeeze it out very well and break into small bits. Heat all but 1 tsp of the lard in a frying pan and fry the bread with the ham and garlic for 5 minutes. Beat the eggs and salt together. Add the bread to the eggs. Heat the remaining fat in the pan and pour in the egg mixture. Cook until set on the bottom, turn out on to a plate, then slide back in to cook the other side.

SERVES 4

SCRAMBLED EGGS WITH WILD MUSHROOMS
REVUELTO DE SETAS

Huevos solos, mil manjares y para todos.

With only eggs, a thousand dishes and something for everybody.

The Basques and the Catalans have a veritable passion for wild mushrooms, collecting many varieties of edible fungi to add interest to local dishes. This one makes an elegant supper dish. It can be made with chanterelles, oyster mushrooms or boletus which sometimes come into the market.

225 g (8 oz) wild mushrooms
3 tbsp olive oil
1 garlic clove, crushed
5 eggs
1 tbsp chopped parsley
1 tbsp water
salt and pepper
fried bread strips
chopped parsley, to serve

Clean the mushrooms very carefully of all grit and discard any which are turning dark or soft. Cut them into small pieces. Heat half the oil in a frying pan and sauté the mushrooms with the garlic. Some kinds give out quite a bit of water, so continue frying until they are fairly dry. Beat the eggs with the parsley, water, salt and pepper. Heat the remaining oil in the pan and, with a wooden spoon, stir the eggs into the mushrooms. Continue stirring the egg mixture until it is just set. The eggs should be creamy-soft. Serve hot with strips of fried bread and a garnish of chopped parsley.

SERVES 2–3

GARLIC-SCRAMBLED EGGS
REVUELTO DE AJETES

Ajetes are young shoots of garlic, which look like skinny spring onions. If not available, substitute spring onions and add a clove of crushed garlic to the eggs.

> **175 g (6 oz) garlic shoots or spring onions and 1 garlic clove, crushed**
>
> **3 tbsp olive oil**
>
> **4 eggs**
>
> **pinch of chopped thyme**
>
> **½ tsp salt**
>
> **1 tbsp chopped parsley**

Clean the garlic shoots or spring onions and chop them. Heat half the oil in a frying pan and sauté the garlic or spring onions very gently, without letting them brown, about 10 minutes. In a bowl, beat the eggs with the thyme, salt and parsley, plus the garlic if using spring onions. Add remaining oil to the pan and pour in the eggs. Stir over a low heat until the eggs are set, but still soft and creamy.

Variation: Add chopped cooked asparagus and cooked prawns to the pan with the garlic.

SERVES 2

SATURDAY NIGHT BACON AND EGGS
DUELOS Y QUEBRANTOS

In the opening lines of the novel about knight errant, Don Quixote, Cervantes introduces us to his character by telling us what he eats: 'a stew with rather more beef than mutton, cold hash most nights, *duelos y quebrantos* on Saturdays, lentils on Fridays and some squab on Sundays for good measure'. *Duelos y quebrantos* means something like 'labours and backbreakers' or 'toil and trouble', so don't try asking in a Spanish market for a dozen *quebrantos*!

> **100 g (3½ oz) bacon or fatty ham, diced**
>
> **1 tbsp olive oil**
>
> **4 eggs**
>
> **2 tbsp water or milk**
>
> **salt and pepper**
>
> **fried bread strips**

Fry the diced bacon or ham in the oil until crisped. Beat the eggs with the water or milk, season with salt and pepper and stir into the pan. Scramble the eggs until soft-set. Serve with strips of fried bread.

SERVES 2

EGGS WITH PEPPERS
PIPARRADA

2 red peppers or 2 tinned pimientos,
    drained

6 tbsp olive oil

4 garlic cloves

1 small onion, shredded

55 g (2 oz) serrano ham, cut in strips

340 g (12 oz) tomatoes, peeled and chopped

8 eggs

salt and pepper

Roast the peppers under the grill until charred. Wrap them in a cloth until cool enough to handle, then peel them. Discard the seeds and stem, then cut the peppers into strips. If you are using tinned pimientos, simply cut them into strips. Heat half the oil in a frying pan and sauté the garlic and onion. Add the strips of ham, then the tomatoes and the peppers. Fry for about 15 minutes until some of the liquid has evaporated. Turn into a bowl and set aside. Beat the eggs with the salt and pepper. Heat the remaining oil in the pan and pour in the eggs. Stir them, cooking very gently, then add the pepper mixture. Cook without stirring until the eggs are set.

SERVES 4

Eggs with Chicken Livers
Huevos con Higadillos

5 tbsp olive oil

250 g (9 oz) chicken livers, cut into pieces

90 g (3 oz) salt pork or bacon, diced

2 tbsp finely chopped onion

1 garlic clove, chopped

6 tbsp dry Sherry

salt and pepper

4 eggs

chopped parsley

Heat 3 tbsp of the oil in a frying pan and sauté the livers with the salt pork, onion and garlic until the livers are browned, but still pink in the middle. Add the Sherry and salt and pepper and cook for another 3 minutes. Remove from the heat and keep warm. Heat the remaining oil in another pan and scramble the eggs. Serve the eggs with the chicken livers, sprinkled with chopped parsley.

SERVES 2

Eggs Poached in Broth
Huevos al Salmorrejo

A dish from Aragón.

8 asparagus spears

2 tsp salt

4 tbsp olive oil

4 garlic cloves, chopped

1 tbsp chopped parsley

1 tbsp wine vinegar

8 eggs

4 slices pork loin

200 g (7 oz) *longaniza* sausage or *chorizo* or salami

Cook the asparagus in boiling water with the salt until limp. Drain and reserve the liquid. In a *cazuela* or deep frying pan heat 3 tbsp of the oil and fry the garlic until soft. Add the parsley, vinegar and reserved asparagus liquid and water to a depth of 2 cm (¾ inch). Bring to a boil, reduce to a simmer and poach 4 of the eggs in the liquid. Skim them out on to 2 plates and poach the remaining four eggs, then remove. Fry the pork slices and sausage in the remaining oil. Serve the eggs with asparagus, pork and sausages.

SERVES 4

FRIED EGGS
HUEVOS FRITOS

Fry eggs in olive oil with chopped garlic. Remove and keep warm while you fry *chorizo* in the same oil. Serve with chips or *migas*, fried croûtons.

FLAMENCO EGGS
HUEVOS A LA FLAMENCA

A speciality of Seville.

3 tbsp olive oil

3 tbsp chopped onion

1 garlic clove, chopped

100 g (3½ oz) serrano ham, chopped

120 ml (4 fl oz) tomato sauce (see page 17)

½ tsp paprika

salt and pepper

70 g (2½ oz) cooked peas

8 eggs

8 asparagus tips, cooked

90 g (3 oz) **chorizo**, sliced

2 artichoke hearts, cooked and quartered

1 tinned red pimiento, cut in thin strips

chopped parsley

fried bread strips

Preheat the oven to 190°C (375°F, gas 5). Heat the oil in a frying pan and sauté the onion, garlic and ham until the onion is soft. Add the tomato sauce, paprika, salt and pepper and cook for a few minutes. Add the peas to the sauce and divide the sauce between 4 ovenproof ramekins. Break 2 eggs into each. Around the eggs place the asparagus, slices of *chorizo* and pieces of artichoke. Lay the pimiento strips over the top. Sprinkle with parsley and bake in the oven until the whites are just set, but the yolks still liquid, about 10 minutes. Serve with strips of fried bread.

SERVES 4

SNACKS AND SANDWICHES

Hefty sandwiches – a whole bread roll split and filled with omelette, sausage, ham or cheese – are the usual snack for the mid-morning break and afternoon tea. These are all variations on the theme of bread with a filling.

FILLED ROLLS
COCS FARCITS

A Menorcan snack. Use leftover cooked meat or fry minced beef.

4 round, day-old bread rolls (each about 90 g/3 oz)

250 ml (8 fl oz) milk

2 tbsp lard, softened (or oil)

175 g (6 oz) cooked, chopped meat, or minced beef

175 g (6 oz) salt pork or ham, chopped

55 g (2 oz) *sobrasada* (soft Mallorca sausage) or *chorizo*, mashed

¼ tsp thyme

salt and pepper

¼ tsp ground cinnamon

pinch of ground cloves

Preheat the oven to 200°C (400°F, gas 6). Cut the tops off the bread rolls and scoop out some of the crumb to leave a shell. Place the milk in a small bowl. Dip the rolls in the milk and soak the crumbs in the remaining milk. Spread or brush the rolls with half the softened lard or oil. Heat the remaining lard or oil in a frying pan and fry the meat, salt pork or ham and Mallorca sausage. Season with thyme, salt and pepper, cinnamon and cloves. Add the soaked breadcrumbs and cook for a few minutes, mashing the meat to a sort of paste. Fill the bread shells with the meat mixture. Press the tops down tightly. Bake in the oven for 25 minutes.

SERVES 4

GALICIAN SAVOURY PIE
EMPANADA GALLEGA

Favourite fare for holiday outings, the *empanada*, a savoury pie, is made by Galician housewives and carried to the village bread oven for baking. The dough often contains some maize and rye flour. Some typical fillings: clams, eel, cod, cockles, tuna, squid, veal, rabbit, hare, mussels, sardines, any fish, pork loin, pigeon, chicken, octopus, scallops, ham – in other words, just about any meat, fish or fowl! A metal paella pan is perfect for shaping and baking this pie.

FOR THE DOUGH

50 g (1¾ oz) fresh yeast or 1 tbsp dried yeast

250 ml (8 fl oz) hand-hot water

pinch of crushed saffron (optional)

600 g (1 lb 5 oz) wheat flour (or use some maize or rye flour) plus additional for flouring board

2 tsp salt

150 ml (¼ pint) olive oil

FOR THE FILLING

500 g (1 lb 2 oz) cooked and boned meat (pork loin, thinly sliced and fried is the best, but fish – including tinned tuna – shellfish, poultry or rabbit can all be used)

3 onions, chopped

200 ml (7 oz) olive oil

50 g (1¾ oz) serrano ham, chopped

5 garlic cloves, chopped

2 tbsp tomato sauce (see page 17)

1 tbsp paprika

cayenne to taste

salt and pepper

pinch of oregano

1 tbsp chopped parsley

2 hard-boiled eggs, chopped

50 g (1¾ oz) tinned or roasted red pimiento

50 g (1¾ oz) stoned olives, chopped

1 egg, beaten with a few drops of water

Dissolve the yeast in 100 ml (3½ fl oz) of the warm water, and leave to stand for 5 minutes. Add the saffron, if used, in the remainder. Combine the flour and salt. Make a well in the centre and pour in the yeast, the oil and the saffron water. Work the dough with the hands, then turn out on a lightly floured board and knead it for 5–10 minutes until the dough is smooth and elastic. Put it in an oiled bowl, turning to coat the ball of dough, then cover the bowl and put in a warm place to rise until doubled in bulk, about 2 hours.

Chop or slice the filling ingredient and put aside. In a frying pan, sauté the onions in the oil until very soft. Add the ham and garlic and fry a few minutes more. Stir in the tomato sauce, paprika, cayenne, salt and pepper, oregano and chopped parsley. Cook for 5 minutes.

Assemble the *empanada* immediately before baking. Preheat the oven to 190°C (375°F, gas 5). Divide the dough into two pieces. Roll, pat and stretch one piece of dough to make a thin bottom crust (30 cm, 12 inches, round or square). Fit it in a shallow baking tin which has been lightly oiled and sprinkled with flour or maize flour. Spread the dough with half the prepared sauce. Arrange on top the sliced or chopped meat, fish, poultry. Add the chopped eggs, strips of red pimiento and chopped olives. Cover with the remaining sauce.

Roll out the remaining piece of dough and fit it over the top. Trim off excess. Crimp together the top and bottom layers to seal the edges. Roll excess dough into long, thin cords and use them to make criss-cross designs on the top crust. Cut two or three steam vents in the top. Brush the top with beaten egg. Place in the oven until the crust is very brown, about 35 minutes. The *empanada* is typically served freshly made, but completely cooled. A good dish for picnic or buffet lunches.

MAKES 8 SNACK-SIZE SERVINGS

ALICANTE 'PIZZA'
COQUES EN LLANDA FASSIDA DE FRITANGAS

Coque or *coca* is how you say pizza in Spanish – or, rather, in Catalan. Essentially, it's the same as the Italian pizza, a crusty, open-faced bread baked with a savoury (sometimes sweet) topping. *Coque* was typically made with pieces of bread dough, with oil kneaded into it, and baked in a wood-fired bread oven. In Almería, *torticas* are similar breads, but made with maize flour. Directions are given here for one *coque* with *fritanga* (somewhat like ratatouille) topping and for one *coque amb espinacs* (spinach topping).

Use one recipe *empanada* yeast dough (see page 223), risen once and divided in half (or substitute frozen pizza dough).

FOR THE FRITANGA TOPPING

3 tbsp olive oil

1 large onion, chopped

1 green pepper, chopped

2 garlic cloves, chopped

1 medium aubergine, peeled and diced

1 tsp salt

pepper

½ tsp oregano

1 tbsp chopped parsley

1 kg (2 lb 3 oz) tomatoes, peeled and chopped

1 small courgette, diced

1 tbsp oil

1 tin tuna or sardines (240 g, 8½ oz), drained

Heat the oil in a pan and sauté the onion, pepper, garlic and aubergine. Fry until the oil is absorbed. Season with salt, pepper, oregano and parsley and add the tomatoes and courgette. Cook, covered, over a medium heat until the vegetables are tender, about 20 minutes. Uncover and cook to evaporate excess liquid.

Preheat the oven to 200°C (400°F, gas 6). Roll and stretch one piece of dough to fit a round or rectangular oven tin that has been lightly oiled. Brush the top of the dough with the remaining oil and spread it with the filling. Top with chunks of the tuna. Bake in the oven until lightly browned, 12–15 minutes. Remove and slice.

FOR THE SPINACH TOPPING

1 kg (2 lb 3 oz) fresh spinach or chard or
    400 g (14 oz) frozen spinach

4 tbsp olive oil

1 onion, chopped

3 garlic cloves, chopped

salt and pepper

200 g (7 oz) soft curd cheese, well drained

2 tbsp pine nuts, toasted

50 g (1¾ oz) cheese, grated

Wash and trim the spinach or chard and cook, covered, until wilted and tender. Drain very well and chop. Heat 3 tbsp of the oil in a pan and sauté the onion and garlic until softened. Add the chopped spinach and fry for several minutes. Season with salt and pepper. Beat the cheese until very smooth. Roll out the remaining piece of dough, brush it with the remaining oil, and spread it with the spinach. Spoon over the soft cheese, sprinkle with the pine nuts and grated cheese. Bake as above.

MAKES 2

FRIED BREADCRUMBS
MIGAS

Migas con tropezones alegran los corazones.

———————

Crumbs fried with bacon bits gladden the heart.

A traditional country dish, eaten throughout Castille, Extremadura, Aragon and Andalusia. Restorative properties are attributed to *migas*, so they're typical for a New Year's Day 'breakfast' after a night of carousing.

450 g (1 lb) stale bread, with crusts, cut in very small dice

½ tsp salt

4 tbsp oil or lard

150 g (5¼ oz) *chorizo*, sliced

150 g (5¼ oz) serrano ham, streaky salt pork or bacon

6 garlic cloves (not peeled)

1 chilli pepper, chopped, or red pepper flakes (to taste)

Put the diced bread in a bowl and sprinkle with salt. Sprinkle with water, then toss them until they are uniformly dampened, but not soaked. Cover tightly and leave to stand for several hours or overnight. In a frying pan or *cazuela*, heat the oil or lard, fry the *chorizo* and ham or salt pork or bacon until lightly browned, then remove. With a mallet or pestle lightly hit the garlic to split them, but don't peel. Add to the fat with the bits of chilli and bread. Fry the 'crumbs', turning with a spatula until they are loose and lightly toasted. Return the *chorizo* and pork fat to the pan, give another few turns and serve.

Accompany the *migas* with any selection of the following: fried pork loin, fried eggs, olives, sardines, melon, radishes, spring onions, fish, fried peppers, pomegranates, salt cod, grapes, raisins or chocolate!

'OLD CLOTHES' (BEEF HASH)
ROPA VIEJA

Nothing is wasted. Food leftover from the midday meal, *sobras,* is used up for supper. Some recycled dishes, including this one, are exceptionally good.Make this with leftover boiled beef or stewing beef. Even the aubergines and potatoes could be left from a previous fry.

450 g (1 lb) cooked beef

1 small onion, chopped

2 garlic cloves, chopped

3 tbsp olive oil

55 g (2 oz) salt pork or bacon, diced

340 g (12 oz) tomatoes, peeled and chopped

225 g (8 oz) aubergine, chopped

2 red peppers, roasted and peeled or tinned pimiento, chopped

340 g (12 oz) any cooked potato, diced

6 tbsp broth or stock

salt and pepper

cooked chickpeas (optional)

Shred the beef and reserve. Fry the onion and garlic in a pan with the oil and salt pork until softened. Add the tomatoes, aubergine and peppers and cook for 5 minutes. Add the shredded meat, potato, broth, salt and pepper and chickpeas, if desired. Cook for 15 minutes.

SERVES 4

4

APPETIZERS

APPETIZERS

Almost all of the dishes, hot and cold, found at Spanish *tapa* bars can also be served as part of a meal – as hors d'oeuvres, starters, even main courses. Similarly, many dishes found elsewhere in this book as starters or main courses can, if dished up in very small portions, be served as tapas.

Examples of both are *pollo al ajillo*, chicken with garlic, which appears in this *tapa* list but can also be served as a dinner dish, and *pescado a la marinera*, fisherman's style fish (see page 152), in which a whole bream or swordfish steak cooked with tomatoes and peppers can be served in *tapa*-size spoonfuls. Even paella rice is served as *tapa*, kept warm over a pot of hot water. While the ones included here are especially typical of *tapa* bars, this is by no means a definitive list, for *tapas* continue to evolve.

Apart from those bars which specialize in just one *tapa* – say, snails, or fried fish – most will serve every midday and evening a variety of tapas, 10–15 different dishes: salads and other cold dishes, fried foods, meat, seafood, plus the usual assortment of ham, sausages, cheese, olives. When most *tascas* – taverns – and bars were family-run, the women usually looked after the kitchen, turning out the *tapas*, and the men poured the wine at the bar.

Tapas are sent out to the bar as they are finished – salads first, then *tapas de cocina*, cooked dishes, including fried ones. Regulars know when to stop in to get the croquettes hot out of the bubbling oil, or which days of the week there's likely to be a special rabbit dish, because they saw the owner come home from the country with a few strung on his belt.

Spaniards aren't so particular about 'hot foods'. A *tortilla*, omelette with potatoes, for instance, is considered perfect when served at room temperature (never chilled!). Of course, nowadays, individual servings can be reheated in the microwave. Some foods, such as grilled prawns or pork cutlet, are prepared to order.

Tapas come with small chunks of bread or breadsticks, which serve in lieu of a spoon for mopping up the sauces.

Although the *tapa* bar culture is very special to life in Spain, the foods are easily adaptable to party meals anywhere. A selection of these *tapa* dishes plus dessert and fruit make a fine buffet spread for any occasion. It is difficult to be specific about the number of servings for each recipe as, like canapés, this depends on how many *tapas* are offered.

Dry *fino* Sherry is the best accompaniment to many *tapas*, especially ham and shellfish.

Beer, red and white wine and, in Catalonia, *cava* (sparkling wine) are other choices.

MOUNTAIN HAM
JAMÓN SERRANO

In many *tapa* bars whole serrano hams hang from the rafters. They are sliced to order, in paper-thin strips. For more about Spanish ham, see page 13.

TOASTED ALMONDS
ALMENDRAS FRITAS

Serve these with dry or medium Sherry.

250 g (9 oz) whole, unblanched almonds

3 tbsp olive oil

1 tsp salt

pinch of ground cumin (optional)

Fry the almonds in the oil, turning until golden, about 5 minutes. Remove and sprinkle with salt and cumin, if desired.

MARINATED OLIVES
ACEITUNAS ALIÑADAS

Aceituna una y si es buena, una docena.

Try one olive; if it's good, try a dozen.

Spain's olives, especially the Seville *manzanillas*, can be found on supermarket shelves the world over. In Spain they come in many more varieties – enormous pink *gordales*, tiny green *arbequines*, pitted *manzanillas* stuffed with anchovy paste, unpitted black ones. In regions where olives grow – about two-thirds of the country! – many families cure their own olives in a traditional way with salt, herbs and garlic. They keep for several months in big crocks and are fished out with perforated wooden dippers. The following marinade gives bottled olives some of the home-cured flavour. Besides being served with aperitifs, olives are usually put on the table as a condiment with dinner or supper.

350 g (12¼ oz) bottled manzanilla olives (not stuffed)

½ lemon, cut in wedges

3 garlic cloves, slivered

sprig of fennel leaves (or a few fennel seeds)

several sprigs of thyme or ½ tsp chopped dried thyme

1 tsp salt

1 tbsp chopped red pepper

1 tbsp virgin olive oil

Drain the olives, rinse and drain again. Put them in a glass jar with the wedges of lemon, slivers of garlic, fennel, thyme, salt and red pepper. Add water barely to cover, then the oil. Cap the jar and shake to blend. Marinate, refrigerated, for 3–4 days. Stand at room temperature for several hours before draining and serving.

POTATO OMELETTE
TORTILLA DE PATATAS

Cut in tiny squares or thick wedges, probably no other *tapa* dish is served more universally than this golden, potato omelette. It can be made in individual servings to order or in huge wheels. Tortilla is also favourite fare for outings to lunch in a park or in the country.

The secret to Spanish tortilla is the slow, slow frying of the potatoes in plenty of olive oil – allow 30 minutes – before the eggs are incorporated. The tortilla should be a thick cake. For the quantity of ingredients given here, use a frying pan 24–26 cm (about 9½–10½ inches) in diameter.

1 kg (2 lb 3 oz) potatoes

5 tbsp olive oil

3 tbsp chopped onion

6 eggs

½ tsp salt

Peel the potatoes and either cut them into slices about 1.5 cm (½ inch) thick, or chop them into 1.5 cm (½ inch) dice. Heat the oil in a non-stick frying pan and cook the potatoes slowly until fork-tender, about 30 minutes, adding the chopped onion towards the end (it burns if added earlier).

Beat the eggs in a bowl with the salt. Place a plate over the potatoes and tip out the excess oil. Combine the potatoes and onion with the beaten eggs. Add the oil to the frying pan and pour in the mixture of eggs and potatoes. Cook the tortilla on a medium heat until set on one side. Shake the pan to keep the tortilla loosened on the bottom. Place a plate on top of the pan. Hold it tightly and reverse the pan, so the tortilla turns out on the plate. If necessary, add more oil to the pan. Slide the tortilla back into the pan to cook on the reverse side. It only needs 5 minutes more. Slide out on to a serving plate.

TAPA SERVINGS 16; LIGHT MEAL SERVINGS 4

BREAD WITH TOMATO
PAN AMB TOMAT

This Catalan preparation is so simple, you can't believe how good it is. The bread must be a dense, country-style loaf, a day or two old, and the oil must be a good quality olive oil. Serve these 'tomato toasts' as an appetizer.

150 ml (¼ pint) olive oil

1 garlic clove, crushed

6 thick slices country bread

2 ripe tomatoes, halved

salt

thinly sliced serrano ham

Combine the oil and crushed garlic. Toast the bread lightly on both sides. Scrub the toasted slices with cut tomato, squeezing out juice and pulp on to the bread. Brush or drizzle the toasts with the oil. Sprinkle with salt and serve topped with sliced ham.

SERVES 6

GARLIC MUSHROOMS
CHAMPIÑONES AL AJILLO

Whether you use cultivated mushrooms or any of the more exotic wild mushrooms, *setas*, so appreciated in Spain, this is a delicious way to prepare them. Chopped ham or prawns can be added to the mixture.

500 g (1 lb 2 oz) mushrooms

6 tbsp olive oil

1 head garlic, the cloves peeled and chopped

1 piece chilli pepper, minced

4 tbsp dry Sherry

½ tsp salt

pepper

2 tbsp chopped parsley

Clean the mushrooms. Slice them if large or quarter them if small. Heat the oil in a frying pan or *cazuela* and sauté the mushrooms slowly, adding the chopped cloves of garlic and the chilli pepper. When the mushrooms are nearly cooked, 10 minutes, add the Sherry and season with salt and pepper. Sprinkle with chopped parsley. Serve hot.

SERVES 6

DEEP-FRIED TAPAS

Almost every *tapa* bar has a few crisp, fried foods – fritters, croquettes, fried fish – as part of its repertoire. Especially in Seville and elsewhere in Andalusia, where olive oil is superb, these are real delicacies. They're best fresh and hot from the oil. If you're preparing a *tapa* party, plan only one or two of these fried foods, which definitely require last-minute attention.

MARINATED FRIED FISH
CAZÓN EN ADOBO

Cazón is dogfish, a kind of shark. But this tasty titbit can also be made with other fish. Choose a solid-fleshed one, such as monkfish, which won't disintegrate. This is best when marinated overnight.

750 g (1 lb 10 oz) fish, such as monkfish or rock salmon

3 tbsp olive oil

5 tbsp wine vinegar

1 tbsp water

3 garlic cloves, chopped

¼ tsp paprika

1 tsp chopped oregano

¼ tsp ground black pepper

pinch of ground cumin

½ tsp salt

flour

olive oil for frying

Cut the fish into 4-cm (1½-inch) cubes, discarding any skin and bone. Put it in a glass or ceramic bowl. Mix together the oil, vinegar, water, garlic, paprika, oregano, pepper, cumin and salt. Pour over the fish and mix well. Marinate for at least 6 hours or overnight. Then drain the fish well, dredge it in flour and fry the pieces a few at a time in hot oil until golden and crisp. Drain on absorbent paper and serve hot.

TAPA SERVINGS 10

Prawns in 'Trenchcoats'
Gambas en Gabardinas

These prawns are dipped in batter – their 'coats' – and crisply fried. Allow about three prawns per person. For easy serving, the prawns can be skewered on to cocktail sticks before battering and frying.

1 egg, beaten

4 tbsp water

½ tsp salt

¼ tsp bicarbonate of soda

100 g (3½ oz) plain flour

a few threads of saffron

500 g (1 lb 2 oz) uncooked jumbo prawns, peeled (25–30 prawns)

olive oil for frying

Make a batter with the egg, water, salt, bicarbonate of soda, flour and saffron. Let it rest for at least 1 hour or, refrigerated, overnight. The batter should have the consistency of pancake batter. Dip the peeled prawns in the batter and fry them in hot oil, turning, until golden on both sides. Drain on kitchen paper and serve hot.

SERVES 8–10

MUSSELS IN CAPES
MEJILLONES ENCAPOTADOS

While the preceding prawns are simply shrouded in raincoats, these mussels are wrapped in heavy capes!

1 kg (2 lb 3 oz) mussels (approximately 24) or tinned mussels

2 bay leaves

5 tbsp water

50 g (1¾ oz) butter or oil

55 g (2 oz) plain flour

250 ml (8 fl oz) liquid (milk plus mussel broth)

salt and pepper

grating of nutmeg

1 egg yolk

55 g (2 oz) plain flour

1 egg, beaten

55 g (2 oz) breadcrumbs

olive oil for frying

Scrape the mussels and remove the beards. Wash well in running water. Put them in a deep pan with the bay leaves and water. Cover and bring to a boil, shaking the pan, until the mussel shells open. Discard any that do not open. Strain the mussels from the liquid, reserving the liquid. Let them cool, then remove from their shells and discard shells. Strain the cooking liquid.

Melt the butter or heat the oil in a pan. Stir in the flour and cook on a low heat for a few minutes. Then whisk in the liquid. This makes a very thick binding sauce, or paste. Season with salt and pepper and nutmeg. Remove from heat and beat in the egg yolk.

Coat each mussel well in paste (unless you're unusually handy with spoons, this is best done by hand). Place on a baking tray and refrigerate for at least 1 hour or overnight.

Dredge each coated mussel in flour, dip in beaten egg, then in breadcrumbs. Fry in deep hot oil until golden. Drain on kitchen paper and serve hot.

MAKES ABOUT 24

'TIGERS' - STUFFED MUSSEL SHELLS
TIGRES

1 kg (2 lb 3 oz) mussels, about 24

40 g (1½ oz) butter or oil

30 g (1 oz) serrano ham or bacon,
    finely chopped

1 tbsp chopped onion

1 garlic clove, chopped

40 g (1½ oz) plain flour

250 ml (8 fl oz) liquid (milk plus
    mussel broth)

¼ tsp paprika

pinch of cayenne

salt and pepper

30 g (1 oz) plain flour

1 egg, beaten

30 g (1 oz) fine breadcrumbs

olive oil for frying

Clean the mussels and steam them open as in the previous recipe. Remove from the shells and save half the shells. Chop the mussel meat. In a pan, heat the butter or oil and sauté the ham or bacon, onion and garlic. Stir in the flour and cook for 1 minute, then whisk in the liquid. Add the paprika, cayenne, salt and pepper and cook, stirring, until sauce is thickened. Add the chopped mussels. Spoon the mixture into the reserved mussel shells, place them on a tray and chill until the sauce is set, at least 2 hours. Dip the mussels, filled side down, into flour, beaten egg and then breadcrumbs and fry them in shallow hot oil until the tops are browned.

MAKES ABOUT 12

FISH BALLS
ALBONDIGAS DE PESCADO

Here's a fine way to use leftover cooked fish. Flake it, discarding skin and bone. Or use frozen fish fillets – hake or cod are perfect.

300 g (10½ oz) fish fillets or leftover cooked fish

salted water plus 1 tbsp wine vinegar

125 g (4½ oz) bread

1 tbsp chopped parsley

1 garlic clove, crushed

¼ onion

1 tsp salt

pinch of cayenne

1 tbsp lemon juice or wine vinegar

flour

beaten egg

breadcrumbs

olive oil for frying

Poach the fish in salted water with the vinegar. Drain, reserving the liquid, and remove any bones. Soak the bread in the reserved fish liquid until the bread is soft. In a blender or processor chop together the parsley, garlic, onion and boned fish. Squeeze out the bread and add to the processor. Season with salt, cayenne and lemon juice or vinegar. Shape the paste into small balls. Place on an oiled baking tray and chill in the refrigerator.

Coat the balls in flour, dip in beaten egg, then coat in breadcrumbs. Fry them in deep hot oil until golden on all sides.

MAKES ABOUT 24

SPINACH FRITTERS
TORTILLITAS DE ESPINACAS

These fritters may be served warm or at room temperature.

400 g (14 oz) spinach or chard leaves
　　or use frozen

2 tbsp olive oil

2 garlic cloves, chopped coarsely

2 eggs, separated

125 g (4½ oz) plain flour

½ tsp baking powder

2 tbsp milk or water

pinch of cumin seed

1 tsp salt

1 tsp wine vinegar

olive oil for frying

If you are using fresh spinach, wash the spinach well and chop it coarsely. In a frying pan, sauté the spinach in the 2 tbsp of oil with the garlic until the spinach is wilted. If you are using frozen spinach, simply drain it well, pressing out excess liquid. In a processor or blender, combine the egg yolks, flour, baking powder and milk or water with the spinach and process until combined (or chop spinach and beat into other ingredients). Season with cumin seed and salt. Beat the egg whites until stiff and add the vinegar. Fold the egg whites into the spinach mixture. Heat enough oil to coat the surface of a frying pan. Over medium heat, drop in spoonfuls of the spinach mixture. Fry slowly until set and lightly browned on the bottom. Turn the fritters and fry slowly on the other side. Remove and serve, or keep warm while you make another batch. Add a little more oil to the pan and continue frying the remaining batter.

MAKES ABOUT 20

SHRIMP FRITTERS
TORTILLITAS DE CAMARONES

Visit an exuberant market in the vicinity of Cádiz – for example, in Jerez, where Sherry is made – and you'll see vendors with baskets of tiny, live shrimp, still jumping around like grasshoppers. Unshelled, these go into a batter and are fried into crisp fritters. Uncooked, the shrimp are grey-brown and translucent. Elsewhere they're found cooked, completely pink. If not available, use any peeled prawn, finely chopped.

1 tbsp finely chopped onion

1 tbsp chopped parsley

100 g (3½ oz) tiny shrimp or peeled prawns, chopped

125 g (4½ oz) plain flour

⅛ tsp baking powder

200 ml (7 fl oz) water

1 tbsp white wine

½ tsp salt

olive oil for frying

Combine the onion, parsley, shrimp or prawns, flour, baking powder, water, wine and salt. The batter should be the consistency of pancake batter. Heat oil in a frying pan and drop spoonfuls of the batter into the hot oil, turning to fry and crisp both sides. Drain the fritters on kitchen paper and serve hot.

MAKES ABOUT 18

Vegetable Fritters

Rebozadas

These can also be served as a side dish with meat or poultry. Cauliflower, separated into florets, is the most usual, but almost any vegetable, blanched crisp-tender, can be used. Try artichoke hearts, chunks of courgette or aubergine, green beans, mushrooms.

For the Batter

1 tbsp finely chopped onion

1 garlic clove, finely chopped

1 tbsp chopped parsley

pinch of crushed saffron (or yellow colouring)

1 egg, separated

150 ml (¼ pint) water (approximately)

½ tsp salt

½ tsp bicarbonate of soda

140 g (5 oz) plain flour

½ medium cauliflower, separated into florets (or other vegetable, cut in cubes or pieces)

olive oil for deep frying

In a bowl, combine the onion, garlic, parsley and saffron. Add the egg yolk, water, salt, bicarbonate of soda and flour. Mix lightly, but do not beat, to make a thick batter. Let it rest for 1 hour.

Meanwhile, boil or steam the cauliflower until crisp-tender, about 8 minutes. Drain and refresh in cold water. Drain.

Beat the egg white until stiff and fold it into the batter. Dip the pieces of cauliflower into the batter and fry them in deep, hot oil until golden. Remove and drain on kitchen paper. Serve hot.

Makes about 24

FRIED PASTIES
EMPANADILLAS

These would be served as an aperitif for a *coctel*, drinks reception, or family fiesta for a christening, communion or wedding. This is a wonderfully 'forgiving' shortcrust dough, crisp and tender no matter what you do to it – probably due to the wine. Use it, too, for baked pies.

FOR THE DOUGH

> 270 g (9½ oz) plain flour
>
> 1 tsp salt
>
> 100 g (3½ oz) butter or lard
>
> 100 ml (3½ fl oz) white wine, chilled

FOR THE FILLING

> 200 g (7 oz) tinned tuna, drained and chopped, or cooked ham or other cooked meat, chopped finely
>
> 3 tbsp tomato sauce (see page 17)
>
> 1 hard-boiled egg, chopped
>
> 1 tbsp chopped parsley
>
> 1 tbsp brandy
>
> salt and pepper
>
> 1 tbsp finely chopped onion
>
> 24 stuffed olives, chopped
>
> cayenne
>
> olive oil for frying

Place the flour and salt in a bowl and cut in the butter or lard until crumbly. Add the wine. Gently press the dough together to form into a ball. Cover with cling film and refrigerate for at least 2 hours.

Mix the tuna or ham with tomato sauce, egg, parsley, brandy, salt and pepper, onion and olives. Season with cayenne.

Roll out the chilled dough on a lightly floured board and cut it into rounds about 10 cm (4 inches) in diameter. Place a small spoonful of filling on each round and fold over the dough to make half-circles. Crimp the edges with a fork. Fry the pies, a few at a time, in hot oil to cover. Drain and serve hot or cold.

MAKES ABOUT 24

FIERCE POTATOES
PATATAS BRAVAS

A *toro bravo* is a fighting bull. These are 'fighting' potatoes, named because of the piquant sauce.

175 ml (6 fl oz) tomato sauce (see page 17)

2 tbsp olive oil or olive oil mayonnaise

1 garlic clove, crushed

1 tbsp wine vinegar

1 tsp paprika

¼ tsp ground cumin

¼ tsp chopped oregano

cayenne or ground chilli

salt to taste

500 g (1 lb 2 oz) potatoes, peeled

olive oil for frying

salt

Combine the tomato sauce, oil, garlic, vinegar, paprika, cumin, oregano and enough cayenne or chilli to make the sauce fierce. Add salt if necessary.

Cut the potatoes into 3 cm (1¼ inch) cubes. Fry them in deep hot oil until browned and tender when pierced with a skewer. Drain them on absorbent paper and sprinkle with salt. Serve the potatoes hot with the sauce spooned over or in a separate bowl for dipping.

TAPA SERVINGS 6

FRIED SANDWICHES
EMPAREDADOS

150 g (5¼ oz) serrano ham or cooked pork
    loin, thinly sliced

150 g (5¼ oz) cheese, sliced

8 slices sandwich bread

100 ml (3½ fl oz) milk

1 egg, beaten

40 g (1½ oz) fine breadcrumbs

olive oil for frying

Layer the sliced ham or cooked pork and sliced cheese on four of the bread slices. Top each with a slice of bread and press them together. Trim off the crusts and cut the sandwiches diagonally into quarters. Dip each piece into milk, then beaten egg, then fine breadcrumbs. Heat enough oil in a frying pan to cover the bottom and fry the sandwiches, a few at a time, until browned on both sides.

MAKES 16

FRIED SQUID RINGS
CALAMARES FRITOS

Favourite *tapa* bar fare, squid is fairly tender if it is fried quickly – overcooking makes it rubbery. Allow 3–4 rings of squid per person. To clean squid, see page 102 (squid in ink sauce).

With scissors, cut the body pouch crosswise into rings 1½ cm (½ inch) wide. Pat them dry. Dredge in flour, then shake off excess. Fry the rings and tentacles in deep, hot oil until golden and crisp. Drain and sprinkle with salt. Serve with lemon wedges.

SALADS AND COLD TAPAS

COUNTRY-STYLE POTATO SALAD
ENSALADA CAMPERA

1 kg (2 lb 3 oz) potatoes

1 small onion, finely chopped

1 large tomato, peeled and chopped

juice of 1 lemon

5 tbsp olive oil

2 tbsp chopped parsley

2 hard-boiled eggs, sliced

60 g (2 oz) tinned pimientos, drained and
    chopped

12 stoned green olives (preferably home-
    cured style)

200 g (7 oz) tinned tuna, drained

mayonnaise (optional)

Cook the potatoes in their skins in water until
just fork-tender. Drain well and cool. When
completely cooled, peel and slice them into a
bowl. Add the onion and tomato, lemon juice,
oil, parsley, eggs, pimientos and olives. Toss
lightly. Garnish with chunks of tuna. If desired,
cover with mayonnaise before garnishing.

SERVES 10–12

RUSSIAN SALAD
ENSALADILLA RUSA

A perennial *tapa* bar favourite, this makes a fine stuffing for tomatoes.

2 medium potatoes, boiled, peeled and diced
    (see previous recipe)

1 large carrot, cooked and diced

60 g (2 oz) peas, cooked

1 red pimiento, chopped

1 tbsp chopped parsley

½ tsp salt

1 tsp wine vinegar

5 tbsp mayonnaise

strips of pimiento for garnish

Combine the potatoes and carrot with the peas, pimiento, parsley and salt. Stir the vinegar into the mayonnaise and blend into the potato mixture. Spread the salad on a platter. If desired, cover it completely with additional mayonnaise. Decorate with strips of pimiento.

TAPA SERVINGS 6

STUFFED EGGS
HUEVOS RELLENOS

8 hard-boiled eggs

60 g (2 oz) tinned pimientos, drained

150 g (5¼ oz) cooked and peeled prawns, chopped

8 green olives, chopped

1 tsp lemon juice

salt and pepper

pinch of cayenne

lettuce leaves

100 ml (3½ fl oz) mayonnaise, preferably made with olive oil and lemon juice

Peel the eggs and cut them in half lengthwise. Remove the yolks and reserve them. Cut 8 strips of pimiento and finely chop the remainder. In a small bowl, combine the prawns with the olives, the chopped pimientos, the lemon juice, salt and pepper and cayenne. Fill the egg whites with this mixture. Arrange the eggs on lettuce leaves on a serving dish. Thin the mayonnaise with a little milk or lemon juice so that it can be spread over the eggs. Top each egg with a strip of pimiento. Sieve the egg yolks and sprinkle over the eggs.

MAKES 16

ORANGE AND COD SALAD
REMOJÓN

This salad has many variations, all of them ravishing to look at. In Granada it's called *remojón*, but in the village where I live, it's called *salmorejo* – which means something very different in Córdoba. In Málaga, the salad includes potatoes (somewhat like the previous *campera* salad) as well as oranges.

150 g (5¼ oz) dry salt cod (see page 110) or tinned tuna

4–6 oranges

1 onion, thinly sliced (red onion looks especially nice)

1 garlic clove, crushed

4 tbsp olive oil

1 tbsp wine vinegar

a few red pepper flakes (optional)

50 g (1¾ oz) green or black olives

Toast the salt cod over a flame or under the grill until it is lightly browned and softened. Put it in a bowl of water while preparing the remaining ingredients. Peel, seed and slice the oranges and combine with the sliced onion on a platter or in a bowl. Whisk the garlic with the olive oil, vinegar and red pepper flakes, if using. Drain the cod and remove all skin and bones. Shred it and add to the salad. If using tinned tuna, drain it well and flake it on to the top of the salad. Sprinkle the dressing over the salad and garnish with the olives.

TAPA SERVINGS 12

MARINATED FRESH ANCHOVIES
BOQUERONES AL NATURAL

For those who have only ever tasted salty, tinned anchovies, these are a revelation – I've had students on my cooking courses who have booked solely to learn how to prepare them! Although the diminutive anchovy (approximately 8 cm/3¼ inches) can sometimes be found in British markets, you may have to substitute sardines, herring or mackerel. In this case, cut the fish, once filleted, into thin strips. Allow time to marinate the fish overnight. Fresh anchovies are also served simply floured and fried or filleted and dipped in a fritter batter and fried. They are indispensable to a Málaga-style mixed fish fry.

1 kg (2 lb 3 oz) fresh anchovies

1 tsp salt

250 ml (8 fl oz) wine vinegar (approximately)

4 garlic cloves, chopped

3 tbsp chopped parsley

3 tbsp olive oil

lemon juice

1–2 spring onions, finely chopped

Cut off the heads and pull out the innards of the anchovies in the same motion. Lift the top of the backbone and pull it down across the belly to release it, then cut it off at the tail, leaving the two fillets attached. Put the fillets in a bowl of water, then rinse them and place in a shallow layer in a glass or ceramic, covered dish. Add salt and enough vinegar to completely cover them. Cover and marinate for 24 hours or longer. The vinegar 'cooks' the anchovies, turning the flesh solid and white.

Before serving, put the fish in a colander and rinse in cold water. Drain well. Open the anchovies and arrange them, skin-side down, on a serving dish. Sprinkle them with garlic, parsley and a little additional salt. Drizzle with olive oil and just a squeeze of lemon juice. Finely chopped spring onion is a good final touch.

FISH ROE SALAD
ENSALADA DE HUEVAS

In the Cádiz Bay area, *corvina* roe is a spring delicacy, wrapped in cloth and poached, so astonishingly fresh that not even lemon juice is added! However, fish roe is usually either fried or dressed with a tangy sauce and served as a salad. Hake or cuttlefish roe is typical, cod could be used instead. Wash the 'packets' of roe, still enclosed in their membranes. Bring a pan of water to a boil and add salt, bay leaf, slice of onion and a slice of lemon. Lower the heat to a simmer and poach the roe very gently for about 10 minutes. Drain well. Set them on a plate and place another plate on top to weight them slightly. Let cool. Slice the roe and arrange on a platter on a bed of shredded lettuce. Spoon over the dressing and garnish the salad with sliced tomatoes.

FOR THE VINAIGRETTE DRESSING

- **1 hard-boiled egg, chopped**
- **1 garlic clove, finely chopped**
- **1 tbsp finely chopped onion**
- **1 tbsp drained capers**
- **¼ tsp salt**
- **½ tsp paprika**
- **3 tbsp wine vinegar**
- **150 ml (¼ pint) olive oil**
- **1 tbsp chopped parsley**

Combine all the dressing ingredients in a bowl and spoon over the salad.

HOT TAPAS

'SADDLED UP'
MONTADITOS DE LOMO

These are thin slices of pork loin or cutlet, fried or grilled and served atop a slice of bread. Use slices of *lomo en adobo*, marinated pork loin (see recipe, page 184), or the following quick marinade.

250 g (9 oz) pork loin, thinly sliced
    (approximately 6 slices)

2 garlic cloves, coarsely chopped

1 tbsp chopped parsley

¼ tsp paprika

salt and pepper

1 tbsp lemon juice

olive oil

6 slices of bread, cut to fit the pork slices

Spread the sliced pork on a large platter or dish in one layer. Sprinkle the garlic, parsley, paprika and salt and pepper over. Add the lemon juice and let the cutlets marinate for 1 hour. Then fry them in a little oil or grill on an oiled griddle. Serve hot on slices of bread.

SERVES 6

KIDNEYS WITH SHERRY
RIÑONES AL JEREZ

Whether made with lambs', pigs' or calves' kidneys, this delectable dish needs slow and gentle cooking so as not to toughen the kidneys.

750 g (1 lb 10 oz) kidneys

lemon juice

4 tbsp olive oil

½ onion, finely chopped

1 garlic clove, chopped

1 tbsp plain flour

120 ml (4 fl oz) dry Sherry

100 ml (3½ fl oz) meat stock

salt and pepper

1 bay leaf

chopped parsley

Peel off the thin membrane encasing the kidney and cut out the core of fat. Cut the kidney into cubes. (Pork or beef kidney can be soaked for several hours in milk, then drained.) Wash the pieces of kidney in water then soak briefly in water with a squeeze of lemon juice added. Pat dry.

Heat the oil in a frying pan and sauté the onion very gently. Add the pieces of kidney and fry gently. Add the garlic and stir in the flour, then the Sherry, stock, salt and pepper and bay leaf. Simmer the kidneys in the sauce for 15 minutes, but do not allow to boil. Serve sprinkled with chopped parsley. The sauce should be velvety, the kidneys very tender.

TAPA SERVINGS 12; MAIN COURSE SERVINGS 4

TRIPE STEW
CALLOS

Perhaps it's because tripe is time-consuming to prepare at home or perhaps it's because people want just a few bites of it rather than a huge bowl, that tripe has become a *tapa* bar speciality from one end of Spain to the other, and especially in Madrid. Now that cleaned and cooked tripe can be found in some butcher's shops the preparation is shorter, and tripe makes hearty fare for winter. In Andalusia, *menudo* is prepared similarly, with the addition of cooked chickpeas and mint to the stew.

1 kg (2 lb 3 oz) cooked calf's tripe, cut into 4 cm (1½ inch) squares

1 calf's foot, cooked, bones removed and chopped (optional)

5 tbsp olive oil or lard

1 onion, chopped

1 carrot, chopped

100 g (3½ oz) serrano ham or bacon, chopped

4 garlic cloves, chopped

1 tbsp paprika or pulp from dried sweet peppers

red pepper flakes or cayenne to taste

¼ tsp ground cumin

3 tbsp tomato sauce (see page 17)

200 ml (7 fl oz) broth reserved from cooking tripe or beef stock

salt and pepper

pinch of ground cloves

1 bay leaf

sprig of thyme

150 g (5¼ oz) *chorizo*

150 g (5¼ oz) *morcilla*

Put the pieces of tripe, and the calf's foot if desired, into a *cazuela* or flameproof casserole. In a frying pan, heat the oil or lard and sauté the onion, carrot, ham or bacon and garlic until the onion is softened. Stir in the paprika, red pepper, cumin, tomato sauce and broth. Season with salt and pepper, cloves, bay and thyme. Pour over the tripe in the *cazuela* and add the pieces of *chorizo* and *morcilla*. Cook slowly for 1 hour. The stew may be left to stand and reheated before serving.

TAPA SERVINGS 12–14; MAIN COURSE SERVINGS 6

GARLIC-SIZZLED CHICKEN
POLLO AL AJILLO

This delicious *tapa* bar favourite has its drawbacks – typically a whole chicken (or rabbit) is hacked into small pieces, which cook quickly but leave dangerous bone chips. This is my own version, made with tiny wing joints, perfect finger food for a *tapa* party. As a main dish, use chicken cut into very small joints. Serve with *patatas fritas*, chips, added to the sauce.

1 kg (2 lb 3 oz) chicken wings
    (about 12 wings)

salt and pepper

paprika

10 garlic cloves

5 tbsp olive oil

1 bay leaf

150 ml (¼ pint) Sherry (*amontillado* or *oloroso seco* or dry Sherry plus a little Brandy de Jerez)

chopped parsley

Cut off the wing tips and discard (use them for stock). Divide each wing into two joints. Rub the chicken pieces with salt, pepper and paprika. Smash 2 garlic cloves without peeling. Heat the oil in a frying pan or *cazuela* and add the pieces of chicken and the 2 garlic cloves. Fry until the chicken is golden. Add the remaining garlic, peeled and coarsely chopped, and continue frying. Then add the Sherry and continue cooking until most of the liquid is absorbed and the chicken is tender, about 20 minutes. Sprinkle with chopped parsley to garnish.

MAKES ABOUT 24

Moorish Kebabs
Pinchitos Morunos

At fiestas throughout southern Spain, a Moor, replete with red fez, fans the braziers on which grills skewered meat, marinated with spices. The kebabs and their seasoning are hardly different from the brochettes of Morocco, just across the Straits of Gibraltar, except that in that Muslim country, the meat would be lamb or veal, whereas in Spain, it's usually pork. So popular are these kebabs that the spices can be purchased already blended – *especias para pinchitos* – but I prefer to mix my own in the old-fashioned way, without monosodium glutamate and other artificial flavourings and colourings. The other 'secret' to tasty *pinchitos* is fresh lemon juice, which both tenderizes and flavours the meat.

FOR THE SPICE BLEND

> 3 tbsp ground cumin
>
> 2 tbsp ground coriander
>
> 1 tsp ground turmeric
>
> 1 tsp ground ginger
>
> 1 tsp cayenne
>
> 1 tsp ground black pepper
>
> 1 tsp salt

FOR THE KEBABS

> 1 kg (2 lb 3 oz) pork or lamb
>
> 4 tbsp chopped parsley
>
> 10 garlic cloves, finely chopped or minced
>
> 1 tsp salt
>
> 2 tbsp blended spices
>
> juice of 3 lemons

Combine the spices. Keep in a tightly sealed jar. (Note: you can substitute 1 tbsp ground cumin combined with 1 tbsp Madras curry powder.)

Cut the meat into 2-cm (¾-inch) cubes. Layer the meat in a bowl with the parsley, garlic, salt, spice mixture and lemon juice. Continue using all the meat. Marinate, covered and refrigerated, for 6–24 hours, turning the mixture 2 or 3 times. Thread 4 or 5 pieces of the meat on to thin metal skewers and grill over charcoal, under a grill or on a griddle until browned on all sides. Serve the skewers with chunks of bread and an additional squeeze of lemon.

TAPA KEBABS SERVINGS 15–16

Saucy Meatballs
Albondigas en Salsa

I can remember bygone days, when times were hard, when in tapa bars we used to take odds on the proportion of meat to bread in these small meatballs. We ate them, nevertheless, for the flavourings make them delectable. So, depending on economics, these meatballs can contain more or less minced meat, more or less bread. (Incidentally, I have re-invented this dish for 'light' cooking, using minced turkey instead of beef, and poaching the meatballs instead of frying them.)

FOR THE MEATBALLS

> 400 g (14 oz) minced beef
> 400 g (14 oz) minced pork or chicken
> 55 g (2 oz) stale bread
> 1 garlic clove, finely chopped
> 3 tbsp finely chopped onion
> 2 tbsp chopped parsley
> ½ tsp salt
> freshly grated nutmeg
> 1 egg, beaten
> flour
> 100 ml (3½ fl oz) olive oil

FOR THE ALMOND-SAFFRON SAUCE

> 50 g (1¾ oz) almonds, blanched and
>   skinned
> 1 slice bread (30 g/1 oz)
> 2 garlic cloves
> 3 tbsp olive oil
> 10 peppercorns
> ½ tsp saffron
> 1 clove

> ½ tsp salt
> 150 ml (¼ pint) white wine
> 250 ml (8 fl oz) meat or chicken stock
> lemon juice
> chopped parsley

Place the minced meats in a bowl. Soak the sliced bread in water or milk to cover until soft. Squeeze out and add to the meat with the garlic, onion, parsley, salt, nutmeg and egg. Knead well to make a smooth mixture. Form into small balls (3 cm/1¼ inches). Roll them in flour and fry very slowly in hot oil until browned on all sides. Remove and drain. The oil can be strained and used for the sauce.

Fry the almonds, bread and garlic in the oil until golden. Remove. In a mortar, crush the peppercorns, saffron, clove and salt. Add the toasted almonds, bread and garlic (or put in processor) with the wine to make a smooth paste. Combine this mixture in the pan with remaining oil, and the stock. Bring to a boil, then add the fried meatballs. Simmer the meatballs for 20 minutes in the sauce, adding a little additional liquid if needed. Immediately before serving, add a squeeze of lemon juice. Serve sprinkled with chopped parsley.

MAKES ABOUT 36

PORK WITH TOMATO
MAGRO CON TOMATE

This dish is served with chunks of bread for mopping up the sauce, or with the pork and sauce spooned on to split bread rolls.

500 g (1 lb 2 oz) boneless pork, cubed

3 tbsp olive oil

3 garlic cloves, chopped

1 kg (2 lb 3 oz) tomatoes, peeled and chopped

2 tsp salt

1 bay leaf

Fry the pork cubes in oil with the garlic until browned. Add the tomatoes, salt and bay leaf. Fry over a high heat for a few minutes, then simmer until the pork is cooked and tomatoes are reduced to a sauce, about 20 minutes.

TAPA SERVINGS 8

SHERRIED SAUSAGES
SALCHICHAS AL JEREZ

500 g (1 lb 2 oz) fresh pork sausage links

2 tsp olive oil

100 ml (3½ fl oz) dry Sherry

With scissors, cut the sausage into 4 cm (1⅝ inch) lengths. Brown them in a little oil, then add Sherry and cook until most of the liquid is absorbed. *Chorizo* can be prepared in the same way, using white wine instead of Sherry.

TAPA SERVINGS 16

VILLAGE FAIR-STYLE OCTOPUS
PULPO 'A LA FEIRA'

This is traditional at fairs in inland villages of Galicia. Itinerant vendors set up their copper cauldrons in the shade of a chestnut tree to cook the octopus, which is served out on wooden plates. In former times, dried octopus was used, though now it's usually frozen. It's so good, that it's served at *tapa* bars all over Spain. You can leave out the potatoes if you prefer.

800 g (1 lb 12 oz) cleaned, cooked octopus
  (if frozen, thaw before use)

1 kg (2 lb 3 oz) medium potatoes

1–2 tsp coarse salt

6 garlic cloves, finely chopped

1½ tbsp paprika

150 ml (¼ pint) olive oil

Simmer the octopus gently for 10 minutes to heat it through. With scissors, cut it into small squares. Boil the potatoes in their skins until tender. Allow to cool, then peel them and cut into quarters. Arrange the octopus and potatoes on wooden plates, and sprinkle with salt. Combine the garlic, paprika and oil and drizzle over the octopus and potatoes.

TAPA SERVINGS 10

SHELLFISH
MARISCOS

A wonderful variety of shellfish are served as *tapas* in very simple ways – boiled in salt water or turned on a grill. They range from unusual ones such as Galicia's famed *percebes*, sea barnacles, and Cádiz's *cañaillas*, whelks, to prawns, crayfish, clams, mussels, crabs, lobster claws, oysters, razor-shells and more. Most are hands-on finger foods – you peel the prawns, suck the heads, scoop clams off the shell, crack crab claws and pick out the sweet flesh. In times not so long past, it was usual for the floors of popular *tascas* to be littered with the debris of discarded shells, pits, picks and napkins, all to be swept up at the end of the day. While that has changed, the excellence of the shellfish has not.

SIZZLING PRAWNS
GAMBAS AL PIL PIL

This is prepared in individual ramekin dishes.

3 tbsp olive oil

1 garlic clove, chopped coarsely

1 piece of chilli pepper, finely chopped,
    or red pepper flakes

10 peeled raw prawns

pinch of paprika

bread

Put the oil, garlic and chilli in a small flameproof ramekin or small pan. Using a heat disperser, put it on the heat until the oil is quite hot. Add the prawns and paprika and cook just until the prawns turn pink and curl slightly. Serve immediately, while still sizzling, with bread for mopping up the sauce.

TAPA SERVINGS 1

GRILLED TINY CUTTLEFISH
CHOPITOS A LA PLANCHA

6 garlic cloves, chopped

1 tbsp chopped parsley

100 ml (3½ fl oz) olive oil

3 tbsp lemon juice

salt

600 kg (1 lb 5 oz) very small cuttlefish
    or squid

The tiny creatures are cooked, ink and all. Make the sauce by combining the garlic, parsley, oil, lemon juice and salt. Brush a griddle with oil, sprinkle it with salt and heat it. Lay the cuttlefish on the griddle until cooked on one side for 4 minutes, turn and cook the other side. Remove them to a platter. Drizzle the sauce over the cuttlefish and serve.

TAPA SERVINGS 10

FISHERMAN'S CLAMS
ALMEJAS A LA MARINERA

Served up at a seaside bar near where the fishermen have beached their boats, these are sensational. The best clams are the big ones from the Bay of Biscay, whereas in Andalusia, tiny *coquinas*, wedge shells, are best. The same dish can be made with mussels. It's customary to eat the clams from a communal dish, with everyone mopping up the juice with chunks of bread.

1 kg (2 lb 3 oz) clams

4 tbsp olive oil

5 garlic cloves, chopped

4 tbsp white wine or dry Sherry

2 tbsp water

2 tbsp chopped parsley

Wash the clams in several changes of water. In a frying pan or *cazuela*, heat the oil with the garlic until it begins to sizzle. Add the clams, over a high heat, then add the wine or Sherry and the water. Cover and cook, shaking the pan, until the shells have just opened. Remove from the heat and stir in the parsley. Sometimes a spoonful of breadcrumbs or flour, and more water, are added to extend the sauce.

TAPA SERVINGS 16; FIRST COURSE SERVINGS 4

Snails
Caracoles

Not seafood, but land-shells, snails are enjoyed in many parts of the country, in Catalonia with rabbit, in Valencia with paella, in Mallorca with *sobrasada* sausage. They are fasted, then cooked with herbs, then put into sauce or stew. Served in bowls, everyone uses a straight pin or pick to extract the snail from its shell. The sauce is worth the trouble! This dish could be made with tinned snails.

100 ml (3½ fl oz) olive oil

1 onion, chopped

4 garlic cloves, chopped

150 g (5¼ oz) diced ham or bacon

150 g (5¼ oz) *chorizo* or *sobrasada* sausage

400 g (14 oz) tomatoes, peeled and chopped

2 tsp paprika

a few red pepper flakes or cayenne

½ tsp ground cumin

salt and pepper

200 ml (7 fl oz) white wine

6–12 dozen snails, cooked (a dozen per person)

chopped mint, fennel or parsley

In a *cazuela* or frying pan, heat the oil and sauté the onion, garlic, ham or bacon and sausage. Add the tomatoes, paprika, red pepper flakes or cayenne, cumin, salt and pepper and wine. Add the snails and cook, covered, for 30 minutes. Serve in bowls, garnished with the choped herbs.

Tapa servings 6–12

5
DESSERTS

DESSERTS

*A*legría – exuberant joyfulness – fills fiestas and happy family gatherings. You hear it in Spanish music and dance. You also savour it in the sweetness of special pastries and confections, with their spicy fragrance and honeyed syrups. They symbolize *alegría*; they're essential to fiesta.

Many typical sweets have saint's names and are made only once a year, for festivities to honour a village's patron saint. Some are so local that they're found nowhere else; others are made in many regions, but often with different names. To confuse things even more, the same name might be used in different regions for completely different sweets!

The best of traditional sweets are made by cloistered nuns, whose confections have been lovingly home-made from recipes which go back centuries. The tradition derives not from the need to earn money for the convent but from former times, when daughters of noble families took vows. Gifts to their families and benefactors of rich cakes and pastries were a way to acknowledge favours to the convent graciously. Many convent sweets are of Moorish or Sephardim origin, particularly those rich with honey, dates, figs, almonds, sesame, rose water, orange blossom water and myriad sweet spices. *Alegría* has its roots in older traditions.

Today many sweets are industrially produced, in particular candied fruits and almonds, marzipan confections, and *turrón*, nougat bars, beloved for Christmas. Yet families and neighbours still enjoy getting together for a festive day of baking or frying favourite sweets.

Traditionally olive oil would be used in preparing these sweets and pastries, but you can substitute any vegetable oil if you prefer.

FRUIT DESSERTS

Frutas y amores, los primeros son mejores.

————————

Fruit and love, the first are best.

In former days, when peasant families lived almost entirely by subsistence farming, refined sugar was a luxury afforded only occasionally, so sweets, puddings and pastries were saved for special festivities. But always there to finish a meal was the natural sweetness of fruit. With fresh fruits abundantly available year-round, this is still the favoured dessert. From springtime's strawberries to early summer's apricots, peaches, cherries and plums, through the melons at the height of summer, with grapes and figs following before autumn's pomegranates, apples, pears, persimmons, custard apples and quince make their appearance, and oranges and tangerines to see the winter through, there is always a delectable fruit available.

Fruit is generally served without embellishment: a whole apple, banana, orange, a slice of melon, a bowl of strawberries. You simply peel and slice the fruit (although there is nothing so enchanting as an orange, speared on a fork by a maestro Spanish waiter, deftly peeled onto a plate, leaving only the sectioned fruit, free of membrane, the sweet juice and ineffable fragrance).

Housewives use various methods to preserve the season's bountiful harvest of fruit for enjoying later. One of the favourites is simply to immerse the fruit in spirits, either anise brandy or wine. Cherries, in particular, are done this way. Later the fruit is served as a dessert and the fruit-flavoured liqueur drunk for holiday meals.

Where sunshine is rampant, drying is a traditional Spanish way of preserving fruits. In the hills above Málaga, sweet *moscatel* grapes are dried in wooden frames on south-facing slopes. The raisins are arguably the sweetest in the world. Figs are spread on a mat to dry, then packed into woven baskets and carried to a fig press.

Another traditional way of preserving fruit, which dates from Moorish times, is in *arrope*, a sweet syrup made of boiled grape must, figs or honey. And, of course, various jams and conserves are made of local fruits.

PEACHES WITH WINE
MELOCOTONES AL VINO

A dish from Aragón, where peaches are superb.

4 large peaches

750 ml (1¼ pints) white wine or Sherry

100 g (3½ oz) sugar

rind of 1 lemon

3 cm (1¼ inch) cinnamon stick

100 ml (3½ fl oz) brandy (optional)

Dip the peaches in boiling water, then remove their skins. Halve them and remove the stones. Combine the wine, sugar, lemon rind and cinnamon and bring to a boil. Remove from the heat and pour over the peaches. Add the brandy, if desired, and steep the peaches for 3 days. Serve them with a little of the syrup. The remaining liquid makes a good basis for *sangria*, wine punch.

SERVES 4

APPLE SAUCE
COMPOTA DE MANZANA

Asturias grows some 250 varieties of apple, most of which are used for traditional cider. This is a lovely by-product.

1 kg (2 lb 3 oz) tart apples

500 ml (16 fl oz) white wine or cider

300 g (10½ oz) sugar

5 cm (2 inch) cinnamon stick

Peel and core the apples and cut them in pieces. Simmer in the wine with the sugar and cinnamon until very tender and the liquid almost cooked off. Serve warm or cold.

SERVES 6

APPLE FRITTERS
BUÑUELOS DE MANZANA

450 g (1 lb) apples

30 g (1 oz) sugar

1 tbsp anise brandy

2 eggs, separated

150 ml (¼ pint) milk

1 tbsp oil

¼ tsp salt

125 g (4½ oz) plain flour

olive oil for frying

sugar

Peel, core and slice the apples. Place them in a bowl and mix with the sugar and anise brandy. In another bowl, beat the egg yolks with the milk, oil, salt and flour until combined. Let the batter rest for 2 hours. Beat the egg whites until stiff, then fold them into batter. Heat the oil until hot but not smoking. Dip the apple slices into the batter and fry them in the hot oil until golden. Drain and sprinkle with sugar. Serve hot.

SERVES 4

ORANGES WITH CARAMEL
NARANJAS AL CARAMELO

Another good sauce with fruit is the *borracho* Sherry sauce (see recipe for drunken cakes, page 282).

6 tbsp sugar

12 tbsp water

4–6 large oranges, peeled and sliced

Cook the sugar with 6 tbsp of water until it has a golden caramel colour. Add the remaining water and stir hard to dissolve the caramel. Pour the sauce over the sliced oranges.

SERVES 6

FIG ROLL
PAN DE HIGOS

Año de higos, año de amigos.

A good year for figs is a good year for friends.

A typical Christmas-time sweet.

1 kg (2 lb 3 oz) dried figs

300 g (10½ oz) hazelnuts, blanched
    and skinned

300 g (10½ oz) almonds, blanched
    and skinned

50 g (1¾ oz) sugar

1 tsp ground cinnamon

½ tsp aniseed, ground

¼ tsp ground cloves

½ tsp ground black pepper

80 g (2¾ oz) sesame seeds, toasted

1 tbsp grated lemon zest

90 g (3 oz) plain chocolate, melted

brandy or anise brandy

30 almonds, blanched and skinned

Finely chop the figs or put them through a mincer. Chop the nuts and add to the figs with the sugar, cinnamon, aniseed, cloves, pepper, 2 tbsp of the sesame seeds and the lemon zest. Mix well with the hands. Add the melted chocolate and just enough brandy or anise to moisten the mixture slightly. It should be quite stiff. When well mixed, divide into pieces of about 200 g (7 oz) and shape them into rolls about 5 cm (2 inches) thick. Roll the logs in the reserved sesame seeds and stud each one with three or four blanched almonds. Store in tightly closed tins or in the refrigerator. The rolls keep for several months.

MAKES 8–10

FRUIT IN SYRUP
ARROPE

A Moorish delight, traditionally, the fruits were preserved first by soaking in slaked lime, then by steeping in syrup made from wine must or boiled figs. This is a simplified version which keeps in the refrigerator for a few days.

2 litres (3½ pints) Málaga Muscatel wine or grape juice

rind of 1 orange, slivered

zest of 1 lemon, slivered

1 cinnamon stick

5 cloves

500 g (1 lb 2 oz) dried figs and/or raisins

1 kg (2 lb 3 oz) various fruits and vegetables (such as melon, pumpkin, aubergine, sweet potatoes), peeled and cut into chunks

140g (5 oz) shelled walnuts or almonds, left whole

Boil the wine or juice with slivered orange and lemon zest, the cinnamon and cloves until reduced by half. Add the figs or raisins and pieces of fruit. Simmer all together until the fruits are tender, about 30 minutes. Add the nuts. Cool. Keep refrigerated.

SERVES 12

QUINCE JELLY
DULCE DE MEMBRILLO

Wash the quinces in water. Put in a pan with water to cover and cook until quite tender, at least 30 minutes. Drain, reserving some of the liquid. Peel and core them and put the fruit through a sieve. Weigh the fruit pulp and put it in a pan with the same weight of sugar and a piece of cinnamon stick. Add a little of the reserved liquid and cook until very thick, stirring frequently so the paste doesn't scorch. Pour the jelly into shallow rectangular moulds and cool. The jelly should set up solid enough to slice.

GRAPES OR QUINCE JELLY WITH CHEESE
UVAS O MEMBRILLO CON QUESO

Uvas con queso saben a beso.

Grapes with cheese taste like a kiss.

Serve slices of quince jelly with mild white cheese, such as Burgos or Villalón. If you can't obtain these try cottage cheese or ricotta, though the texture is different. If desired, cheese can be drizzled with a little honey and a few walnuts sprinkled on top.

PUDDINGS

CATALAN CUSTARD
CREMA CATALANA

This luscious pudding, with its crackly topping of caramelized sugar and scented with lemon and cinnamon, is especially loved for the holiday of San José, Father's Day, in March. You need a salamander – not a mythical beast, but an iron disk on a rod – heated red-hot, to caramelize the sugar. You can improvise by putting the puddings under a hot grill.

6 egg yolks

200 g (7 oz) sugar

750 ml (1¼ pints) plus 120 ml (4 fl oz) milk

zest of 1 lemon

5 cm (2 inch) cinnamon stick

3 tbsp cornflour

Beat the egg yolks and 150 g (5¼ oz) of the sugar in a bowl. Put 750 ml (1¼ pints) of the milk in a saucepan with the lemon zest and cinnamon stick. Bring to a boil. Remove from heat and strain it into the eggs, whisking them constantly. Dissolve the cornflour in the remaining milk and stir it into the custard mixture. Pour the mixture into the pan and cook on a low heat, stirring constantly, just until it starts to bubble. Remove from the heat and pour into a shallow pudding bowl or into individual dishes. Let the custard cool. Before serving, sprinkle the top of the puddings with the remaining sugar. Heat the salamander on the hob until very hot. Set it on to the sugar and hold in place long enough for the heat to caramelize the sugar, about 20 seconds. Immediately wipe the salamander surface on a damp cloth before reheating it. Puddings can also be placed beneath a hot grill. The sugar should turn brown and bubbly.

SERVES 8

CREAMY CUSTARDS
NATILLAS

This egg-rich pudding is typical during *Semana Santa*, Holy Week and Easter.

500 ml (16 fl oz) plus 3 tbsp milk
1 cinnamon stick or vanilla pod
zest of 1 lemon
4 egg yolks
100 g (3½ oz) sugar
1 tbsp cornflour
biscuits or sponge fingers
1 tsp ground cinnamon

Place the 500 ml (16 fl oz) milk, cinnamon stick or vanilla pod, and the lemon rind in a pan. Bring to a boil, simmer for 2 minutes, then remove from the heat. Let it sit until slightly cooled, then strain it. Beat the egg yolks and sugar in the top of a double-boiler or bain-marie. Combine the cornflour with the 3 tbsp milk until very smooth, and stir into the yolks. Whisk the hot milk into the yolk mixture. Stirring constantly, cook the custard over boiling water until thickened, about 10 minutes. It should be thick enough to coat the back of a spoon. Remove and cool. Pour into 4 individual pudding dishes. Put 2 or 3 biscuits or sponge fingers around the edges and sprinkle the top with cinnamon. Chill. The custard thickens to the consistency of very thick cream. If desired, 2–3 egg whites can be used for meringues (see recipe, page 290) to top the puddings.

SERVES 4

SWEET BREAD FRITTERS
TORRIJAS

While *torrijas* would be served as a dessert or sweet course in Spain, those who enjoy sweets such as pancakes or 'French toast' with syrup for breakfast would also like this dish.

6–8 thick slices of day-old bread, crusts removed (about 300 g/10½ oz)

250 ml (8 fl oz) sweet Sherry or Málaga wine (or milk with sugar)

2 eggs, beaten

olive oil for frying

sugar or honey

ground cinnamon

Cut each slice of bread, corner to corner, into 4 triangles. Soak them in the sweet wine until the bread has absorbed the liquid. Dip the pieces into beaten egg and fry them in oil, turning to brown both sides. Sprinkle with sugar or dip in honey which has been heated until thinned. Sprinkle with cinnamon. Serve hot or cold.

SERVES 6

RICE PUDDING
ARROZ CON LECHE

200 g (7 oz) medium-grain rice

250 ml (8 fl oz) water

5 cm (2 inch) cinnamon stick

zest of 1 lemon

100 g (3½ oz) sugar

¼ tsp salt

1¼ litres (2 pints) milk

sugar

ground cinnamon

Put the rice and water to cook in a saucepan. Bring to a boil, cover and simmer until the water is absorbed, about 8 minutes. Then add the cinnamon stick, lemon zest, sugar, salt and milk. Again, bring to a boil, then turn heat to very low (an asbestos pad is useful to prevent scorching). Cook until the rice is very tender, about 30 minutes more. Remove the cinnamon and lemon zest. While still hot, ladle the pudding into a serving bowl or into individual dishes. Sprinkle with a little sugar and dust thickly with ground cinnamon. Allow to cool.

SERVES 6–8

'HEAVENLY BACON' — RICH CUSTARD SQUARES
TOCINO DE CIELO

This is a sweet made in wine-making regions such as Jerez, where Sherry is made. Egg whites were used in the clarification of new wine and the yolks, in vast quantities, were contributed to convents where nuns made sweets such as these. The 'heavenly' name probably derives both from the convent origin and because the pudding, with its dark caramel topping, looks quite like a slab of bacon. Unlike real bacon, prohibited on church fast days, this sweet was allowed during Holy Week.

FOR THE CARAMEL
> 200 g (7 oz) sugar
> 150 ml (¼ pint) water

FOR THE CUSTARD
> 250 g (9 oz) sugar
> 400 ml (14 fl oz) water
> 1 piece vanilla pod
> 12 egg yolks

In a heavy saucepan, boil the sugar and water until the mixture turns golden. Cook it a little longer to caramelize and immediately pour the liquid caramel into a mould (approximately 16 × 16 cm or 7 × 7 inches). Tip the mould to coat it evenly with the caramel.

Preheat the oven to 150°C (300°F, gas 3). In a heavy saucepan, heat the remaining quantity of sugar, the water and vanilla pod. Cover for a few minutes, then uncover and boil the syrup to the thread stage, 10–15 minutes. A drop of the syrup, cooled, will spin a thread off the tip of a spoon. Stir the yolks together and pass them through a fine sieve. Remove the vanilla pod and whisk the syrup into the yolks. Pour the mixture into the prepared mould. Cover with foil and stand the mould in an oven dish. Partially fill with boiling water and cook in the oven until the custard is just cooked, about 25 minutes or when a thin skewer comes out clean. Let it cool for 15 minutes, then turn the custard out on to a serving dish. Cut into about 8 squares.

SERVES 8

ALMOND BREAD PUDDING
CUAJADO DE ALMENDRA

You can make this dessert either with or without the caramel.

FOR CARAMEL (OPTIONAL)
250 g (9 oz) sugar
200 ml (7 fl oz) water

300 g (10½ oz) stale sponge cake or
    sweet rolls
500 ml (16 fl oz) milk
lemon rind
5 cm (2 inch) cinnamon stick
4 eggs
200 g (7 oz) sugar
200 g (7 oz) almonds, blanched and
    skinned, toasted and chopped
50 g (1¾ oz) raisins or candied fruit
    (optional)

Preheat the oven to 150°C (300°F, gas 3). If using a caramelized mould, prepare a caramel by boiling the sugar and water until the mixture turns golden. Cook it a little longer to caramel and immediately pour it into a mould 18 × 30 cm (7 × 12 inches) or 22 × 22 cm (8¾ × 8¾ inches). Tip the mould to coat it evenly with caramel. Otherwise butter a mould.

For the pudding, tear the rolls into bits. Place a piece of lemon rind and the cinnamon stick in the milk and heat until almost boiling. In a bowl, whisk the eggs with the sugar. Beat in the hot milk, then the crumbs, almonds and raisins or fruit. Pour into the prepared mould. Stand the pudding mould in a larger pan. Add very hot water to the pan until it comes halfway up the sides of the mould. Bake in the oven until the pudding is set, about 45 minutes. Allow to stand for 15 minutes, then loosen edges and turn the pudding out onto a serving dish.

SERVES 6

'FRIED MILK'
LECHE FRITA

How do you fry milk? First convert it into a sweet custard, then cut it into pieces, coat with egg and breadcrumbs and fry. This pudding is lovely with a fresh fruit purée or a spoonful of strawberry preserve.

500 ml (16 fl oz) milk

rind of 1 lemon

5 cm (2 inch) cinnamon stick

50 g (1¾ oz) cornflour

5 eggs

100 g (3½ oz) sugar

125 g (4½ oz) plain flour

100 g (3½ oz) fine breadcrumbs

olive oil for frying

30 g (1 oz) sugar

ground cinnamon

Put all but about 4 fl oz of the milk in a pan with the lemon rind and cinnamon stick. Bring to a simmer and cook for 5 minutes. Strain the milk and wipe the pan clean. Meanwhile, stir the cornflour into the reserved cold milk until smooth. Beat three eggs in a bowl with the sugar and stir in the cornflour. Whisk in the hot milk and return the custard mixture to the pan. Cook, stirring constantly, until very thick and smooth. Spread the custard in an oiled pan 18 × 30 cm (7 × 12 inches) or 22 × 22 cm (8¾ × 8¾ inches) and chill it for several hours.

Beat the remaining 2 eggs and place in a shallow dish. Put the flour and breadcrumbs in dishes. Cut the custard into squares, triangles or diamonds. Dip each piece into flour, then beaten egg, then breadcrumbs. Place them on a tin and chill. Shortly before serving, heat oil in a heavy frying pan and fry the pieces of custard until browned on both sides. Drain on absorbent paper. Sprinkle the fried custard with sugar and ground cinnamon. Serve warm.

SERVES 8

CHEESE CUSTARD
QUESADA PASIEGA

The Valley of Pas in Cantabria is famous for its cheeses. This sweet is made from fresh, soft, white cheese. Any unsalted white curd cheese, such as cottage cheese, could be substituted. Similar to the Cantabrian pudding are *flao* of Ibiza, spiced with aniseed and mint, and Andalusian *cuajada*, with cinnamon. Any of these can be turned into cheesecake by baking in a crumb crust.

500 g (1 lb 2 oz) white curd cheese, drained well

125 g (4½ oz) butter, melted and cooled

250 g (9 oz) sugar

4 eggs

3 tbsp lemon juice

1 tsp grated lemon rind

200 g (7 oz) plain flour

50 g (1¾ oz) fine breadcrumbs

1 tbsp ground cinnamon

Preheat the oven to 180°C (350°F, gas 4). Beat the drained cheese until very smooth. Beat in the melted butter, sugar, eggs, lemon juice and lemon rind, then the flour. Butter a large cake tin (21 × 36 cm, 8½ × 14½ inches). Sprinkle with the breadcrumbs and cinnamon and pour in the custard mixture. Bake in the oven until set and a skewer inserted in the centre comes out clean, about 30 minutes. Cool for 10 minutes, then unmould and cut the pudding into 24 squares.

MAKES 24

WALNUT CREAM
INTXAURSALSA

In the Basque Country, this dish is served on Christmas Eve. A similar cream, made with almond paste, is typical for Christmas meals in Castille–La Mancha. In Galicia, chestnuts are cooked with milk and fennel until very soft, then sprinkled with sugar and grated chocolate.

150 g (5¼ oz) shelled walnuts

60 g (2 oz) toasted bread

2 litres (3½ pints) milk

300 g (10½ oz) sugar

ground cinnamon

Grind the walnuts and the toast. Add the milk and sugar and cook, stirring frequently, for about 40 minutes. Serve cold in small cups, sprinkled with cinnamon.

SERVES 8

RENNET PUDDING
MAMIA

In Navarre and the Basque Country this might be made with ewe's milk, heated in the traditional milk pail with hot stones. Another unusual milk pudding, traditional in goat-herding families in Andalusia, is *calostros*, made with the first milk that comes after kids are born, cooked with bread, sugar and cinnamon.

1 tsp rennet powder

1 litre (1¾ pints) milk

sugar, honey or fruit jam

Heat the milk to 36°C (66°F). Add the rennet powder and whisk. Divide between small bowls or crockery pots and leave to set for 2 hours. Chill. Serve with sugar, honey or jam.

SERVES 6–8

MILK PUDDING
GACHAS DULCES

120 ml (4 fl oz) olive oil

2 slices bread, cubed

150 g (5¼ oz) plain flour

1 tsp aniseed

300 g (10½ oz) sugar

1 litre (1¾ pints) milk

ground cinnamon

molasses or honey

Heat the oil in a pan and fry the bread cubes until golden. Remove them. Stir in the flour and toast it lightly, then add the aniseed. Remove from the heat and stir in the sugar, then whisk in the milk. Return to the heat and cook, stirring constantly, until the pudding is thickened. Butter a pudding bowl and put the fried bread cubes in it. Pour in the pudding and dust the top thickly with cinnamon. Serve cooled with molasses or honey to add to each serving.

SERVES 6–8

Cakes, Biscuits, Tarts and Pastries

Sponge Cake
Bizcocho

In *pueblo* homes, a gift of *bizcocho* was considered very special, a heart-felt present. *Hecho con huevos*, 'made with eggs', as one dear friend said, beaming, as she presented me with one as a going-away gift. A dozen eggs, sugar, flour – and a loving hand to beat the eggs for a long time, incorporating air to make the cake rise.

The village housewife would take her fresh eggs to the store and weigh them, then purchase the same weight of sugar, and flour equal to half the weight of the eggs. Served for special occasions such as christenings and communions, the cake is normally presented in its simple glory. Before whipped cream became commonplace, it might be filled with a thick syrup with raisins and nuts and topped with meringue. It can also be split and filled with jam, whipped cream, etc. The cake is excellent with fresh fruit compotes.

8 medium eggs (500 g/1 lb 2 oz), at room temperature, separated

500 g (1 lb 2 oz) sugar

1 tsp grated lemon rind

250 g (9 oz) plain flour, sifted

Preheat the oven to 180°C (350°F, gas 4). Have ready a large cake tin (28 cm/11 inches diameter and at least 6 cm/2½ inches deep), greased, and the bottom lined with a buttered round of paper.

Place the egg whites in a large bowl and, with an electric mixer, beat them until stiff. In a separate bowl, beat the yolks until light, then beat in the sugar and continue beating for 2 minutes until the yolks are thick and creamy. Add the lemon rind. Beat the yolk mixture into the whites. By hand, fold the flour lightly into the sponge.

Pour the batter into the cake tin and bake in the oven until a skewer inserted in the centre comes out clean, about 45 minutes.

Loosen the sides with a knife and invert the cake on to a rack to cool.

Serves 8

MAIZE-FLOUR CAKE
BIZCOCHO DE MAIZ

In Galicia, maize thrives and wheat does not, so this yellow flour (Americans call it cornmeal) was traditionally used in many breads and cakes. It is sieved, but not sifted, so is slightly coarse in texture. If possible, purchase fresh, stone-ground maize-flour from a mill or health food store. Keep it in a jar with a lid in the refrigerator and use within a few months.

The cake can be served plain, with just a dusting of icing sugar. Or split it and fill with a chocolate or chestnut pastry cream. Galicia, incidentally, was a centre for the chocolate industry in the 19th century, so it's only fitting that these two New World ingredients – maize and chocolate – come together in this cake.

6 eggs, separated

225 g (8 oz) lard or butter

225 g (8 oz) sugar

250 g (9 oz) maize-flour

¼ tsp salt

Preheat the oven to 180°C (350°F, gas 4). Beat the egg whites until stiff and reserve. In another bowl, cream the lard or butter until light and fluffy. Beat in the sugar a little at a time, then beat in the egg yolks. Stir in the maize-flour and salt, and fold in the egg whites. Pour the batter into a greased spring-form mould (23 cm/9 inches diameter) and bake in the oven until a skewer inserted in the centre comes out clean, about 40 minutes. Cool and unmould.

Variation: *bolos de millo*, corn cakes. Traditionally, these were baked on a fig leaf. Use the batter, above, and make rounds on a greased baking tin. Bake until golden.

SERVES 8–10

LEMON-SCENTED TEA CAKES
MAGDALENAS

These are related to French *madeleines*, but the Spanish version, said to have originated with the Magdalen nuns, is made with oil, not butter. Serve *magdalenas* with breakfast (delicious dunked in coffee) and with afternoon tea.

3 eggs, at room temperature
150 g (5¼ oz) plain flour
½ tsp baking powder
150 g (5¼ oz) sugar
1 tsp grated lemon zest
150 ml (¼ pint) sunflower oil

Preheat the oven to 180°C (350°F, gas 4). Have ready small paper cups (6 cm, 2½ inches), lightly oiled, on a baking tray. Before cracking open, place the eggs into hot tap water to warm them slightly. Sift together the flour and baking powder. With an electric mixer, beat the eggs and sugar for 10 minutes until increased in volume (30 minutes by hand). Stir in the lemon rind, then fold in the flour. Stir in the oil. Fill the paper cups two-thirds full of batter. Bake in the oven until the cakes are golden, about 15 minutes.

MAKES ABOUT 20

DRUNKEN CAKES
BORRACHOS

The perfect way to use up stale sponge cake, you can also make these with store-bought sponge.

1.5 kg (3 lb 5 oz) sponge cake

200 g (7 oz) sugar

200 ml (7 fl oz) water

zest of 1 orange

200 ml (7 fl oz) Sherry (*amontillado* or *oloroso seco*)

almond flakes

If possible, use a thin, rectangular sponge layer. Otherwise, slice the cake horizontally into 3 cm (1¼ inch) thick slabs. Place it in a flat dish or tray in one layer and prick it all over with a skewer. Boil together the sugar, water and orange rind for 5 minutes. Remove from the heat and add the Sherry. Spoon half the Sherry syrup over the cake. Leave to stand for 30 minutes. Cut the sponge into small squares (about 4 cm/1½ inches). Put a few almond flakes on top of each. Spoon over the remaining Sherry syrup. When the sponge has absorbed most of the syrup, place the squares in fluted paper cups.

MAKES ABOUT 30 SMALL SQUARES

PINE NUT HONEY CAKES
PIÑONATA

I first sampled this dense, spicy sweetmeat at Jimena de la Frontera, a village inland from the Straits of Gibraltar. When I requested the recipe I was told, *'es muy complicado!'*, it's very complicated. So I crossed it off my list. When, later, I was researching Moorish contributions to Spanish food, I came across an almost identical recipe dating from 1100. So I asked my friends Carmen and Angeles if they would show me how to make the typical *piñonata*. It's not really complicated, but, yes, old-fashioned, in that it takes a leisurely afternoon. The more hands, the better – and more fun. In the old days, a whole gaggle of women would get together to make this much-loved sweet, the occasion becoming a fiesta itself. In the days before store-bought sweets, this was served as a wedding cake. It's also favoured for Christmas and other festivals.

The old way of measuring called for topping off the egg shell and filling it with an equal number of shell-fulls of oil and, for every three of oil, one of *aguardiente*, anise brandy. Of course, only olive oil is used. Then flour is incorporated until the dough no longer sticks to the fingers.

350 g (12 oz) almonds, blanched, skinned and toasted

1 cinnamon stick, toasted

12 cloves

3 tbsp sesame seeds, toasted

2 tbsp grated orange zest

7 eggs, separated

100 ml (3½ fl oz) anise brandy

7 eggshells of olive oil (350 ml/12 fl oz)

plain flour (about 650 g/1 lb 7 oz + 350 g/ 12¼ oz)

olive oil for frying

150 g (5¼ oz) pine nuts, toasted

1 litre (1¾ pints) honey

'hundreds and thousands', for decoration

Have ready 5 or 6 moulds. These are typically square wooden frames (12 × 12 × 5 cm/5 × 5 × 2 inches). Otherwise, use tins well greased or lined with baking paper.

Save a few almonds and sesame seeds for decorating the cakes and grind together the remaining almonds and sesame seeds with the cinnamon, cloves and orange zest. (In former days, these ingredients would be ground in a mortar. Nowadays, it's quickly done in a coffee grinder or spice mill.) Beat the egg whites until stiff. In another bowl, beat the egg yolks until light, then beat in the anise brandy and oil, then combine with the egg whites. Add 4 tbsp of the ground almond and spice mixture to the yolks, then add about 650 g (1 lb 7 oz) of the flour, little by little, to make a smooth dough which doesn't stick to the hands. Take walnut-sized balls of the dough and roll them into thin cords, about the thickness of fat spaghetti. Fry these cords in hot oil until golden. Skim them out and drain. When all the dough is fried and cool, break into small pieces and place in a large bowl. In a frying pan (or in an oven tin) toast the remaining flour very slowly, stirring, until lightly golden. Save a few pine nuts for decorating and grind the remainder coarsely. Put the honey to boil in a saucepan. When the flour is toasted, combine it with the fried dough, the remaining almond-spice mixture and the ground pine nuts. Cook the honey until a spoonful dropped into cold water doesn't run, but forms a soft ball. Put a quarter of the honey syrup to one side for later. Gradually add about three-quarters of the remaining hot honey syrup to the fried dough, combining well. Working quickly, scoop the mixture into prepared moulds, pounding it down with a mallet or pestle. Before it cools completely, press the mixture out of the moulds onto foil or greaseproof paper. Spoon the reserved honey syrup (reheat if it becomes too thick) over the squares. Decorate them with sesame seeds, almonds, pine nuts and a sprinkling of 'hundreds and thousands'. Makes 5–6 squares, 12 × 12 × 5 cm (5 × 5 × 2 inches). Let the squares cool completely, then wrap in cling film and foil. They keep for several months.

MAKES 5–6

SANTIAGO ALMOND TORTE
TORTA DE ALMENDRAS SANTIAGO

This delectable Galician torte is usually finished by placing a template of the cross of Santiago de Compostela on top of the cake, then dusting thickly with icing sugar. Brush sugar off the pattern and remove it.

450 g (1 lb) almonds, blanched and skinned (or ground almonds)
150 g (5¼ oz) butter
500 g (1 lb 2 oz) sugar
7 eggs
150 g (5¼ oz) plain flour
juice and grated zest of 1 lemon
icing sugar

Preheat the oven to 180°C (350°F, gas 4). Toast the almonds in the oven, then grind them finely. Cream the butter with the sugar until fluffy, then beat in the eggs, one at a time. Stir in the flour and the ground almonds. Add the grated zest of the lemon. Put in a buttered spring-form tin and bake in the oven until a knife inserted in the centre comes out clean, about 1 hour. Cool for 10 minutes, then prick the surface of the torte and sprinkle with the juice of the lemon. Remove from the mould and cool on a rack. Sprinkle the top with icing sugar. Good served with tart raspberry or plum purée.

SERVES 12

WALNUT TORTE
TORTA DE NUECES

This is an easy cake to make to use up egg whites after you've indulged in one of the yolk-rich puddings such as Catalan cream or 'heavenly bacon'.

125 g (4½ oz) plain Marie biscuit crumbs (*galletas Marias*)

4–5 egg whites

175 g (6 oz) sugar

1½ tsp baking powder

200 g (7 oz) walnuts, chopped

Preheat the oven to 180°C (350°F, gas 4). Biscuits are easily crumbed in a processor or place them in a plastic bag and roll with a rolling pin. Beat the egg whites until stiff. Fold in the crumbs, sugar, baking powder and chopped nuts. Pour into a buttered pie dish and bake in the oven until golden, about 25 minutes.

SERVES 8

Canary Islands Banana Cake
Torta de Plátanos, Islas Canarias

Bananas are an important commercial crop in the Canary Islands, a Spanish archipelago situated off the coast of West Africa. If you cannot find Málaga raisins, use the best quality you can find.

300 g (10½ oz) underripe bananas

115 g (4¼ oz) lard or butter
    (or a combination)

250 g (9 oz) sugar

4 eggs

125 g (4½ oz) plain flour, sifted

2 tsp baking powder

1 tsp aniseed

1 tsp ground cinnamon

grating of fresh nutmeg

80 g (2¾ oz) ground almonds

100 g (3½ oz) Málaga raisins, seeded

Preheat the oven to 180°C (350°F, gas 4). Butter and flour a rectangular baking tray (approximately 20 × 30 cm, 8 × 12 inches). Without peeling, boil the bananas in water for 5 minutes. Drain, peel and mash the pulp with a fork. Cream the lard or butter with the sugar until fluffy. Beat in the eggs one at a time, then add the banana pulp. Combine the flour, baking powder, aniseed, cinnamon and nutmeg and stir into the egg batter with the ground almonds and raisins. Spread the batter evenly in the tin and bake in the oven until a skewer inserted in the centre comes out clean, 40–45 minutes. Cool. Cut the cake into squares.

Serves 8

WALNUT ROLLS
CASADIELLES

Pastries made with *hojaldre*, leafy puff pastry, are very popular in Spain. In most regions, the puff paste would be made with lard, rather than butter. Today, of course, it's easy to buy frozen puff pastry in supermarkets, so no recipe for the *hojaldre* is given.

200 g (7 oz) shelled walnuts
100 g (3½ oz) sugar
3 tbsp Sherry or anise brandy
120 ml (4 fl oz) water
1 tsp ground cinnamon
strip of lemon zest
500 g (1 lb 2 oz) puff pastry, thawed
1 egg, beaten

Finely chop or grind the walnuts in a processor. Combine the sugar, Sherry or brandy, water, cinnamon and lemon rind in a pan and bring to a boil. Cook until the syrup is thick. Remove the lemon zest and add the ground walnuts. Cook for 5 minutes. Preheat the oven to 220°C (425°F, gas 7).

Roll out the puff pastry and cut into 10 cm (4 inch) squares. Spread a tablespoonful of the walnut mixture on each square. Fold the top edge to the centre and the bottom edge to meet it and pinch together. Crimp the ends with the tines of a fork and put the packets, seam side down, on a lightly buttered oven tin. Brush with beaten egg and bake until golden, about 10 minutes.

Variation: roll out two-thirds of the puff pastry and fit in a flan ring with removable sides. Spread it with a thin layer of fruit jam and cover with the walnut mixture (or almonds prepared in the same way). Roll out remaining pastry dough. With a sharp knife or pastry wheel cut it into thin strips and make a lattice over the filling. Brush with egg and bake until the pastry is golden (about 25 minutes). When cooled, decorate the top with a few candied cherries and figs.

MAKES ABOUT 15

ANGEL'S HAIR PASTRY
PASTEL DE CABELLO DE ANGEL

Angel's hair, fine golden strands of candied fruit, is made from the flesh of the *sidra*, a type of large squash, striated in green and yellow, which seems to be used for nothing else but this sweet. The pulp is cooked first, then weighed and cooked again with an equal weight of sugar to make a stringy jam. It's used in many sweets, such as the above variation on *casadielles* and in the filling of *empanadillas*, fried pasties. In Spain you can purchase tinned *cabello de angel*, angel's hair. Otherwise, you can substitute any fruit jam or else apple sauce to which sugar has been added. The *dulce de batatas*, candied sweet potatoes, (see page 300), mashed, could also be used. In Córdoba, the pastry is sometimes served in thin wedges topped with sliced serrano ham.

500 g (1 lb 2 oz) puff pastry, thawed
400 g (14 oz) angel's hair or fruit jam
grated lemon zest
1 egg, beaten
ground cinnamon sugar

Divide the puff pastry in half. Roll out one half into a circle (23 cm/9 inches across) and place it on a baking tray. Spread with the angel's hair or jam and sprinkle with grated lemon rind. Roll out second sheet of pastry and cover the filling. Roll the edges together to seal the pie. Chill for 20 minutes. Preheat the oven to 220°C (425°F, gas 7). Brush the pastry with some of the beaten egg, prick it with a skewer in several places and bake until golden, 20–25 minutes. Remove and brush again with egg. Sprinkle with cinnamon sugar and return to the oven for a few minutes to dry.

MAKES 8

ALMOND PUFFS
SOPLILLOS

These fragile biscuits are typical of Granada, where almonds grow on many hillsides.

**250 g (9 oz) almonds, blanched and
skinned, slivered or chopped**
4 egg whites
juice and grated rind of 1 lemon
400 g (14 oz) sugar

Preheat the oven to 150°C (300°F, gas 3).
Lightly oil 36 small fluted paper cups and place
on a baking tray. Toast the slivered or chopped
almonds in a heavy frying pan or in the oven,
stirring frequently so they do not scorch.
Remove and cool. In a bowl, beat the egg whites
until stiff. Beat in the lemon juice and grated
rind, then the sugar, a little at a time. Fold in the
almonds. Spoon the mixture into the paper cups.
Bake the puffs in the oven, about 40 minutes.
Turn off the oven and let them dry overnight in
the oven. The almond batter can also be
spooned straight on to baking trays (preferably
coated with non-stick spray or lined with baking
paper). They will flatten somewhat as they bake,
so leave space between them.

MAKES 36

MERINGUE KISSES
MERENGUES

Make this with leftover egg whites when you've used the yolks for puddings..

250 g (9 oz) sugar

120 ml (4 fl oz) water

2 tbsp strong coffee (optional)

6 egg whites

24 sponge fingers (optional)

Preheat the oven to 130°C (275°F, gas 1). Make a syrup with the sugar and water (and coffee, if desired). Bring to a boil, cover the pan for a few minutes, then uncover and boil until a drop of syrup will form a soft ball when dropped into cold water. Whisk the egg whites until stiff. Beat the sugar syrup into the whites. Grease a baking tray, sprinkle it with water and with sugar (or line with baking paper) and pipe mounds of the meringue on to it with a piping bag. Alternatively, place sponge fingers flat side up on tins and pipe meringue on to them. Bake the meringues in the oven for 30 minutes. Turn off the heat and let them dry overnight in the oven.

MAKES 24–36, DEPENDING ON SIZE

CINNAMON RINGS
ROSQUILLAS

One version of these is called *listas y tontas*, smarties and dumbies. The 'smart' ones, topped with white icing, have a hole in the centre; the 'dumb' ones have baked closed. *Rosquillas* are holiday sweets, specially for saint's day festivities.

4 whole eggs

2 eggs, separated

100 g (3½ oz) sugar

6 tbsp olive oil

520 g (1 lb 2¼ oz) plain flour

1 tbsp ground cinnamon (or aniseed, toasted and ground)

250 g (9 oz) sugar, for icing

A SHOWIER ICING IS AS FOLLOWS:

225 g (8 oz) sugar

120 ml (4 fl oz) water

1 tsp lemon juice

Boil together the 4 eggs and 2 yolks. Remove 1 tbsp of the beaten egg and reserve.. Add the sugar and beat until light, then beat in the oil. Stir half the flour and the cinnamon into the egg mixture. Continue adding flour, kneading it into the dough with the hands. The dough will be very sticky. Add the remaining flour and work the dough until it is smooth and no longer sticks to the hands. Let it rest for 20 minutes. Preheat the oven to 180°C (350°F, gas 4).

Lightly oil a baking tray. Divide the dough into walnut-sized balls (about 40g/1½ oz). Poke a finger through the middle and stretch them into little rings. Place on the baking tray. Add a few drops of water to the reserved tbsp. of beaten egg. Paint the tops of the rings with beaten egg. Bake in the oven until lightly coloured, about 25 minutes. Remove and cool on a rack.

For the topping: a very simple version is to make a meringue with the remaining 2 egg whites, beaten with 250 g (9 oz) of sugar. Spoon this over the rings and put them in a very low oven to dry.

Or, for a showier icing: boil together the sugar and water until syrup spins a fine thread off the tip of a spoon. Meanwhile, beat the egg whites until stiff, then beat in the lemon juice. Pour the syrup slowly into the whites, beating constantly. Spread the icing over the cooled rings. Allow to dry completely before storing.

MAKES ABOUT 12

ANISE DOUGHNUTS
ROSCOS DE ANÍS

While nowadays, many of the typical Christmas sweets are store-bought and packaged, these fried doughnuts are still typically made at home, often in enormous quantity as they disappear quickly. If you like a strong anise flavour, use anise brandy for some of the liquid.

200 ml (7 fl oz) olive oil

20 g (¾ oz) aniseed

grated zest of 1 small lemon

450 g (1 lb) sugar

200 ml (7 fl oz) liquid (milk, orange juice, white wine, anise brandy or a combination)

2 tsp ground cinnamon

1 kg (2 lb 3 oz) plain flour

2 eggs, separated

3 tsp bicarbonate of soda

olive oil for deep frying

Put the oil in a frying pan and heat until hot but not smoking. Add the aniseed and cook a few minutes just until the spice is fragrant. Remove and cool the oil. In a large bowl, mix the lemon rind, 185 g (3 oz) of the sugar, the liquid, cinnamon and the oil with aniseed. Add 2 cups of the flour, then beat in the egg yolks and bicarbonate of soda. Beat the egg whites until stiff, then fold them into the batter. Gradually add the remaining flour, using the hands to work it in. At first the dough will be very sticky. Continue adding flour until it forms a soft dough which doesn't stick to the fingers. Take a small ball of the dough and roll it into a thick cord about 12 cm (5 inches) long. Pinch the ends together to form a circle. Continue forming the rings. Heat oil in a fryer or deep frying pan until hot but not smoking and fry the rings, a few at a time, until golden brown. Remove with a skimmer, drain briefly and, while still hot, dredge them in the remaining sugar.

MAKES 72

CHEESE FRITTERS
ALMOJÁBANAS

Bien sobre bien, bollo en mantecado mojado en miel.

Good on top of good, sweet buttery buns bathed in honey.

While there are quite a few versions of this, all derive from a Moorish sweet made with fresh cheese.

200 g (7 oz) soft curd cheese, well drained

2 eggs, separated

200 g (7 oz) sugar (or half honey)

1 tbsp chopped mint

pinch of salt

200 g (7 oz) plain flour

2 tsp baking powder

olive oil for frying

sugar and cinnamon, for dusting

In a mixer or processor, cream the cheese until smooth. Beat the egg whites until stiff. Fold into them half the sugar, the egg yolks, mint, salt, flour and baking powder to make a soft dough. Break off pieces of about 40 g (1½ oz) and shape into small ovals or rings. Fry them in hot oil, turning to brown both sides. Drain. Boil the remaining sugar with 100 ml (3½ fl oz) water to make a syrup. Pour it over the fritters. Serve hot or cold, dusted with additional sugar and cinnamon.

MAKES 16

GALICIAN CRÊPES
FILLOAS

Perhaps descrying their common Celtic ancestry, crêpes are as popular in the northern Spanish regions of Galicia and Asturias (where they're called *frixuelos*) as they are in Brittany. In Galicia, *filloas* (from the Latin *folio*, meaning leaf) are favourite fare for summer *romerías*, pilgrimages to country shrines. They're also made during the winter pig slaughtering, incorporating pig's blood and fried in lard. Some variations are made with maize flour or rye. *Filloas queimadas* are crêpes flambés, usually with rum or herb liqueur. The *filloas* may be served folded into quarters and sprinkled with sugar and cinnamon, or folded around a filling. This recipe includes a sweetened soft cheese filling. Other sweet alternatives are confectioner's custard or sweetened chestnut purée. Use the crêpes too with savoury fillings such as seafood, *grelos* (turnip tops), or ham.

3 eggs
100 ml (3½ fl oz) milk
100 ml (3½ fl oz) water (approximately)
60 g (2 oz) plain flour
pinch of salt
15 g (½ oz) butter, melted
additional fat for the pan
sugar
ground cinnamon

FOR THE CHEESE FILLING
200 g (7 oz) soft cheese (*queso fresco* or *requesón*) or cottage cheese, well drained
200 ml (7 fl oz) double cream
55 g (2 oz) sugar
1 tsp grated lemon zest

Beat together the eggs, milk, water, flour, salt and melted butter. Let the mixture rest for 30 minutes before using. Heat a heavy frying pan. Use a swab of cotton speared on a fork and dipped in melted butter, or a cube of pork fat, to grease the frying pan. Pour in enough batter to make a thin film (about 3 tbsp). When it is set, turn it with the fingers or a thin spatula. The edges will crisp slightly, but don't let the crêpe brown. Remove. Grease the frying pan before adding batter for the next one.

Beat the cheese until smooth. Whip the cream, fold in the sugar and lemon zest and fold it into the softened cheese. Spoon this mixture on to the crêpes and fold them like an envelope.

To flambé the *filloas*: sprinkle the crêpes with sugar. In a small saucepan, combine 2 tbsp of sugar and 2 tsp of lemon juice. Add 175 ml (6 fl oz) of gold rum, brandy or anise brandy. Set alight and let burn for a few seconds, then pour the burning liquid – carefully – over the crêpes.

MAKES 12

FRIED CAKES
PESTIÑOS

In Spain, *frutas del sartén*, fruits of the frying pan, are famous. Some of them are made with special moulds and irons which shape the frying batter – such as *florones*, flowers; *hojuelas*, leaves, and *rosas*, roses. Others, filled and unfilled, are easily made at home without special tools.

100 ml (3½ fl oz) olive oil

½ tsp aniseed

100 ml (3½ fl oz) white wine

pinch of salt

250 g (9 oz) flour plus additional for
    rolling out

olive oil for deep frying

200 g (7 oz) honey

3 tbsp water

sugar

Heat the oil in a pan until hot, but not smoking. Add the aniseed and heat a few seconds longer. Remove and cool. Combine the cooled oil, wine, salt and 250 g (9 oz) of flour or enough to make a soft dough which can be gathered into a ball. Don't overwork the dough. Cover and chill the dough for 1 hour.

On a lightly floured board, roll out the dough thinly. Cut it into strips or 5 cm (2 inch) squares. Fold opposite ends or corners together and pinch together. Fry the pieces in deep hot oil until they are golden. Remove and drain on absorbent paper.

Put the honey and water in a pan, bring to a boil and simmer 5 minutes to make a thick syrup. Dip the fried pastries into the honey syrup then put them on a rack. Sprinkle them with sugar and let dry. (Alternatively, the honey can be omitted and the pastries, while still hot, can be dredged in sugar.)

Variation: *empanadillas*, little pasties: roll out the dough, cut into circles and put a dab of fruit jam or mashed candied sweet potatoes (see recipe page 300) in the centre of each circle. Fold over, seal the edges with a fork, then fry the tiny pasties. These are usually just dredged in sugar. *Empanadillas* are one of many Christmas treats.

MAKES ABOUT 48

SPICED OIL CAKES
TORTAS DE ACEITE

These thin, flaky disks, studded with aniseed and sesame, are consumed for breakfast or with afternoon tea, and go nicely with sweet wine as well. For another version, see the section on Bread.

250 ml (8 fl oz) olive oil

1 tbsp aniseed

1 tbsp sesame seeds

120 ml (4 fl oz) water or white wine

125 g (4½ oz) sugar

460 g (1 lb) plain flour

¼ tsp bicarbonate of soda

3 tbsp honey

3 tbsp sugar

3 tbsp water

sugar

Heat the oil in a small frying pan. When hot but not smoking, add the aniseed and sesame seeds and heat for another minute until the spices are fragrant. Remove and cool completely.

Combine the cooled oil and spices with the water or wine and sugar. Add the flour and bicarbonate of soda to make a soft dough. Do not knead more than necessary to combine. Form into a ball and chill for 1 hour. Preheat the oven to 200°C (400°F, gas 6). Form the dough into balls the size of eggs (70 g/2½ oz). Pat them out very thinly on baking tins (about 14 cm/5½ inches diameter). Bake in the oven until lightly golden, about 15 minutes.

Have ready a syrup made by boiling for 3 minutes the honey, sugar and water. Remove the *tortas* from the tin to a flat surface or rack. Brush the tops with the honey syrup and sprinkle them with sugar. Allow to cool thoroughly.

MAKES 11

Sweet Lard Cakes
Mantecados

Winter's pig butchering, with the preparation of hams and sausages, starts after the feast of St Martin (November 11) and ends in February with the beginning of Lent, and thus, coincides with Christmas festivities. Pigs destined for sausages are fattened on cereals, potatoes, acorns, beets, chestnuts, table scraps and yield a higher percentage of fat than those raised for fresh meat. Many of the favourite Christmas cakes and biscuits are confected with fresh, pure white lard. So popular are these cakes that now their production is an important industry. Towns such as Estepa (Seville) are redolent with the sweet smells of cinnamon and aniseed in the months preceding Christmas.

500 g (1 lb 2 oz) plain flour

125 g (4½ oz) almonds, blanched and skinned

250 g (9 oz) white lard

200 g (7 oz) sugar, sifted

½ tsp ground cinnamon

1 tbsp sesame seeds, toasted (optional)

icing sugar

Preheat the oven to 150°C (300°F, gas 3). Spread the flour in an oven tin and toast it in the oven until lightly coloured, stirring frequently so it browns evenly. Toast the almonds lightly, then chop finely or grind (a processor works well for this). Cool the flour and combine with the ground almonds. Beat the lard until smooth and fluffy. Beat in the sugar and cinnamon, then add the flour and almond mixture a little at a time and the toasted sesame seeds, if using. The dough will be quite crumbly. Pat it to a thickness of 1 cm (⅜ inch). Cut into 5 cm (2 inch) circles and place on a baking tray. Bake in the oven until the cakes are dried, about 30 minutes. Let them cool, then dust with icing sugar and wrap them individually in tissue paper, if desired.

Makes about 36

'DUST' CAKES
POLVORONES

As for *mantecados*, these can be dusted with icing sugar when cooled and wrapped in tissue.

125 g (4½ oz) lard

150 g (5¼ oz) sugar

300 g (10½ oz) plain flour, sifted

2 tsp cinnamon

icing sugar (optional)

Preheat the oven to 150°C (300°F, gas 3). Cream the lard with a wooden spoon until light. Blend in the sugar gradually, then add the sifted flour and the cinnamon. Knead lightly, just to blend. Roll or pat out the dough to a thickness of 2 cm (¾ inch). Cut into circles or ovals of about 4 cm (1½ inches). Place on an ungreased baking tin and bake in the oven for about 25 minutes.

MAKES ABOUT 24

PUFFS
BUÑUELOS

These fritters, as insubstantial as a breeze, are favourites during *cuaresma*, the Lenten season and Holy Week. Sometimes friends set up a vat of oil on a street corner and fry the little puffs for the whole *barrio*, neighbourhood.

240 ml (8 fl oz) milk or water

70 g (2½ oz) butter

1 tbsp brandy or anise brandy (optional)

30 g (1 oz) sugar

pinch of salt

125 g (4½ oz) plain flour

4 eggs

olive oil for deep frying

sugar

Place the milk, butter, sugar and salt in a heavy pan and heat until it just boils. Lower the heat and add the flour all at once, beating it hard with a wooden spoon until it forms a smooth ball of dough. Remove from the heat and beat in the eggs one at a time. Beat until cool and very smooth. Heat the oil in a deep fryer or heavy pan. Put in a cube of potato – when potato is nicely coloured, the oil is hot enough to fry the *buñuelos*. Drop the balls of batter, by teaspoons, into the hot oil. Fry until golden and puffed up. Remove, drain and sprinkle the puffs liberally with sugar. The puffs can also be split and filled with jam or confectioner's custard.

MAKES ABOUT 24

CONFECTIONS

CANDIED SWEET POTATOES
DULCE DE BATATAS

Unlike the candied sweet potatoes Americans enjoy as a vegetable side dish with roast turkey, this Spanish interpretation, typical of Málaga, really is a sweet. Serve it with bland *requesón*, a fresh, curd cheese, or with whipped cream. Mashed, the sweet potatoes are used for filling *empanadillas*, little fried pies.

1½ kg (3 lb 5 oz) sweet potatoes or yams

1 kg (2 lb 3 oz) sugar

5 cloves

zest of 1 orange

3 cm (1¼ inch) cinnamon stick

500 ml (16 fl oz) water

2 tbsp brandy (optional)

Cook the whole sweet potatoes in water to cover until they are only just tender. Drain and cool. Peel and scrape them smooth. Cut into equal-size chunks or slices. In a large pan, combine the sugar, cloves, orange zest, cinnamon and water. Bring to a boil and cook for 5 minutes. Add the chunks of sweet potato and reduce the heat so the liquid just bubbles. Cook, uncovered, about 40 minutes. Do not let the sweet potatoes overcook or they will disintegrate. Remove them to a tall jar or covered bowl. If the syrup seems too thin, boil it a little longer. Add the brandy, if desired, and pour the syrup over the sweet potatoes. Cover the jar and cool.

SERVES 10

TOMATO JELLY
DULCE DE TOMATE

What do you do with dozens of tomatoes at the end of the summer? Try this unusual jelly. It's very pretty in glass jars. Spoon it over ice cream, serve with cream cheese, or for breakfast with croissants.

2 kg (4 lb 6 oz) tomatoes (approximately)
sugar (see method)
1 vanilla pod
5 cloves
zest of 1 small lemon

Dip the tomatoes into boiling water for a few seconds. Remove and slip skins off. Cut out the cores. Cut the tomatoes in half and with a spoon scoop out all the seeds and liquid. Chop coarsely, weigh the tomatoes and put them in a pan with the same weight of sugar, the vanilla pod, cloves and lemon zest, cut into small pieces. Bring to a boil, then cook on a medium heat until the jelly is thick and doesn't run when spooned on to a cold plate, about 1 hour.

MAKES ABOUT 5 × 250 ML (8 FL OZ) JARS

EGG YOLK CANDY
YEMAS

Made in convents, this sweet varies somewhat in shape and consistency from one region to another. One famous sort is from the San Leandro nuns in Seville, made of candied threads of eggs. They require a special utensil, a *hilador*, a sort of funnel with six or more tiny spouts from which the yolk mixture is spun into the boiling sugar syrup. This version is quick and easy and a good way to use leftover yolks.

225 g (8 oz) sugar
200 ml (7 fl oz) water
1 tsp grated orange zest
12 egg yolks, lightly beaten and strained
50 g (1¾ oz) icing sugar

In a heavy pan, bring to the boil the sugar, water and orange zest. Cover the pan and cook for 3 minutes. Then uncover and cook, without stirring, until the syrup forms a soft ball when dropped into cold water, about 10 minutes. Using a wooden spoon, beat in the egg yolks, little by little. Continue beating the syrup on a medium heat until it thickens and leaves the sides of the pan. Remove from heat and continue beating as the syrup cools. Sprinkle some of the icing sugar on a marble slab (or on a tray covered with baking paper) and spread out the yolk candy. Leave to cool. Dust the hands with additional icing sugar and form small balls of the paste (about 15 g/½ oz) into little cones or cylinders. Roll them in icing sugar. Chill. The sweets can be individually wrapped in tissue paper.

MAKES ABOUT 18

GLOSSARY OF SPANISH WORDS

Aceite, aceite de oliva. Oil, olive oil.

Aceituna. Olive.

Adobo. A marinade with vinegar and herbs for uncooked foods.

Aguardiente. Distilled liquor, often flavoured with anise. **Aguardiente de orujo.** A clear grape brandy, similar to French *marc* or Italian *grappa*.

Alioli. Garlic and oil sauce, but often garlic mayonnaise.

Almíbar. Sugar syrup.

Almirez. Brass mortar for grinding spices and nuts.

Almuerzo. Lunch or a light meal.

Bacalao. Dry salt cod.

Bizcocho. Sponge cake.

Bocadillo. Sandwich in a roll.

Bodega. Wine cellar, winery.

Bollo. A bun or small bread roll.

Brasa, a la. Food grilled over coals.

Buñuelo. Fritter, beignet.

Butifarra. A Catalan sausage.

Cabrito, choto or chivo. Baby goat, kid.

Caldereta. A fish or lamb stew cooked in a deep pot.

Caldo. Broth or stock.

Cava. Sparkling wine made by the Champagne method.

Caza, mayor, menor. Game, large (e.g. venison, boar); small (rabbit, partridge).

Cazuela. Earthenware casserole.

Cena. Supper, evening meal.

Cerveza. Beer.

Cerdo. Pork.

Chacina. Cured meats, sausages.

Chorizo. Sausage flavoured with garlic and paprika.

Churro. Breakfast fritter.

Cochinillo. Baby suckling pig.

Cocido. One-pot meal of soup, meat, chickpeas and vegetables.

Cocina. Kitchen, cuisine.

Comida. Principal midday dinner, meal.

Cordero, cordero lechal. Lamb, baby suckling lamb.

Cortijo. Farm, country estate.

Cuaresma. Lent, Lenten meals without meat.

Desayuno. Breakfast.

Embutido. Sausage.

Empanada. Savoury pie.

Empanado-a. Breaded, coated in breadcrumbs.

Encurtido. Pickle.

Entremeses. Selection of hors d'oeuvres.

Escabeche. Marinade for cooked food.

Feria. Fair, holiday.

Fideos. Thin vermicelli noodles.

Fiesta. Feast day, holiday.

Finca. Small farm, smallholding.

Fino. A dry aperitif Sherry.

Frito. Fried food.

Garbanzo. Chickpea.

Grelo. Flowering turnip green (Galician).

Haba. Broad bean; fava bean.

Hojaldre. Puff pastry.

Horchata. Sweet, milky drink made of tiger nuts.

Jamón, jamón serrano. Ham, salt-cured 'mountain' ham.

Lacón. Salt-cured pork shoulder.

Manteca. Lard.

Manzanilla. A dry Sherry wine from Sanlúcar de Barrameda. Also a type of olive.
   Infusion de manzanilla. Chamomile tea.

Marisco. Shellfish.

Matanza. Pig slaughtering.

Mazapán. Marzipan.

Mollete. Flat roll, bap.

Morcilla. Black pudding, blood sausage.

Navidad. Christmas.

Noche Buena. Christmas Eve.

Olla. Tall, pot-bellied cooking pot.

Pacherán. Distilled liqueur flavoured with sloeberries and anise.

Parilla. Grill (usually over coals).

Pasa. Raisin. **Ciruela pasa.** Prune.

Pascua; Pascua de resurrección or **florida.** Christmas; Easter.

Pastel. Pie, pastry.

Pescado. Fish.

Piquillo. Pointy, slightly piquant peppers.

Plancha. Griddle, grill.

Potaje. Thick soup, usually with pulses.

Puchero. Cooking pot; one-pot meal cooked in it.

Revuelto. Eggs scrambled with vegetable, ham or seafood.

Reyes. Feast of the Three Kings, January 6, Epiphany.

Romesco. Sauce of sweet peppers, nuts and oil.

Rosco, rosquilla. Ring, doughnut.

Semana Santa. Holy Week preceding Easter.

Sofrito. Sauce of fried onion and tomatoes.

Tapa. Tiny serving of aperitif food.

Tarta. Cake, tart.

Tasca. Tavern.

Ternera. Veal, but also young beef.

Tortilla. Omelette, usually with potatoes or other vegetables, served round and flat.

Torta. Round flat cake or biscuit.

Turrón. Nougat candy made of nuts.

Venado. Venison.

BIBLIOGRAPHY

Benavides Barajas, L.
Al-Andalus – La Cocina y Su Historia
(Ediciones Dulcinea, Motril, 1992).

Brenan, Gerald
South from Granada
(Penguin Books, Middlesex, 1963).

Cunqueiro, Alvaro and Filgueira Iglesias,
Araceli
Cocina Gallega
(Editorial Everest, León, 1982).

Davidson, Alan
Mediterranean Seafood
(Penguin Books, Middlesex, 1972)

Las Raíces del Aceite de Oliva
(Ministerio de Agricultura y Alimentacion,
Madrid, 1983)

Lujan, Nestor and Perucho, Juan
Cocina Española – Gastronomía e Historia
(Ediciones Danae, Barcelona, 1970)

Martinez Llopis, Manuel M.
Historia de la Gastronomía Española
(Alianza Editorial, Madrid, 1989)

Root, Waverly
Food
(Simon and Schuster, New York, 1980)

Sevilla, María José
Life and Food in the Basque Country
(Weidenfeld and Nicolson, London, 1989)

Williams, Mark
The Story of Spain
(Santana Books, Málaga, 1990)

INDEX

Aceitunas Aliñadas 231
aceitunas aliñades caseras 15
Acelgas a la Malagueña 77
adafina 6
Ajo Blanco con Uvas 42
Ajo Colorado 63
Ajo Pringue 118
Ajo-aceite sauce 128–9
Ajoharina Jienense 91
Albondigas de Bacalao 117
Albondigas de Pescado 239
Albondigas en Salsa 256–7
Alcachofas Rellenas 72
Alcachofas Salteadas con Jamón 73
Alicante 'pizza' 224–5
Almejas con Faves 100
Almejas a la Marinera 260
Almendras Fritas 230
Almería 5, 55, 63, 176
Almojábanas 293
almonds
    almond bread pudding 274
    almond puffs 289
    Catalan-style chicken 173
    chicken in almond sauce 168–9
    monkfish with almond sauce in casserole 121
    noodles with pork chops 189
    pine nut honey cakes 282–4
    Santiago almond torte 284

saucy meatballs 256–7
savoury almond soup 48
skinning 14
sweet lard cakes 297
toasted 230
white garlic soup with grapes 42
almuerzo 212
'altogether' pot 136
Amanida 37
anchovies
    casseroled 161
    marinated fresh 249
Andalusia 26, 52, 61, 63 65, 135, 141, 145, 226, 253, 260
    Al-Andalus 4–5
Andalusian gazpacho 40
Andalusian hash 191
Andalusian salad 32
Andalusian vegetable pot 138
Andalusian-style asparagus 74
Andalusian-style larded pot roast 206
Andrajos con Liebre 175
angel's hair pastry 288
Angulas al Pil Pil 97
anise doughnuts 292
aniseed
    fried cakes 295
    spiced oil cakes 296
Apicius 4
apple fritters 266
apple sauce 265

Aragón 71, 154, 171, 220, 226, 265
Aragón-style beans and rice 59
Arrope 268
Arroz con Leche 272
Arroz Negre 132
Arroz en Paella a la Marinera 125–126
Arroz Rosetxat 130
artichokes
    flamenco eggs 221
    sautéed with ham 73
    spring-time vegetable stew 71
    stuffed 72
asparagus
    Andalusian-style 74
    eggs poached in broth 220
    Flamenco eggs 221
Asturias 65, 100, 151, 203, 265, 294
Asturian beans 139
Asturias-style salmon 164
Asturias-style stuffed sardines 95–6
Atascaburras 111
Atún en Conserva 158
Atún Mechado 156
aubergines
    aubergine pudding 78
    Catalan stuffed 80
    Catalan-style grilled vegetables 76
    with cheese 81

Mallorcan aubergine
    casserole 79
medley of summer
    vegetables 87
Murcia omelette 214–5
avocados 7

bacalao see dry salt cod
Bacalao al Pil Pil 115
Bacalao con Coliflor a la
    Gallega 113
Bacalao a la Vizcaina 112
bacon
    Saturday night bacon and
        eggs 218–9
    see also ham
baked fish 148
baking powder 14
Balearic Islands 36, 52
bananas
    Canary Islands banana cake
        286
barbecued lamb chops with
    alioli sauce 199
Basque *cocido* 135
Basque country, Basques 9,
    102, 112, 115 147, 149,
    157, 162, 217, 277
Basque-style hake 143
Basque-style spider crab 104
beans
    Andalusian vegetable pot
        138
    Aragón-style beans and rice
        59
    Asturian 139
    clams with 100
    'cobblestones' – rice with
        beans 131

dried 16
puré of white beans 58
Uncle Lucas's bean pot 56
Valencia paella rice 124
see also broad beans;
    green beans
beef 203–10
    'altogether' pot 136
    Andalusian hash 191
    Andalusian-style larded pot
        roast 206
    big beef chop 205
    braised beef tongue 210
    braised oxtail 208
    meal-in-a-pot 134–5
    meat and tomatoes 207
    'old clothes' (beef hash)
        227
    onion-braised 203
    stew 207
    stuffed cabbage 88
    stuffed peppers 84-5
Berenjenas con Queso 81
Berenjenas Rellenas a la
    Catalana 80
Bertons Rellenos 88
Berza 138
Besugo al Txacolí 147
Besugo a la Espalda 149
Besugo a la Madrileña 150
Biscay salt cod 112
biscuits 12
    almond puffs 289
Bizcocho 279
Bizcocho de Maiz 280
black pudding *see morcilla*
black rice 132
bocadillo 20

Boquerones al Natural 249
Borrachos 282
braised beef tongue 210
braised oxtail 208
brandy 12
bread 12, 24–8
    country bread 27
    filled rolls 222
    fried breadcrumbs 226
    making 14
    ovens 10, 25
    regional variations 26
    starter dough 14, 24
    sweet bread fritters 272
    sweet oil breads 28
    with tomato 233
bread cake 216–7
breadcrumbs 12
breaded veal cutlets 205
bread pudding, almond 274
breakfast 20–8
bream
    grilled 'on its back' 149
    Madrid-style 150
    with white wine 147
broad beans
    Catalan-style 70
    cuttlefish with 103
    with ham 69
    spring-time vegetable stew
        71
Bronze Age 2–3
broth 46
    with chopped ham 45
Buñuelos 299
Buñuelos de Manzana 266
butifarra 17
    Catalan salad 37

Catalan-style broad beans 70
Valencian rice and lamb casserole 130

Caballa con Fideos 160
Caballas Rellenas 159
cabbage
    chopped cabbage and potatoes 86
    Mallorcan 'dry' soup with cabbage 49
    partridge with cabbage 180
    stuffed 88
cabello de angel 288
Cachorreñas 61
Cádiz 3, 4, 9, 61, 121, 138, 141, 148, 156, 241, 250, 258
cakes
    Canary Islands banana cake 286
    drunken cakes 282
    'dust' cakes 298
    lemon-scented tea cakes 281
    maize-flour cake 280
    pine nut honey cakes 282–4
    Santiago almond torte 284
    spiced oil cakes 296
    sponge cake 279
    sweet lard cakes 297
    walnut torte 285
    see also pastries
Calabaza Guisada 84
Calamares Fritos 245
Caldeirada 162
Caldera de Langosta a la Menorquina 68

Caldereta de Cordero 196
Caldero Murciano 128–9
Caldillo 46
caldo 44
Callos 253
calostros 277
calves' liver in vinegar sauce 209
Canary Islands
    banana cake 286
    cocido 135
    green sauce 50–1
    'scalded' soup 50
candied sweet potatoes 300
Cangrejos del Rio 107
Caracoles 261
Carne Entomatada 207
Carthaginians 3
Casadielles 287
casseroled anchovies 161
casseroles 12
Castille 48, 107, 192, 226, 277
Castillian-style roast baby lamb 194
Catalan, Catalonia 86, 117, 132, 155, 180, 217, 277
    chicken with vegetables 172
    custard 270
    escudella 135
    fishermen's soup 66
    potage 57
    salad 37
    seafood grill with Catalan pepper sauce 142
    stuffed aubergines 80
Catalan-style broad beans 70

Catalan-style chicken 173
Catalan-style grilled vegetables 76
cauliflower
    Galician-style salt cod and cauliflower 113
    Mule-driver's style garlic cauliflower 78
cava (sparkling wine) 18
Cazón en Abodo 235
Cazuela de Arroz con Cigalas y Langosta, a la Sevillana 129
Cazuela de Bocartes 161
Cazuela de Boda 200–1
Cazuela de Esparragos a la Andaluza 74
Cazuela de Judías Verdes con Chorizo 82
Cazuela de Lentejas 56
Cazuela de Rape con Almendras 153
Cazuela Tio Diego 99
Champiñones al Ajillo 234
cheese 12–3, 193
    aubergines with cheese 81
    custard 276
    fried sandwiches 245
    fritters 293
    Galician crêpes 294
    grapes or quince jelly with 269
chestnuts 9
    Galician chestnut soup 51
    Galician-style duck 174
    purée, in Galician crêpes 294
    skinning 14

chicken
  in almond sauce 168–9
  Catalan chicken with
    vegetables 172
  Catalan-style 173
  garlic-sizzled 254
  meal-in-a-pot 134–5
  with olives 170
  roast 166
  stuffed 166–7
  with sweet peppers 171
chicken livers, eggs with 220
chickpeas
  Andalusian vegetable pot
    138
  Catalan potage 57
  meal-in-a-pot 134–5
  spinach with chickpeas 54
Chipirones en su Tinta 102–3
chocolate 7
  Catalan-style chicken 173
  drinking 22
  introduced to Spain 7
  maize-flour cake 280
  in savoury dishes 168
Chocolate a la Taza 22
Chocos con Habas 103
Chopitos a la Plancha 259
chopped cabbage and
  potatoes 86
choricero peppers 15, 190
chorizo 17, 183, 190
Christmas 48, 166, 263, 267,
  277, 283, 292, 295, 297
  Catalan *escudella* 135
Chuletas de Cordero a la Brasa
  199
*Chuletas de Cordero a la
  Navarresa* 198

Chuleton de Buey 205
Churros 20, 21
cinnamon
  'dust' cakes 298
  rings 291
  sweet lard cakes 297
clams
  with beans 100
  clam and pine nut soup
    from Las Marismas 64
  fish soup with orange 61
  fisherman's 260
'cobblestones' – rice with
  beans 131
coca 26
Cochifrito de Cordero 195
Cochinillo Asado 192
cocido 6, 133
Cocido Español 134–5
Cocs Farcits 222
cod *see* dry salt cod
Coliflor al Ajo Arriero 78
Columbus, Christopher 6, 7
comida, la 30
Compota de Manzana 265
Conejo a la Campera 177
Conejo a La Mallorquina 178
confections 300–2
  candied sweet potatoes 300
  egg yolk candy 302
  tomato jelly 301
  see also sweets
conger eel, mule-driver's-style
  124
Congrio al Ajo Arriero 154
*Coques en Llanda Fassida de
  Fritangas* 224–5
Cordero a la Miel 197

Córdoba 41, 208, 248
  angel's hair pastry 288
Cortez, Hernando 7
country bread 27
country-style potato salad 246
country-style rabbit 177
courgette pudding 78
crab
  Basque-style spider crab
    104
  bisque 65
crayfish
  river crayfish 107
creamy custards 271
Crema Catalana 270
crêpes, Galician 294
cuajada 276
Cuajado de Almendra 274
Cuajado de Berenjenas 78
Cuaresma 299
cuttlefish
  with broad beans 103
  grilled tiny 259
  with peas 155

Don Quixote (Cervantes) 133,
  200–1, 218–9
doughnuts, anise 292
drinking chocolate 22
drunken cakes 282
dry salt cod *(bacalao)* 9, 13,
  108–117
  Biscay salt cod 112
  buying 109
  cod fritters with molasses
    116
  cod and potato purée 111
  codfish balls 117

Galician-style salt cod and cauliflower 113
'little soldiers' cod fritters 114
orange and cod salad 248
preparation 110
sizzling cod 115
duck, Galician-style 174
Duelos y Quebrantos 218–9
Dulce de Batatas 288, 300
Dulce de Membrillo 269
Dulce de Tomate 301
'dust' cakes 298

Easter 28, 271
eggs 213–221
bread cake 216–7
with chicken livers 220
egg soup 47
egg yolk candy 302
flamenco eggs 221
fried 221
garlic-scrambled eggs 218
Jaén-style spinach 75
with peppers 219
poached in broth 220
Saturday night bacon and eggs 218–9
scrambled eggs with wild mushrooms 217
stuffed 247
see also omelettes
elvers sizzled with garlic 97
Emblanco 62
Empanada Gallega 223–4
Empanadas 26
Empanadillas 243, 295
angel's hair filling 288
sweet potato filling 300

Emparedados 245
Empedrado 131
Encebollado de Ternera 203
Ensaimadas 22–3, 26
Ensalada Andaluza 32
Ensalada Campera 246
Ensalada de Huevas 250
Ensalada de la Serranía 33
Ensalada de Perdiz 34
Ensalada de Pimientos Asados 38
Ensalada mixta 31
Ensaladilla Rusa 246–7
entremeses 121
Escaldón 50
Escalivada 76
Espinacas con Garbanzos 54
Espinacas Estilo Jienense 75
Estofado de Carne 207
extra virgin olive oil 15
Extremadura 226

Fabada 16, 139
fava beans *see* broad beans
fennel
potage with wheat and fennel 55
Fideos con Cerdo 189
Fideuá 126–7
fierce potatoes 244
fiestas 11, 263
fig roll 267
Filetes de Ternera Empanadas 205
filled rolls 222
Filloas 294
Filloas queimadas 294
fish 140–64
baked 148

balls 239
Catalan fishermen's soup 66
elvers sizzled with garlic 97
fish roe salad 250
fisherman's wife's vegetable and fish dish 92–3
Galician fish stew 162
grilled fish with garlic dressing 141
marinated 94
marinated fried 235
mixed fish fry 141
Murcia rice and fish pot 128–9
red garlic fish soup 63
seafood grill with Catalan pepper sauce 142
seafood starters 92–107
soup with orange 61
stock 61
stuffed peppers 84–5
white fish soup 62
in yellow sauce 146
see also dry salt cod; names of individual fish; seafood
fisherman's clams 260
fisherman's wife's vegetable and fish dish 92–3
fisherman's-style swordfish 152
flamenco eggs 221
Flamenquines 119
flao 276
flour 13
fried breadcrumbs 226
fried cakes 295
fried eggs 221

'fried milk' 275
fried pasties 243
fried sandwiches 245
fried squid rings 245–6
fritanga topping for Alicante 'pizza' 224–5
Frito Mallorquín 202
fritters
    apple 266
    cheese 293
    churros 20, 21
    cod fritters with molasses 116
    puffs 299
    shrimp 241
    spinach 240
    sweet bread 272
    vegetable 242
fruit, preserving 264
fruit desserts 264–69
    apple fritters 266
    apple sauce 265
    fig roll 267
    fruit in syrup 268
    oranges with caramel 266
    peaches with wine 265
    quince jelly 269
fruit in syrup 268
frutas del sartén 295

Gachas Dulces 278
Galianos de Pastor de La Mancha 179
Galicia 9, 26, 52, 88, 95, 101, 137, 203, 258, 277, 280, 284, 294
Galician chestnut soup 51
Galician crêpes 294
Galician fish stew 162

Galician savoury pie 223–4
Galician-style duck 174
Galician-style salt cod and cauliflower 113
Galician-style scallops 98
Gambas al Pil Pil 259
Gambas en Gabardinas 236
game
    country-style rabbit 177
    La Mancha-style shepherd's stew 179
    Mallorca-style rabbit 178
    pasta with hare stew 175
    pasta with rabbit 176
    see also partridge
garlic 13
    elvers sizzled with garlic 97
    garlic-scrambled eggs 218
    garlic-sizzled chicken 254
    grilled fish with garlic dressing 141
    Jaén-style garlic potatoes 91
    Mule-driver's-style garlic cauliflower 78
    mushrooms 234
    paté 118–119
    red garlic fish soup 63
    roasting 13
    sizzling cod 115
    soup 52
    white garlic soup with grapes 42
garum 3, 4, 5, 156
Gazpacho Andaluz 40
gazpacho cream 41
gazpacho soups 39–43
    Andalusian gazpacho 40

gazpacho cream 41
toasted gazpacho 43
white garlic soup with grapes 42
Gazpacho Tostado 43
Gazpachuelo 47
gordal (queen olive) 15
Granada 5, 69, 215, 248, 289
grapes
    white garlic soup with grapes 42
Greeks 3
green beans
    omelette 216
    and sausage casserole 82
    with tomato 82
green peppers *see* peppers
grilled fish with garlic dressing 141
grilled tiny cuttlefish 259
Guadalquivir River 2, 3, 64, 92, 120, 121
Guiso de Mejillones y Patatas 106
Gurullos con Conejo 176

Habas con Jamón 69
Habas a la Catalana 70
hake
    Basque-style 143
    chiclana-style hake 145
    fried hake in wine marinade 144
ham 15
    artichokes sautéed with ham 73
    broad beans with ham 69
    broth with chopped ham 45

meal-in-a-pot 134–5
roast fresh ham or pork
    shoulder 186
see also serrano ham
hare
    La Mancha-style shepherds'
      stew 179
    pasta with hare stew 175
hazelnuts
    skinning 14
'Heavenly Bacon' – rich
    custard squares 273
herbs 13
Hígado de Ternera en Adodo
    209
hilador 302
hojaldre 287
honey
    lamb with 197
    pine nut honey cakes
      282–4
Huelva 2, 103
Huevos a la Flamenca 221
Huevos al Salmorrejo 220
Huevos con Higadillos 220
Huevos Fritos 221
Huevos Rellenos 247
Intxaursalsa 277

Jaén 3, 34, 175
Jaén-style garlic potatoes 91
Jaén-style spinach 75
Jamón o Lacón Asado 186
Jamón Serrano 230
Jews 5–6, 263
Judías a lo Tío Lucas 56
Judías Verdas con Tomate 82

kid 193
kidneys
    Sacromonte omelette 215
    with sherry 252
kitchens 10

Lacon con Grelos 137
La Mancha 34, 107, 118,
    136, 277
La Mancha-style shepherds'
    stew 179
lamb 193–202
    barbecued lamb chops with
      alioli sauce 199
    Castillian-style roast baby
      lamb 194
    with honey 197
    Moorish kebabs 255
    Navarre-style lamb chops
      198
    in pepper sauce 195
    stew 196
    Valencian rice and lamb
      casserole 130
    wedding stew 200–1
lamb's kidneys
    Sacromonte omelette 215
lamb's liver, Mallorcan-style
    202
lard 13
larded and pot roasted tuna 156
leavening 14
Lechazo Asado al Castellano
    194
Leche Frita 275
leek soup 53
leftovers 226
lemon-scented tea cakes 281

Lengua de Ternera Guisada
    210
Lent 108, 299
lentils
    'cobblestones' – rice with
      beans 131
    lentil pot 56
León 154, 192
Levante 25, 126, 214
listas y tontas 291
'little soldiers' cod fritters 114
liver
    calves' liver in vinegar sauce
      209
    eggs with chicken livers
      220
    lamb's liver Mallorcan-style
      202
lizards 107
lobster
    Menorca-style lobster pot
      68
    Seville-style rice with
      prawns and lobster 129
*Lomo de Cerdo Relleno con
    Pinones* 185
Lomo embuchado 17
Lomo en Adobo 184
Lubina con Sidra 151

mackerel
    fisherman's wife's vegetable
      and fish dish 92–3
    marinated fish 94
    and noodle casserole 160
    stuffed 159
Madrid 52, 253
Madrid-style bream 150

Madrid-style omelette with
    pickled fish 214
Magdalenas 281
Magdelanian culture 2
Magro con Tomate 257
maize-flour cake 280
Málaga 5, 116, 141, 148,
    249, 264
Málaga-style chard 77
Mallorca 65, 188
    Mallorcan aubergine
        casserole 79
    Mallorcan 'dry' soup with
        cabbage 49
    Mallorcan sweet rolls 22–3,
        26
Mallorca-style rabbit 178
Mallorcan-style lamb's liver
    202
Mamia 277
Mantecados 297
marinated fish 94
marinated fresh anchovies 249
marinated fried fish 235
marinated olives 231
marinated oysters 101
marinated pork loin 184
Mariscos 258
Marmitako 157
meal-in-a-pot 134–5
meat
    Galician savoury pie 223
    garlic paté 118–9
    and tomatoes 207
    see also beef; lamb; pork
meatballs
    Andalusian 5
    meal-in-a-pot 134–5
    saucy 256–7

medley of summer vegetables
    87
Mejillones Encapotados 237
Melocotones al Vino 265
Menestra de Primavera 71
Menorca-style lobster pot 68
Merengues 290
merienda 212
meringue kisses 290
Merluza Frita al Vino 144
Merluza a la Chiclanera 145
Merluza a la Vasca 143
Migas 226
milk pudding 278
minced meat
    Catalan stuffed aubergines
        80
    stuffed cabbage 88
    stuffed peppers 84–5
mint 13
mixed fish fry 141
Mojete 35
Mojo Verde 50–1
monkfish with almond sauce
    in casserole 153
Montaditos de Lomo 251
Moorish kebabs 255
Moors 4, 5, 6, 24, 42, 48, 80,
    87, 120, 168, 170, 197,
    263, 264, 268, 282, 293
morcilla 17, 183
mortars 10, 14
mountain ham 230
Mule-driver's-style conger eel
    154
Mule-driver's-style garlic
    cauliflower 78
Murcia 4, 55, 120, 121
Murcia omelette 214–5

Murcia rice and fish pot
    128–129
Murcia salad 35
mushrooms
    garlic mushrooms 234
    scrambled eggs with wild
        mushrooms 217
mussels
    in capes 237
    in paella 125–6
    and potato stew 106
    shellfish cocktail 105
    'Tigers' – stuffed mussel
        shells 238

Naranjas al Caramelo 266
Natillas 271
Navarre 6, 71, 171, 277
Navarre-style lamb chops 198
Navarre-style trout 163
Neolithic Age 2–3
New Year's Eve 25, 45, 187,
    226
noodles
    mackerel and noodle
        casserole 160
    meal-in-a-pot 134–5
    noodle paella 127
    with pork chops 189
nuts 14
octopus, village fair-style 258
'old clothes' (beef hash) 227
olive oil 15
    in paella 122
    in Roman times 3
olives 15
    chicken with olives 170
    marinated 231
Olla de Trigo con Hinojo 155

olla podrida 133
omelettes 213–6
  green bean omelette 216
  Madrid-style omelette with
    pickled fish 214
  Murcia omelette 214–5
  potato omelette 232
  Sacromonte omelette 215
one-pot dishes 134–5
  'altogether' pot 136
  Andalusian vegetable pot
    138
  meal-in-a-pot 134–5
  olla podrida 133
  pork shoulder with greens
    137
onion-braised beef 203
orange
  and cod salad 248
  fish soup with 61
  oranges with caramel 266
  pork fillet with 187
Ostras en Escabeche 101
oxtail, braised 208
oysters, marinated 101

paella 120, 121–7
  ingredients 122–3
  noodle paella 127
  pans 15, 121
  procedure, quantity and
    timing 122–3
  with seafood 125–6
  Valenciana 124
  see also rice
Pan amb Tomat 233
Pan de Campo 27
Pan de Higos 267
paprika 15

Parrillada de Pescados y
  Mariscos con Romesco 142
parsley 13
partridge
  broth 46
  with cabbage 180
  salad 34
  stewed with beans 181
  Toledo-style marinated 182
pasta
  with hare stew 175
  with rabbit 176
Pastel de Cabello de Angel 288
pastries
  angel's hair pastry 288
  walnut rolls 287
Patatas Bravas 244
Patatas en Salsa Verde 90
Patatas a lo Pobre 89
Patatas Viudas 90
Pato a la Gallega 174
peaches with wine 265
peas
  spring-time vegetable stew
    71
peppers 15–16
  'Altogether' pot 136
  Catalan-style grilled
    vegetables 76
  chicken with sweet peppers
    171
  choricero 15, 190
  Biscay salt cod 112
  eggs with peppers 219
  introduced to Spain 7
  lamb in pepper sauce 195
  Murcia omelette 214–5
  roasted pepper salad 38

skinning 16
stewed peppers with tuna
  76
stuffed 84–5
Perdices con Coles 180
Perdiz en Escabeche a la
  Toledana 182
Perdiz Estofado con Alubias
  181
Pescado al Horno 148
Pescado en Amarillo 146
Pescado en Escabeche 94
Pescado a la Plancha 141
Pesca'ito Frito 141
Pestiños 295
Pez Espada a la Marinera 152
Phoenicians 3
picada 117
Picadillos a la Andaluza 191
pig's liver
  garlic paté 118–9
pimientos see peppers
Pimientos Rellenos 84–5
Pinchitos Morunos 255
pine nuts
  clam and pine nut soup
    from Las Marismas 64
  pine nut honey cakes
    282–4
  pork loin stuffed with 185
Piñonata 282–4
Piparrada 219
Pipirrana Jienense 36
Pisto 87
Pisto a la Marinera 92–3
Pollo a la Catalana 173
Pollo al Ajillo 254
Pollo al Chilindrón 171

Pollo Asado 166
Pollo, Capon o Pavo Relleno 166–7
Pollo con Aceitunas 170
Pollo en Pepitoria 168–9
Pollo en Samfaina a la Catalana 172
Polvorones 298
pomegranate
    pork fillet with pomegranate sauce 188
'poor folk's' potato casserole 89
pork 183–92
    Andalusian hash 191
    Andalusian vegetable pot 138
    Catalan stuffed aubergines 80
    chops with noodles 189
    fillet with orange 187
    fillet with pomegranate sauce 188
    loin stuffed with pine nuts 185
    mantanza (pig butchering) 183
    marinated pork loin 184
    meal-in-a-pot 134–5
    Moorish kebabs 255
    roast fresh ham or pork shoulder 186–7
    roast suckling pig 192
    rolls 119
    'saddled up' 251
    sausages 183–4
    shoulder with greens 137
    stuffed artichokes 72
    stuffed cabbage 88

stuffed peppers 84–5
with tomato 257
see also chorizo; morcilla
potage with wheat and fennel 55
Potaje a la Catalana 57
potajes 133
potatoes 7, 89–91
    cod and potatoe purée 111
    chopped cabbage and potatoes 86
    country-style potato salad 246
    fierce potatoes 244
    in green sauce 90
    Jaén-style garlic potatoes 91
    mussel and potato stew 106
    patatas fritas 89
    'poor folk's' potato casserole 89
    potato omelette 232
    vegetable shake-up 83
    'widowed' 90
prawns
    in paella 125–6
    Seville-style rice with prawns and lobster 129
    shellfish cocktail 105
    sizzling 259
    in 'trenchcoats' 236
    Uncle Jim's prawn casserole 99
puddings 270–8
    almond bread pudding 274
    Catalan custard 270
    cheese custard 276
    creamy custards 271
    'fried milk' 275

'Heavenly Bacon' – rich custard squares 273
    milk pudding 278
    rennet pudding 277
    rice pudding 272
    sweet bread fritters 272
    walnut cream 277
    see also sweets
puff pastry 287
puffs 299
Pulpo 'a la Feira' 258
pulses 16
    stews and soups with 54–9
pumpkin
    stewed 84
Pure de Judías Blancas 58
purée of white beans 58
Purrusalda 53
Purim 28

Quesada Pasiega 276
quince jelly 269

rabbit
    country-style 177
    La Mancha-style shepherds' stew 179
    Mallorca-style 178
    pasta with 176
Rabo de Toro 208
Rebozadas 242
Recao de Binefar 59
red garlic fish soup 63
red peppers *see* peppers
Remojón 248
rennet pudding 277
Revuelto de Ajetes 218
Revuelto de Setas 217
rice 18–9, 120–32

black rice 131

'cobblestones' – rice with
    beans 131

Murcia rice and fish pot
    128–9

for paella 122–3

pudding 272

Seville-style rice with
    prawns and lobster 129

Valencian rice and lamb
    casserole 130

see also paella

Riñones al Jerez 252

Rin Ran 76

Rioja 6, 154

river crayfish 107

roast chicken 166

roast fresh ham or pork
    shoulder 186

roast suckling pig 192

roasted garlic 13

roasted pepper salad 38

Rollitos de Ternera 204

Romans 3–4, 24

Romesco 142

Ropa Vieja 227

Roscos de Anís 292

Rosquillas 291

Russian salad 246

Sacromonte omelette 215

'saddled up' 251

saffron 16

    in paella 120, 122

salads 31–8

    Andalusian 32

    Catalan 37

    country-style potato salad
        246

fish roe 250

    mixed 31

    Murcia 35

    orange and cod 248

    partridge 34

    roasted pepper salad 38

    Russian 246–7

    Sierra 33

    summer salad from Jaén 36

    tapas 246–50

salchicha 17

Salchichas al Jerez 257

salchichón 17

salmon, Asturias-style 164

Salmon a la Ribereña 164

Salmorejo Cordobes 41

Salpicón de Mariscos 105

salt-pork 16

Sanlúcar 92

Santander 161

Santiago almond torte 284

Santiago de Compostela 6, 98

Sardinas con Tomate 96

*Sardinas Trechadas a la
    Asturiana* 95–6

sardines

    Asturias-style stuffed
        sardines 95–6

    Murcia salad 35

    in tomato sauce 96

Saturday night bacon and
    eggs 218–9

sauces

    ajo-aceite 128–9

    alioli 199

    apple 265

    Canary island green sauce
        50–1

Catalan pepper 142

    green, potatoes in green
        sauce 90

    tomato 17–8

saucy meatballs 256–7

sausages 16–7

    eggs poached in broth 220

    sherried 257

    see also chorizo; morcilla

scallops, Galician-style 98

scrambled eggs with wild
    mushrooms 217

sea bass cooked with cider
    151

seafood

    grill with Catalan pepper
        sauce 142

    paella 125–6

    Seville-style rice with
        prawns and lobster 129

    shrimp fritters 241

    soups 61–8

        Catalan fishermen's soup
            66

        clam and pine nut soup
            64

        crab bisque 65

        fish soup with orange 61

        Menorca-style lobster
            pot 68

        red garlic fish soup 63

        seafood soup 66–7

        white fish soup 62

    starters 92–107

        Asturias-style stuffed
            sardines 95–6

        Basque-style spider crab
            104

clams with beans 100
cuttlefish with broad
beans 103
elvers sizzled with garlic
97
fisherman's wife's
vegetable and fish dish
92–3
Galician-style scallops 98
marinated fish 94
marinated oysters 101
mussel and potato stew
106
river crayfish 107
sardines in tomato sauce
96
shellfish cocktail 105
squid in ink sauce 102–3
Uncle Jim's prawn
casserole 99
tapas 258–61
fishermen's clams 260
grilled tiny cuttlefish 259
shellfish 258
sizzling prawns 259
village fair-style octopus
258
see also crab; lobster;
prawns; squid
Sepia amb Pesols 155
serrano ham 13
Andalusian salad 32
artichokes sautéed with
ham 73
Catalan salad 37
fried sandwiches 245
gazpacho cream 41
mountain ham 230
Seville 2, 3, 41, 54, 120, 121,

208, 221, 231, 302
Seville-style rice with prawns
and lobster 129
sheep 5
shellfish 258
cocktail 105
see also seafood
sherried sausages 257
sherry 18
kidneys with sherry 252
shrimp fritters 241
sidra 288
Sierra salad 33
sizzling cod 115
sizzling prawns 259
snails 108, 124, 261
sobrasada 17
Soldaditos de Pavia 114
*Solomillo con Salsa de
Granadas* 188
*Solomillo de Cerdo a la
Naranja* 187
Sopa de Ajo 52
*Sopa de Almejas con Pinones,
Las Marismas* 64
Sopa de Almendras 48
Sopa de Cangrejos del Mar 65
Sopa de Castañas 50
Sopa de Pescados y Mariscos
66–7
Sopa de Picadillo 45
Sopas Mallorquinas 49
Soplillos 289
soups 44–53
broth 46
with chopped ham 45
Canary islands 'scalded'
soup 50
egg soup 47

Galician chestnut soup 50
garlic soup 52
gazpachos 39–43
leek soup 53
Mallorcan 'dry' soup with
cabbage 49
with pulses 54–9
savoury almond soup 48
seafood 60–8
spiced oil cakes 296
spices 5, 8, 17
spider crab, Basque-style 104
spinach
with chickpeas 54
fritters 240
Jaén-style 75
topping for Alicante 'pizza'
224–5
sponge cake 279
spring-time vegetable stew 71
squid
fried squid rings 245
in ink sauce 102–3
in paella 125–6
starter dough 14, 24
stewed peppers with tuna 76
stewed pumpkin 84
stews and soups with pulses
54–9
Aragón-style beans and rice
59
Catalan potage 57
lentil pot 56
potage with wheat and
fennel 55
purée of white beans 58
spinach with chickpeas 54
Uncle Lucas's bean pot 56
stuffed artichokes 72

stuffed cabbage 88
stuffed chicken, capon or
    turkey 166–7
stuffed eggs 247
stuffed mackerel 159
stuffed peppers 84–5
sugar cane 5
summer salad from Jaén 36
Suquet del Pescador 66
sweet bread fritters 272
sweet lard cakes 297
sweet oil breads 27, 28
sweet potatoes 7
    candied 288, 300
sweets 6, 263
    anise doughnuts 292
    cheese fritters 293
    cinnamon rings 291
    fried cakes 295
    Galician crepes 294
    meringue kisses 290
    see also confections;
        puddings
Swiss chard
    Málaga-style chard 77
swordfish, fisherman's-style
    152

tapas 229–61
    deep-fried 235–47
    hot 251–61
    salads 246–50
Tartessos 2
*Ternera Mechada a la
    Andaluza* 206
'Tigers' – stuffed mussel shells
    238
Tigres 238
toasted almonds 230

toasted gazpacho 43
Tocino de Cielo 273
Tojunto 136
Toledo-style marinated
    partridge 182
tomato sauce 17–8
    fierce potatoes 244
    flamenco eggs 221
    sardines in 96
tomatoes 7, 17
    Andalusian gazpacho 40
    bread with tomato 233
    green beans with tomato
        82
    meat and tomatoes 207
    Murcia omelette 214–5
    pork with tomato 257
    tomato jelly 301
Torrijas 272
Torta de Almendras Santiago
    284
Torta de Nueces 285
*Torta de Plátanos, Islas
    Canarias* 286
Tortas de Aceite 26, 28, 296
*Tortilla de Escabeche a la
    Madrileña* 214
Tortilla de Judías Verdes 216
Tortilla de Pan 216–7
Tortilla de Patatas 232
Tortilla Murciana 214–5
Tortilla Sacromonte 215
tortillas 213
*Tortillitas de Bacalao con Miel
    de Caña* 116
Tortillitas de Camarones 241
Tortillitas de Espinacas 240
tostada 20
Trinxat 86

tripe stew 253
trout, Navarre-style 163
Truchas a la Navarra 163
Tumbet 79
tuna fishing 3, 5
tuna (fresh)
    conserve 158
    larded and pot roasted 156
    and potato stew 157
tuna (tinned)
    country-style potato salad
        246
    fried pasties 243
    Madrid-style omelette with
        pickled fish 214
    mixed salad 31
    Murcia salad 35
    stewed peppers with tuna
        76
turkey 8
    salad 34
    stuffed 166–7
turrón 14
Txangurro 104
Uncle Jim's prawn casserole
    99
Uncle Lucas's bean pot 56

Valencia 162
    meal-in-a-pot 134–5
    paella rice 121, 124
    rice growing 120
Valencian rice and lamb
    casserole 130
veal 203
    breaded veal cutlets 205
    rolls 204
vegetable fritters 242

vegetables
  Andalusian vegetable pot
    138
  Catalan chicken with 172
  Catalan-style grilled
    vegetables 76
  fisherman's wife's vegetable
    and fish dish 92–3
  medley of summer
    vegetables 87
  in paella 122–3
  spring-time vegetable stew
    71
  starters 69–89
  vegetable shake-up 83

Vieiras a la Gallega 98
village fair-style octopus 258
vinegar 18
virgin olive oil 15

walnut cream 277
walnut rolls 287
walnut torte 285
wedding stew 200–1
wheat
    potage with wheat and
      fennel 55
white fish soup 62
white garlic soup with grapes
    42

'widowed' potatoes 90
wine 18
wine making 6–7

yeast 14
Yemas 302
Zarangollo 83